THE FACE BEFORE
I WAS BORN

A Spiritual Autobiography

LLEWELLYN VAUGHAN-LEE

THE GOLDEN SUFI CENTER

First published in the United States in 1997 by
The Golden Sufi Center
P.O. Box 456, Point Reyes, California 94956
www.goldensufi.org

© 1997 by The Golden Sufi Center
Second Edition © 2009 by The Golden Sufi Center

Third printing, 2012.

Cover Illustration by Tennessee Dixon
Printed and bound by McNaughton & Gunn, Inc.

Library of Congress Cataloging-in-Publication Data

Vaughan-Lee, Llewellyn.
  The face before I was born : a spiritual autobiography / by
  Llewellyn Vaughan-Lee. -- 2nd ed.
      p. cm.
  Includes bibliographical references.
  ISBN 978-1-890350-18-5 (pbk. : alk. paper)
  1. Vaughan-Lee, Llewellyn. 2. Sufis--Biography. 3. Spiritual
life. I. Title.
  BP80.V39A3 2009
  297.4092--dc22
  [B]
                                              2009011222

THE FACE BEFORE I WAS BORN

A Spiritual Autobiography

CONTENTS

He who was lost has come Home.

FOREWORD

Every journey great or small begins with the first step, says a Chinese proverb. What leads the human being to make this inner journey in order to realize the Truth? "Truth is God," said Mahatma Gandhi. Sufis conceive God as "Ultimate Reality," "in which everything is and nothing is outside it."

Each person will find his or her individual way and attract the circumstances for the inner development, which is very personal, very lonely, and absolutely unique. There will be signposts along the way, but one must be ever alert to read the directions.

In each of us there is a strange and mysterious longing, a faint echo. We hear it and hear it not, and sometimes the whole life can pass without us knowing what this call is. I asked one of my teacher's disciples to translate a Persian song, and it went like this:

> I am calling to you from afar
> Since aeons of time,
> Calling, calling, since always.
> "I can't hear"—so you say
> "Who is calling and why?"

Sometimes a very young child begins to ask questions about the meaning of life and the purpose of creation: "Who is God? How did the world come about? Why am I here?" Parents *be careful*. Don't answer these questions glibly or facetiously. It may be, just maybe, the first signpost. The first step leading us much later to the great inner journey.

Llewellyn came to our group very young. I think he was nineteen. He arrived wounded by life. His wings were clipped. Had his life much meaning? I don't think so. But he stayed and grew. He meditated. He worked upon himself. He watched, willing to surrender to his own Light. He persevered.

It is not easy to understand that the purpose of spiritual training is to help the human being to control, to diminish the ego. Our teacher, Bhai Sahib, said, "Two cannot live in one heart. Make yourself empty; when your cup is empty something else can fill it." But the taming of the ego is a painful process. It is a crucifixion. One does not lose anything. "You cannot become anything else but what you already are," said Carl Jung. We just learn to control our lower self and it becomes our servant, not our master. The master is the Real Us, our soul, and the real wisdom *is* in the soul.

Llewellyn caught the meaning, the subtle essence of the spiritual training. He understood the pressing urge, that Something within the human heart, which drives the human being mercilessly on and on, no matter the sacrifice, sometimes with superhuman effort, at least to try to reach the ultimate Goal.

May our revered Teacher's blessing be with him always, and may my love be his companion on the way.

Irina Tweedie, London, June 1989[1]

INTRODUCTION
TO FIRST EDITION

*Don't be satisfied with stories, how things
have gone with others. Unfold
your own myth, without complicated explanation,
so everyone will understand the passage,*
We have opened you.

Rûmî[1]

When I visited my teacher in the late summer of 1995, she told me that I should write and lecture more about my own personal spiritual experiences. Until then I had been reluctant to talk too much about my experiences, fearing that the ego might get hold of them. But as her teacher said to her, "Orders are orders," and this book is a direct result of her instructions.

I was sixteen when the path was awakened within me, when the long journey Home began. Over the years I have recorded a few important dreams and visions, but I have never kept a diary or journal, because I loved the invisible, hidden nature of the path. This story of my journey comes from memory, from how I see the path as it unfolded within me. But spiritual experiences carry an intensity that impacts them into consciousness, and because they do not belong to the mind or the personality, they keep their original quality. Also, many experiences need time to reveal their real significance, to bring into consciousness the depth of their meaning. Only now do I begin to appreciate many of the experiences I have been given over the years.

The spiritual path is unique for each of us; in the words of a Sufi saying, "There are as many ways to God as human beings, as many as the breaths of the children of men." This story is how the path unfolded within me, the outline of a transformation whose real nature can never be put into words. Many things have been omitted, because they have been forgotten or are too personal. Also, on the Sufi path most of the transformation happens beyond the threshold of consciousness, deep in the unconscious and on the level of the soul. But what has always remained is the intensity, wonder, and majesty of this soul's journey, of the way my heart was opened.

When I first came upon the path, all I knew was my need, a hunger that drove me. It was a long and arduous journey which strained every fiber of my being. I have tried to recapture the rawness, the intensity, the desolation, and the fragility of those early years on the path, the sense of a life that was fragmentary, without any hint of wholeness, in which I was held together only by will power and an inborn desire for truth. But it is difficult to fully recall what it was like before love was present, before His companionship replaced the deep loneliness. Now I have drunk the wine for which I longed. I have been opened to the beyond and life has begun to show its deeper purpose. For so many years there was only a dream haunting me, an inner conviction that called me.

One of the many miracles of the path is that it is always just beginning; the horizon is always beckoning. The Sufi Dhû-l-Nûn once asked a woman whom he met on the seashore, "What is the end of love?" She replied, "Love has no end, because the Beloved has no end." Yet on this endless journey there comes a time when the wayfarer has come Home, "back to the dwelling place of his desires." Through the guidance of my teacher and the grace of my Sheikh[2] I have been allowed to taste the feeling of coming Home, the knowing that I am where I belong. The spark that was planted within my heart has burnt away many of the veils between the two worlds, revealing much that was hidden. I have been taken beyond the boundaries of the known into the spinning center of my own self, and then further, into the unknown emptiness that is the real home of the mystic. My heart is filled with gratitude for all those who have gone before, and whose footsteps have guided me. For my teacher and my Sheikh there are no words to express my feelings, just an echo of an ancient song of belonging. In the circle of oneness the heart melts and everything is made empty.

Llewellyn Vaughan-Lee, 1997

INTRODUCTION
TO SECOND EDITION

Many events have taken place in the inner and outer worlds since I wrote this spiritual autobiography. Most noticeably my teacher, Irina Tweedie, passed away in August 1999, over twenty-six years since I first met her. At her funeral, at her request, I played Louis Armstrong singing "What a Wonderful World," a celebration of the world of the Beloved whose colors, tastes, fragrances, and experiences she had so loved. I also read a simple poem from Rûmî which she had meditated on for many years:

> When I am dead, look for my resting place
> Not in the earth, but in the hearts of men.

Who can say how much she changed and influenced me, laid out the stages of the journey. And yet the journey continues, and the teacher whom I knew as a white-haired old woman living in North London has remained present within the consciousness of the heart. The transition we call death has led to a deeper connection, even more alive, more potent and more loving.

Other important transitions have taken place. Her passing gave me more responsibility in the inner and outer world, as I took up the work of the tradition that she left behind, and also a deeper knowing began to emerge. I began to experience and understand more fully how the soul looks towards God, and how the real work of the path belongs to the soul, to the depths of the heart, rather than to the person whom we think we are. I also began to glimpse the larger dimension of spiritual work that belongs to our path, what is called the work of the masters, or of the *awliyâ*, the friends of God. This is the dimension of spiritual work that looks after the spiritual well-being of the world, rather than just the development of the individual wayfarer.

My own writings and teachings also went through a fundamental transition. Until the year 1999 the focus of my teachings was on the Journey Home, the traditional journey of the Sufi wayfarer. I wrote and lectured about the psychological and spiritual dynamics of this journey, paying particular attention to dreamwork, which has always been a central part of our Naqshbandi Sufi tradition. I attempted to give a contemporary understanding to this tradition and the inner processes of the path, in order to make it more accessible to people living and practicing in the West.

In the spring of 2000 all these teachings were taken away, as if my mind was a computer being reprogrammed. Instead I began to be given through meditation a series of teachings about the evolving consciousness of oneness and the part this has to play in our contemporary time of global crisis and transition. For eight years I was given a detailed impression of teachings on this subject of oneness, which I wrote and lectured about, and also made available in films on the internet (www.workingwithoneness.org). Then, last year in 2008, that too ended. The transmission of teachings on oneness was complete.

So this new edition comes at an interesting time, when once again the path within me is changing. I could continue this autobiography and try to describe the inner and outer changes over the past years, what has been revealed and what has been taken away. But I am reluctant to do so. This book, written at the request of my teacher, belongs to the years I sat with her. In the time since her passing the path as I knew it within me has dissolved completely. If I look within there is just an empty space. I feel always the presence of my Sheikh, the Sufi master Bhai Sahib who was also Irina Tweedie's teacher. I feel his grace and the grace of the tradition, the transmission of love that comes from the Source. I know that is what has supported and held me through everything that has happened since I first turned towards the Truth.

Therefore I have decided to leave this story as I told it, knowing it is only footprints in the sand leading to the shore of the ocean. At the end I have added an epilogue that points beyond the shore, and gives my present image of the path I trod. Part of the wonder of the journey is how it is always changing, and no doubt in years to come it will again appear very differently. But this is my story as I saw it then, how through the grace of my teacher and my Sheikh something came alive within me, how I came Home.

Llewellyn Vaughan-Lee, 2009

PART 1

———

He travels with whoever looks for Him,
and having taken the seeker by the hand,
He arouses him to go in search of himself.

Al-Ansârî

AWAKENING

The longest journey begins with a single step.

Lao Tsu

AWAKENING TO WILD GEESE

My journey Home began in the London underground. In the summer when I was sixteen I was traveling back from boarding school for a weekend break with an American student who was, for a short time, a boyfriend of my sister. Sitting in the half-crowded tube train, I noticed that he was reading a book on Zen Buddhism. At this time in the late sixties Zen was becoming quite popular in certain hippie circles, and intrigued, I asked to look at the book. Turning the pages, I came across a Zen saying,

> The wild geese do not intend to cast their
> reflection,
> The water has no mind to receive their
> image.

Reading this saying was like lifting a curtain. There, in the morning tube train, I felt a joy I had never before experienced, a moment of intense exhilaration. Now I know that this was the moment of the heart's turning towards God, the moment the door to the journey Home opened.

This joy stayed with me for weeks. There was a sense of laughter, a feeling of seeing the joke within creation. A world that had seemed grey sparkled with a hidden light. I laughed at everything I saw. My boarding school was beside a river, and there was a beautifully tended garden on the riverbank where one could sit, away from the sports fields and any noise. Those summer afternoons, when schoolwork was over, I would come to this garden and watch the river, full of wonder, full of delight. The flowing water, the ripples in the current, the reflections sang to me. There was no desire in me to understand the reason for this sudden change, this inner opening. In such states of grace there is no questioning; the moment is too full.

Looking back, I realize that this deep joy came from the soul, which flooded my life with its sunlight. My soul knew that the journey Home had begun, the ancient quest that one carries from lifetime to lifetime. The Sufi says that there are three journeys, the Journey from God, the Journey to God, and the Journey in God. The Journey from God is the journey of the exile in which we come into this world and forget our real nature, our real Home. I had been traveling this journey of forgetfulness for sixteen years, not even knowing that there was a journey. Born into a middle-class English family, I had gone to church every Sunday and read the Bible. I had sung hymns and recited prayers. But nowhere was there the slightest suggestion of spiritual life, of any reality beyond the world of the senses.

Suddenly this Zen saying opened a doorway which I never even knew existed, and my heart rejoiced. Many years later I discovered that this same saying about the wild geese was a favorite of the Sufi master Bhai Sahib, the being whom I came to know as my Sheikh. He would often compare his line of Sufism with Zen Buddhism, and when asked to describe the path would point to wild birds in the sky, saying, "Can you trace the path of their flight?" The saying about the wild geese led me through an ancient doorway, back onto the path to which my soul belonged. Those summer weeks were like the taste of a first love; they were unexplained magic and I looked for no reason.

I borrowed the book on Zen and discovered a simple meditation technique, to sit with closed eyes and meditate on nothing. I practiced this meditation and immediately had inner experiences. The most powerful experience was of being enormously large, spreading into infinite space, and at the same time being very small, incredibly dense, with a feeling of great power and compactness. These absolute opposites were experienced simultaneously, and although it must have lasted for just a few moments, there was no sense of time. Outside of space and time the experience was very tangible and intensely real. There was also an exhilaration, the exhilaration of going beyond the limitations of the outer world, for the first time consciously knowing an inner dimension so different from the boarding-school world around me. I remembered that I had had this same experience a number of times as a young child just before falling asleep. As a child I was terrified and told no one. Now I welcomed it, for it was a taste of an inner reality which was very potent and deeply satisfying. Years later I asked about the meaning of this experience and was told that it was an experience of the Self, "larger than large and smaller than small...boundless power, source of every power." I had brought with me into this life this stamp of the Self, this inner consciousness of transcendence, and through meditation it was being awakened. To a child this reality was frightening; there was no context for an experience of this deeper being.[1] But now it was a wonderful confirmation of what was waiting within.

In the evenings I would sit and meditate and find myself inwardly expanding beyond my physical self. Again there was no questioning of these experiences, which seemed both natural and miraculous. I just knew that I had found something very precious. Later I discovered that while the most common Zen meditation is to sit with open eyes, the meditation I had read and was practicing was very similar to the Sufi meditation that was to become my central spiritual practice. The door had opened onto the one spiritual path that was to take me Home, although it was more than three years before I made the outer connection.

EMPTY MIND

Although I had been awakened to spiritual life, I was still confronted by the difficulties of adolescence, by all the psychological and emotional turbulence of growing up. I also added to these everyday problems by giving an interview in a school magazine about Buddhism, in which I mentioned my experiences in meditation. I had to learn that it is usually wisest to keep silent about spiritual experiences. With the naivety and enthusiasm that come from having just discovered something wonderful, I wanted to share it. Of course I was ridiculed. One does not talk about spiritual truth in a high school magazine at an English boarding school! A boarding school is a small, contained environment with strict codes of what is acceptable. Only too easily does one evoke the collective shadow. I learned the painful lesson of silence, and for a number of reasons was very glad when, a year later, I was seventeen and high school was finished. I then had the opportunity to travel for a year before starting college. But before I left I went to a talk given by the Zen teacher Paul Reps, whose books *Zen Telegrams* and *Square Sun Square Moon*, full of koan-like images, I had found deeply inspiring. They pointed beyond the logic of the mind into the silence and humor of life's deeper mysteries, as in Reps's simple sketch of a cucumber with the caption: "cucumber unaccountably cucumbering." Paul Reps was the first "enlightened" person I had ever encountered and he had a profound effect. He began his talk back to front by first asking if there were any questions. I asked a question, but as I was speaking I suddenly experienced the space from which the question came. I called this space the "not answer" to the question, because it was beyond the opposites of question and answer. His presence had thrown me beyond the mind and its normal thinking patterns. Like the wild geese reflected in the water, I experienced an emptiness of intention that was both exhilarating and refreshing.

Zen was opening me to an inner world beyond any preconceptions. My travels also took me to a world beyond anything I could have imagined. My father had arranged a job for me on a coconut plantation in New Guinea. Seventeen and just out of boarding school, I arrived at a small tropical island to take up a job helping to oversee a work force of two hundred New Guinea Highlanders, who are some of the most primitive people in the world. Their grandparents had been headhunters, and they still carried the wildness of the warrior spirit. Furthermore, the men in their culture had no work ethic, as in the villages the women did all the work; but they had agreed to a two-year work contract on the plantation partly induced by the free airplane ride the company provided to bring the workers in! This was at the very end of Australian colonial rule and there were two Australians overseeing the work on the plantation—my boss who very rarely spoke to me, and an ex-army sergeant just back from Vietnam.

I spent the days walking or riding over the island inspecting the work. The environment was both primitive and breathtakingly beautiful, with a myriad of butterflies and wild parrots screeching in the trees. For the first time in my life there was little mental input. Without television, books, or conversation, my mind became increasingly empty. For the first weeks my mind would occupy itself with past incidents or relationships, but as the days passed these thoughts lost their intensity and interest. Significantly, my present environment was so different from my previous life that there was little external context for these thought patterns. This was poignantly illustrated one mid-January afternoon when I rode my horse down to the jetty to meet the little boat from the mainland that brought the mail. I found that I had a letter, posted two months earlier, which was an invitation to a Christmas ball in London. The idea of a formal dance in London belonged to a very different world from the one where I now stood, looking out over the deep blue tropical waters, seeing the rainbow-colored fish flash beneath the surface. Lacking any meaningful context to support them, the thoughts which related to my other life drifted away, and during those days I experienced the deep peace of an empty mind. Seeing a storm coming, watching it bend the palm trees, I was able to experience the storm without any thoughts intruding on its power and beauty.

The days passed and the emptiness deepened. During this time I wrote many haiku-like poems, for they reflected an experience of life that just *is*. The moon on the water, a spider's thread shining in the sun, a coconut lying on the beach, these images caught a quality of life without psychological or mental distortion. The dragonflies in the sunlight are just dragonflies. This is a mystery in which nothing is hidden.

I had stopped meditating regularly since leaving England, travel and then my work schedule of rising well before dawn having thrown off any imposed discipline. But I was discovering a different way of being. Externally I was a seventeen-year-old trying to adjust to a life harsh and beautiful, relating to my one colleague whose only enjoyment seemed to be getting drunk, and to the New Guinea Highlanders, whose tribal life was more innocent and brutal than anything I had ever encountered—there were different tribes working together and their old tribal histories could easily spill into violence, spear fights at night. I learned to speak pidgin English, the collective language, and to perform basic first aid. I also discovered a quality of aloneness and inner stillness that had been unobtainable in ten years of boarding school and family life. When the external patterns of life are lifted so abruptly, a deeper quality of being is allowed to emerge. Possibly this stillness and aloneness had always been there, only covered by the confusion and clamor of my external life, people, family, school.

I also found my values of life and death changing. After two or three months on this island I realized that my own life was of relatively little significance— whether I lived or died seemed to matter far less than it did when I was living in Europe. Possibly I was influenced by the tribal people with whom I was working. In the tropics life expectancy is far shorter than in the West. Men and women are old by their mid-thirties. A cut easily becomes infected; without medicine disease can kill quickly. Also, in a tribal culture the individual is of less importance than the tribe. For example, these Highlanders had little understanding of personal possessions; everything belonged to the tribe. (Sadly, under the influence of Western values, one of the first things these Highlanders bought with their wages was a box with a lock.) For myself it was very freeing to feel the importance of personal life slipping away, together with the need to achieve or be valued. A deeper sense of life that underlies the individual was there instead, life that is always present. The coconut lying on the beach does not need us to notice it; the spider is always spinning its web.

MACROBIOTICS, YOGA, AND *KUNDALINI*

After a few months on this island I left to travel in the Far East. I had been given a taste of a quality of life that belongs to the moment, far distant from our goal-oriented, time-possessed culture. Nature had evoked an inner stillness and detachment that I carried with me as I wandered through the villages, towns, and temples of the East. I had been intending to find my way along the hippie trail to India, but never got that far. After spending some time in Chiang Mai in northern Thailand, where there seemed to be more Buddhist temples than houses—the washing lines were full of orange robes drying in the sun—I decided it was time to return to Europe.

On the way home I stayed with some friends in Switzerland who introduced me to macrobiotics, a

Japanese-based diet that balances food according to its yin or yang nature. A diet that focused on grains and had a simple Zen-like quality was very appealing to me, providing an external form to contain the inner simplicity I had found in the Far East. I did not want to lose this simple sense of essence amid the myriad impressions of the Western world I was now reentering.

I experienced a month-long "high" when I started this diet. At the time I did not realize that it was a result of a physical detoxification and purification. Growing up before nutrition or health foods became a part of the collective consciousness, I had all my life eaten without thinking about the nature or quality of the food. "Meat and two vegetables" was the criterion for a basic meal, and at school the vegetables were usually boiled until all the goodness had been removed. Suddenly my body was being fed whole grains and organic vegetables, and it rejoiced. Unfortunately I mistook this physical high for the spiritual effect of this diet, and thought that it would continue indefinitely!

Practiced with balance and understanding, macrobiotics can be a healthy diet. I only had youthful enthusiasm and an intensity to live the spiritual life that was surfacing within me. The initial high did not continue, but I was caught in the conviction that brown rice, carrots (carrots are very yang), and unleavened bread would help me to realize something. I practiced chopping vegetables and making whole-wheat pastry with the intensity of a devotee. At the same time I discovered Hatha Yoga, which was just becoming popular. Again the initial experience of Hatha Yoga was intoxicating as energies started to flow through my body. In particular I loved the relaxation meditation after an hour of *asanas*, as I felt my consciousness expand beyond my physical body. For over a year I practiced yoga for half an hour every morning and attended classes every week, often jealous of the young girls who could easily move their bodies into any position as I strained my muscles and joints.

Yoga advocates fasting, which also can produce a natural high. Beginning the day with just an orange, rather than cereal, toast, and eggs, can be an intoxicating change! I enjoyed walking with a clear head and my feet hardly touching the ground, so different from the heaviness of my boarding-school years. However, fasting, eating a macrobiotic diet, practicing yoga, I was putting pressure on my physical body with my soul's desire for Truth. My body could not take the intensity of the inner drive that had now become ignited. After the initial high from the macrobiotic diet and fasting had passed, I began to get thinner and thinner. I did not realize that basic minerals, vitamins, and reserves of fat were being used up and not replenished. I found I had less and less physical energy. My knee became damaged after practicing the full-lotus position for too long. But I did not stop, because I had nowhere else to put this unknown spiritual drive.

Today, if you walk into any bookshop you will find a confusing multitude of books about different spiritual paths and techniques. In the early seventies in England there were relatively few books on yoga and Buddhism that outlined a spiritual path. I had read *The Secret of the Golden Flower*, a Taoist classic that describes the creation of the spirit-body and the circulation of the inner light. This book was wonderfully inspiring but it did not offer practical guidance for the path. Yoga and macrobiotics were tangible. They had produced results for me, a natural high and a sense of purification.

Unfortunately my body was not up to the physical pressure. The lines of the song "You can't get to heaven in a rocking chair, 'cause a rocking chair don't rock that far" can equally be applied to the physical body's inability to take us to God. But I was unaware of this simple wisdom, and was straining my body to produce spiritual results. Knowing nothing of the real process of inner purification, the work of "polishing the mirror of the heart," I was stumbling along, trying to purify and enlighten my soul through brown rice and fasting.

Without a teacher or guide, or the help of common sense, I was a serious student making myself ill from the lack of ordinary nourishment. But not only was my body getting weaker, Hatha Yoga had inadvertently awakened my *kundalini*.[2] This powerful inner energy, which should only be awakened under the guidance of a spiritual master,[3] was to cause me problems for a number of years. I have met other people without a teacher whose *kundalini* has been unexpectedly awakened by chanting or other spiritual practices. It can result in cosmic experiences and psychological breakdown. In my case it was not so extreme. At first I was just aware of an increased energy within me that could be felt as a warmth along the spine. I knew that it was not just physical, because when my body was tired I would also be full of energy.

After doing yoga *asanas* and then lying down, I could feel the energy flow through my body. But this energy buildup could also make me very nervous, and combined with an unbalanced diet, it affected my stomach. Later I was to learn the simple techniques, like wearing leather-soled shoes (as rubber insulates one from the earth) and taking physical exercise, that can help with the *kundalini*. I learned that any form of yoga or breathing exercise increased the *kundalini* and the discomfort.

I spoke to my yoga teacher about this awakening energy, but she had no experience or understanding of *kundalini*, and so I was left alone with the problem. I continued with Hatha Yoga though it would have been far better to have stopped. The *kundalini*, my diet, and various psychological problems began to stretch me tauter and tauter. I was putting pressure on my physical body with an intense inner drive that finally resulted in a neurosis about food and continual stomach problems that were both physical and psychological. But this drive to *find something*, to *reach somewhere*, could not be diluted, could not be put aside. Somewhere I knew that whatever it cost, whatever it took, I had to seek. The difficulty was that I had not yet found the right container. I had not yet made physical contact with my spiritual tradition.

KRISHNAMURTI

I had been introduced to Hatha Yoga by the elder sister of a schoolfriend whom I had visited soon after I returned from the East. My friend lived in a cottage on the Welsh coast where I unexpectedly found a library of mysticism, Chinese philosophy, and yoga books that his sister had collected. Here I discovered *The Secret of the Golden Flower*, *The Tibetan Book of the Dead*, and other classics that pointed to a reality beyond the physical. I would sit on the grass in their little Welsh garden, transported into the mysteries of Taoism, and then walk along the paths overlooking the sea, my whole being held in the wonder of this other world. I was enthralled by this library and by my friend's sister who had collected it. When I met Sarah we became friends and would discuss Taoism and other esoteric subjects for hours. My study of Zen had been very solitary, but now I had met someone with whom I could share this awakened mystery. For the first time in my life I enjoyed spiritual companionship.

Along with Hatha Yoga and Taoism, Sarah introduced me to Krishnamurti's writing. Krishnamurti's sense of a pathless path beyond the struggles of the mind had a Zen-like quality that was very appealing. Each summer Krishnamurti would visit England to lecture at his school, and that summer I attended his lectures. Many people camped in the school grounds for the weekend. Not having a tent, I made myself a shelter from hay bales in a nearby field. I remember waking up in the early morning with the mist still over the fields, seeing a red postal van driving down a nearby country lane. For many years, especially when life was very intense, I would imagine being a country postman, delivering mail to the farms and hamlets. This seemed an ideal, simple way to be.

I don't remember Krishnamurti's lectures that day, only the white tent and how his presence drew me into a different dimension. For that morning I experienced the freedom of the space from which he was speaking, a space beyond the mind, beyond any seeking. Just as Paul Reps had thrown me beyond the duality of question and answer, Krishnamurti's presence took me into a place of pure being.

Krishnamurti's message, as I understood it then, was that although there was no path and no teacher that could help the seeker realize his or her own freedom, realization could happen. He seemed to say that it was necessary to go beyond ideas and concepts, to go beyond all "doing." Having briefly experienced this inner freedom in his presence, I wanted to return to it, but because, according to him, there was "no way," I felt stranded. But when, during the following spring, I had the opportunity to be alone for two weeks in my father's house in the countryside, I decided to try to follow his "teaching" of non-doing. Apart from cooking and walking, I would do nothing but sit for hours, letting the mind get empty. Sometimes I would just stare at a wall, watching my thoughts, not realizing that I was practicing a Buddhist meditation! It was a very intense two weeks during which I became more and more sensitive, more and more acutely observant.

I would walk in the early morning along the river-bank watching the birds and waterfowl. I would study insects and the buds breaking on the trees. I sensed something but did not know what it was. There was a feeling of presence to which I was being awakened, a sense of something beyond the outer activities of life. A oneness and harmony in nature were there at the borders of consciousness, but as yet I did not have the inner container to fully appreciate such an experience.

This acute sensitivity became painful to bear. When people came to visit I could not cope with their presence, and would even lock myself in the bathroom in order to sit on the floor undisturbed. I still did not have the right vehicle for the intensity of my inner drive, and when I saw Krishnamurti the next summer I felt nothing. His presence had opened me, his writings inspired me, but I needed a deeper connection.

SACRED GEOMETRY AND CHARTRES CATHEDRAL

Studying Zen, meditating, practicing yoga, reading the few books that were then available, I felt that there were spiritual truths and something called "enlightenment," but I had no knowledge of any esoteric or mystical paths to lead the seeker to this different reality. In the early seventies most esoteric groups were still very secretive. Apart from the Buddhist society, or the Maharishi's Transcendental Meditation, neither of which appealed to me, no spiritual paths appeared open. I had met a few people who had been to Japan to spend time in a Zen monastery, but I had become an architectural student and although I was very attracted to Zen, I had no feeling to go to Japan.

However, spiritual destiny follows its own unexpected way, and I discovered that at my architectural college there was a course on sacred geometry. The course was taught by Keith Critchlow, who was later to become well known for his work on this subject. Keith Critchlow taught us about the geometric patterns in nature and how these are reflected in the geometry of sacred buildings. We studied mandalas and the rose windows of Gothic cathedrals. During my second year he became course-tutor to a small group of students, and we were able to study this sacred science in more depth. We discovered the geometric designs of St. Paul's Cathedral and how simple, one-room Welsh cottages have mandalas in the patterns of their flint floors. We studied Stonehenge and the domes of mosques, deciphering their beautiful geometry. I became excited and fascinated seeing this sacred science open in front of me, sensing the esoteric knowledge that had formed the basis of so many civilizations. We felt the poverty of our own age that no longer lived according to these ancient principles, and with the idealism of the early seventies felt we could restore these principles to daily life, reintroduce the sacred wisdom of the ancients.

Keith Critchlow was very inspiring, and there was always the feeling of mysteries being uncovered, secrets being revealed. We were students at the dawn of a new era, using the tools of the ancients. My own hunger for truth was briefly nourished by the wonder that I felt opening around. I read all the esoteric books I could find, about Tibet and the Holy Grail, about Egypt and the pyramids, about the inner laws of the universe. Without much discrimination I filled my mind and my life with whatever was available, whatever books I could afford to buy or was able to borrow. My studies were a way of seeing what was hidden in the outer world. The sacred geometry pointed to an inner meaning of life so different from the material values of my childhood and conditioning.

My girlfriend, Beba, who was an artist, used to laugh at my need to find wisdom in books. When I would excitedly tell her of some spiritual idea I had just discovered, like the chakras, or the "subtle body," she would respond with, "You don't have to read books to know that." With the innate wisdom of the feminine she intuitively knew many of the ideas I was just discovering. There is a Sufi saying, "Why listen to secondhand reports when you can hear the Beloved speak Himself?" But at this time all I knew were secondhand reports, the knowledge I was finding in books. I did not have my girlfriend's feminine understanding. Furthermore, nobody suggested that one could have a direct relationship with the invisible source whose beauty and harmony were reflected in the geometric designs, echoed in this "esoteric knowledge."

My studies were all I had, and they were filling my mind with ideas and concepts, fascinating and intoxicating. But the study of sacred geometry also gave me something that went deeper than the mind, for its patterns reflect the inner structure of life and the universe. At the beginning of these studies I also had an experience that unexpectedly helped me. In the late spring of my first year of architectural studies I was part of a group of students who went to Chartres Cathedral to work with an architect who was writing a book about its geometry. For two weeks we were allowed full run of the cathedral. We were a mixed group of students, some interested in the cathedral from an historical point of view, a few fascinated by its sacred geometry. At the end of the two weeks we had all been deeply touched, each in our own way.

The trip to Chartres came immediately after my two-week retreat of not-doing. I was in a heightened state of sensitivity when I arrived. I was also cold. That spring in England had been especially warm, with sun-filled days. Without thinking I assumed that the warm weather would continue in France, and so took only a few thin clothes. The town and cathedral of Chartres are on the top of a hill surrounded by a large plain of wheat fields. It seemed that a cold wind was always blowing across these fields. We stayed in an unheated stone building, an old nunnery next to the cathedral. We spent all day in the stone cathedral and never seemed to get warm. My macrobiotic diet had also removed what little fat I had had on my body. For two weeks I was both cold and overwhelmed.

Most people visit Chartres for a few hours. They are struck by its beauty, its perfect stained-glass windows, its sculptures which are some of the finest medieval art. They sense the holiness of this ancient pre-Christian site which belonged to the Earth Mother, the Black Virgin, before it was dedicated to the Virgin Mary. But to spend two weeks inside this sacred space is a very different experience. Chartres was the "blueprint cathedral" for the Gothic movement, and is an almost perfect geometric and harmonic creation. (There was an esoteric school at Chartres, which was one of the spiritual centers of medieval Europe and taught sacred geometry as well as sacred music.) Chartres Cathedral is an instrument designed to attune the worshiper to the spiritual energies that flow through the earth. The medieval masters had created a space of inner harmony to help the worshiper contact the soul.

Chartres is also like the Great Mother, always present, watching over her children. One early morning I was sitting in the nave and saw a schoolboy enter from the south door and walk through to the north door. I realized that this was his shortcut to school. I felt the cathedral accept him as fully as the most ardent worshiper. To each of us students she gave a sense of the sacred, communicating it to us each in our own way. The experience she gave me was that of *knowing* that the esoteric mysteries I had been reading and studying were really true. After those two weeks I *knew* that they were not just ideas in a book, but a living reality. The cathedral gave me this sense of *knowing*, a deep affirmation that my inner convictions were true. I returned home with a "yes" singing within me.

On a physical level my task for those two weeks was to accurately measure the maze, a circular mandala-pattern, forty feet in diameter, depicted in blue and white stones near the west door. Working with a fellow student I was able to move the chairs and spend hours following this ancient circuitous pattern that images the journey of the soul, the path to the center of the psyche.[4] Medieval pilgrims would kneel their way round the maze until they reached the center where they would turn and look up at the magnificent west rose window, whose twelve-fold mandala form images the Self with luminous beauty.

At this time I knew nothing of psychology, nothing of the inner states and fluctuations of the path. Later, over the years, I was to walk this inner path of the soul that would take me deep into the unconscious. The path would turn me this way and that, continually changing, continually unexpected, but even in the most confusing and difficult times always leading to the center. In earlier centuries there had been a picture of the Minotaur at the center of the Chartres maze,[5] and this primal beast, the dark shadow, I would also encounter, before finally turning to behold the endless wonder and light of the real Self.

INTRODUCTION TO SUFISM

During my second and what was to be my last year of architectural studies I was an avid student of sacred geometry. The one building I designed was a Japanese teahouse built according to sacred Japanese principles. I also became fascinated by Islamic patterns, the flowing, interweaving geometric shapes that cover the walls of mosques. Because figurative representation is not allowed in Islam, some of their finest artists and minds had put their understanding of man and his place in the universe into these star-bursts and continually flowing mandalas.

I did not want to understand these patterns intellectually. I wanted to draw them, and would spend hours at my drawing board tracing patterns from books, completing patterns that were only half-imaged. I now realize that this was like a meditation practice. My psychological life during this time was under intense pressure, and these patterns were able to contain and transcend my difficulties. They gave me peace, a focus, and a tranquility which I badly needed. I had no psychological tools or container to deal with my personal difficulties, with powerful shadow dynamics that were surfacing within me, anger and resentment that were breaking through my English reserve. Drawing these patterns hour after hour was intoxicating and reassuring. The Islamic geometric forms described an order that I knew was somewhere, but was very much lacking in my own personal life.

At this time I was living with my girlfriend, Beba, in my mother's house, in an atmosphere swirling with psychic difficulties of which I was only partly aware. When I first started architectural school I had shared a flat with an acquaintance, but he didn't like my obsessive macrobiotic cooking, and so I had returned home, where Beba joined me. There I discovered what had been hidden from me for the many years of my boarding-school life, the degree of my mother's drinking and depression. I had sensed a chaos beneath the surface when I was fourteen and my parents separated one dramatic night with my mother trying to kill herself. My father could no longer cope. Somehow my mother's emotional burden landed on my shoulders, and I went from child to parent that one weekend.

After the separation she would come to school each Sunday afternoon, and we would walk in a nearby park as she would tell me her problems. But then, with an adolescent's survival instinct, I was able to compartmentalize this chaos—I focused instead on the freedom and rebellion offered by the hippie movement, and remained unaware of the real nature of my family shadow.

Now, as spiritual life was opening me, awakening a deeper sensitivity, I was being confronted by the intensity of my mother's problems and the family shadow dynamics in which her depression played a central role. Every family has its psychological patterns of repression and denial. The moment we step beneath the surface, beneath the socially accepted norms, we enter the dark craziness of what has been repressed. The demons of this inner world are real and terrible, the more powerful because they have been unacknowledged. Without any outer support, without any knowledge of psychology, I was engulfed by both my mother's pain and an underworld of chaos very different from the polite exterior my family presented to itself and the world.

The veneer of middle-class conditioning that had given me some semblance of normality was beginning to break under the pressure of these unconscious forces. At the same time the atmosphere in the house surrounding my mother's alcohol and depression became almost unbearable. But when Beba and I decided to leave, my mother pleaded with us to stay, to help her stop drinking. Foolishly we agreed, and over the next few months I had to realize the painful lesson that trying to help someone else with her problems is a recipe for disaster. Later I would learn how to resist the unconscious vortex that can pull one into another's problems. But at that time I just felt trapped in the unspoken tensions and the web of her depression.

I could not confront the situation, because talking to my mother just drew me further into her psychological confusion and endless pain. And so we lived like shadows, Beba and I not speaking to my mother, avoiding her. These tensions, combined with my anger and desperation, built up to such a degree that when my mother went away for her summer holiday we left the house and I didn't talk to her for over a year.

During these months my nerves were being strung out by my macrobiotic diet and the psychic tensions swirling around me. I felt the insidious and destabilizing nature of all of this darkness, difficulty, and denial, and yet lacked the ability to express or contain it. Trying to hold my own struggling sense of identity in this treacherous, twisted chaos was almost beyond me. My newly awakened spiritual self was being bombarded by the psychic darkness emanating from my mother's pain and my family's denial.

Looking back, I also wonder whether one of my deepest problems was that I had been born into an environment in which spiritual reality was nonexistent. My father was a sincere, practicing Christian, and I was brought up regularly attending church and reading the Bible, but in my childhood there was not even the concept of different levels of consciousness, of any existence apart from the physical world. What was most fundamental to me, what was the core of my meaning in life, received no echo from the world around as I grew up. I have met many others who have had a similar experience. Some people as children have had a deep connection with God, but because there was no echo, they buried this spiritual connection until later in life when it could safely surface. The price they paid was to live during the intermediate years without any conscious connection to the one thing that could give their life real meaning. Often they would try to fit into a world in which they felt a stranger, sometimes wounding themselves in the process. The story of the ugly duckling always resonated deeply with me, because it tells this tale of how the bird painfully and unsuccessfully tries to be a "duckling," only to finally discover that he is a beautiful swan.

I do not remember as a child having any spiritual connection, except the frightening experiences of the Self I have already mentioned. Maybe I knew that I would have to wait sixteen years before my spiritual self could come alive. I was long overdue as a baby, reluctant to arrive in this world! But I have since recognized that I carried a resentment against an ordinary world that does not support spiritual life. As soon as I felt the freedom of the inner world, the vistas opened by meditation and the spiritual path, an anger came up in me that tried to break the cage of my conditioning. You only know that you are imprisoned, when the window opens and you can see the landscape and the sunshine. Only then do you try to escape.

Much of my path has been coming to terms with the value and importance of everyday life, accepting the limitations of this world. But during those early years of seeking I felt suffocated and tightly strung. I sensed a spiritual life for which I longed and which I had been denied. As I awoke to these feelings, I also became aware of the darkness that surrounded my mother's drinking, and sensed my family's shadow dynamics and patterns of repression. I was torn between my love and compassion for her and the anger I felt at seeing the truth, at being burdened with an awareness I could hardly bear. I felt more and more a stranger, isolated and under pressure from conflicts whose origins were more complex and deeper than I could have realized. Drawing Islamic patterns was a temporary relief, and it also turned my attention towards Sufism.

I went to a few Sufi gatherings. College friends of mine were involved with a Sufi group based upon the teachings of Ibn 'Arabî. There was beautiful music and chanting of the *dhikr*, but for me there was no inner resonance. I began to consciously look for a meditation practice as my previous Zen meditation was no longer effective. A need to find a real spiritual teacher and a living tradition began to push itself into consciousness. For the first time in my life I began to actively look around, but found nothing. Then, one cold February, Keith Critchlow gave a weekend course on Plato in a country house in the west of England. I hitchhiked down in the rain and dried out in front of an open fire in the living room. As I was sitting in front of the fire with a few fellow students, a young man and woman entered the room. My attention was drawn to them and suddenly I felt the *kundalini* explode in fire all over my back. I did not know it then, but I had found the path that was to take me Home.

MEETING THE TEACHER

Coming home...my heart was singing.... I felt light, free and happy, as one would feel when coming home after a long absence.

Irina Tweedie,
arriving at her teacher's house for the first time.[1]

LESS THAN THE DUST AT THE FEET OF THE TEACHER

A few weeks after this encounter by the fireside, my new friends, as they had become, invited me to a spiritual talk on mathematics. Listening to the talk, I noticed an old woman with white hair tied in a bun sitting directly in front of me. After the talk my friends introduced me to her in the aisle. She gave me one look from piercing blue eyes. In that instant I had the physical experience of becoming just a speck of dust on the ground. Then she turned and walked away and I was left, empty and bewildered.

I was nineteen and very arrogant, proud of my spiritual learning. I had read books and practiced yoga. In one instant all this identity crashed to the floor. I was nothing. I was nowhere. In that moment my whole self was crushed; all feelings of self-value disappeared. I was just left stunned, overwhelmed not by love or devotion, but by the power of annihilation, the destruction of the ego.

There is a Sufi saying that the disciple has to become "less than the dust at the feet of the teacher." We have to be ground down until there is nothing left, just a speck of dust to be blown hither and thither by the wind of the spirit. Only when we have lost our sense of self, the values of the ego, can we carry His sweet fragrance, as in the words of a Persian song:

> Why are you so fragrant, oh dust?
> I am a dust people tread upon,
> But I partake of the fragrance of the
>   courtyard of a Saint.
> It is not me, I am just an ordinary dust.[2]

At the time I had no understanding of this experience. I had no framework within which to assimilate it. It just happened, and I mentioned it to no one. Years later I realized that it was a foretaste of the path. When we meet the teacher, when we first tread upon the path, we are given a glimpse of where this will take us. In visions, dreams, or inner experiences, the wayfarer is shown what this journey will mean, for there is a saying that "the end is present at the beginning." The Sufi path is a closed circle of love and everything is present in the first moment.

Often wayfarers are given glimpses of bliss or unconditional love. I was thrown into *fanâ*, the state of annihilation. I was shown how I would lose everything, all sense of myself. This was not so much a warning as a statement. There was no sense of free will or of deciding anything. I did not even consciously know that this was to be my spiritual future. I had looked into the eyes of a white-haired old woman whom I had never seen before, and become a piece of dust on the floor. I did not either understand or question the experience. One does not question sun-light or the wind.

A SENSE OF BELONGING

When I was introduced to Irina Tweedie in that lecture hall I did not know that she was a Sufi teacher. I only knew that she was connected to the friends I had met at the weekend course on Plato a few weeks earlier. The explosion of my *kundalini* had attracted my attention to the young couple who were artists, and I had spent the weekend walking the wet fields and lanes of the countryside with them. The lectures suddenly held little interest for me. My attention had been turned elsewhere, away from the mind towards a different world.

I met up with these friends again in London, at cafés for lunch or tea. They seemed to belong to a small group that shared a common interest, but this interest was only hinted at, never spoken of directly. I just inferred that there was a deeper connection than that of art-school friends. At that time Irina Tweedie's Sufi group was secret and never spoken about in public. One had to be invited to the group, and Mrs. Tweedie (as she liked to be called[3]) had to ask her teacher in meditation if the new person could come. When I had met these friends she was actually away in the Philip-pines, where she was having psychic surgery to heal a heart valve, but no one knew where she had gone. She had just "disappeared" and her group meetings were closed until further notice. But on her return the meetings reconvened, and one of the friends, feeling the intensity of my spiritual quest, asked if I might come.

29

After meeting with Mrs. Tweedie at the lecture hall, I was invited to the meditation group. So one Tuesday late-afternoon I arrived at a north-London house with Beba. Beba had also been at the lecture on mathematics and thought that we were going to visit the old lady we had met there for tea. I didn't know what to think. I had never been to a meditation group. I had absolutely no preconceptions and so had said nothing to Beba. We had not discussed it. Looking back I realize that it is significant that I did not talk or even think about how the group might be, in the same way that my initial meeting with Mrs. Tweedie had left no mental residue—only years later did I think about the experience of being made to feel like a speck of dust. At the time the experience did not evoke any thoughts, nor did the invitation to the group. There was nothing to say or think except that we were going to visit the old lady. Meeting the teacher, meeting the path, did not belong to my mind.

Mrs. Tweedie lived in a studio flat, what the English call a "bed-sit." It was a small, second-floor room, looking out over the street, containing a bed, chest of drawers, wardrobe, table, chair, sink, cooker, and small refrigerator. On the other side of the street was an above ground tube- and train-track, and every five minutes or so the room would shake with the noise of a train passing. The twelve or more people attending the group sat on the bed, against the bed, against the chest of drawers, wherever there was space. Mrs. Tweedie sat beside the sink, and after the meditation, served us all with tea and biscuits. What I remember from that first meeting was a feeling of "coming home," of for the first time in my life being where I belonged. I also remember being offered a selection of chocolate biscuits, and being told "Sugar is good for you." I had long identified spirituality with healthy eating, and the worst sin was pure sugar. That first afternoon, what had become one of my central preconceptions about spiritual life was thrown aside by the offer of a biscuit. Later Mrs. Tweedie elaborated on this, quoting a saying of her teacher, Bhai Sahib: "You cannot reach God through your stomach."

This small room beside the train tracks contained a power and energy I had never before experienced. It was alive with the intensity of a different dimension. Leaving our shoes in the corridor, we would enter the intense aura of meditation and dynamic love. Here was a presence that spoke directly of the mysteries I had heard hinted at in the books I had read, a fragrance of an inner reality beyond the mind and the senses. And I belonged here, in this inner space enclosed by the small room and the noise of the trains.

The sense of belonging was tangibly real. It was so definite and distinct that the mind was not allowed to argue. I was a drowning man who had just discovered that there was ground under his feet, and I could now stand with my chin above the water. This was the first real ground that I had ever felt—not the shifting sands of the world of appearances, but something ancient and present. Again what was significant was that this experience was so direct it bypassed the mind and any judgment. After the first meeting I did not consider whether I would come back. I did not think about the experience at all. I just came to the next meeting, and the next.... If you are where you really belong there is no before and no after, no sense of arrival and no possibility of departure.

This little room in north London became my real home, psychologically and spiritually. The members of the group became my family, an inner family of friends with whom I shared the deepest bond of belonging and a commitment to find the Truth. For the first time in my life there was an echo of my real being. What was most important to me, what had been hidden in the very depths of my being, resonated in the room around me. A teacher, friendship, and the power of the path—I had found the container to take me Home.

THE AUTHORITY OF THE TEACHER

Twice a week I would go to the meetings, twice a week feel this presence, this energy, this belonging. The meetings became the focal point of my life. I lived from meeting to meeting. When I could I would spend time in between with friends from the group, people with whom I could share this hidden secret, this obsession. We were of a similar age, interested in art, music, and the heart's call to God. We would meet, talk, drink tea, listen to music, and meditate. I liked the silence of meditation and the shared, unspoken understanding.

I don't remember any "teachings" at the meetings. I remember sitting in a chair just in front of where Mrs. Tweedie sat on the floor, and how, when she stood up, she would tousle my hair with her hand and how I didn't like it. I remember intense physical discomfort when we meditated and the energy started to flow through my body. My body had become very nervous from too much yoga, fasting, and the pressure of psychological problems. Meditation did not help. The energy was intense, the longing desperate, and the body just seemed a hindrance, an obstacle.

One of the effects of *kundalini* is to make you want to urinate. The moment we began the meditation, the *kundalini* would be activated and I would want to go to the bathroom. Even if I went to the bathroom just before the meditation the effect would be the same. Should I remain for the whole meditation trying to hold myself, or should I disturb everyone in that small, crowded room by getting up? I felt trapped and embarrassed, and would often sit in torment for the whole meditation, surrounded by people with heads bowed in deep silence. I longed to be normal, to just sit in silence and peace. I had looked forward to the meeting, but only suffered.

I think that the group was very tolerant. I had arrived with a large burden of problems weighing me down, and an intensity that was not easy to bear even for myself. It was a small group meeting in a small space, but I never received any criticism, only love. Mrs. Tweedie would say that one of the special qualities of a Sufi group is that we are allowed to be ourselves, "warts and all," and in that space I was accepted for myself without conditions. At the time I was aware only of my own needs and my own insecurities, but the group responded to these needs and gave me the support of real acceptance.

Mrs. Tweedie would talk about her Sufi teacher, Bhai Sahib, her time with him in India. Her book, describing her training with him, was not to be published for a few years, but her time in his presence and her continued inner relationship with him permeated the meetings. Although he was no longer physically alive, she had a direct, inner connection with him and could contact him in meditation. At times she would give people messages that she had received from him. She always insisted that she was not a teacher, only a disciple, just his representative here in the West. She was full of fire, passion, and love in its two sides, tenderness and the cold knife of love that cuts away illusions. But in those early meetings I most remember her being someone who lived what I dreamed of. She lived in the inner reality for which I longed. Until I met her I never knew that it was possible. I had read books about masters in the Himalayas, but here was a white-haired Russian woman, who lived beside the train-tracks in north London, and whose eyes were not of this world.

She would not allow any form of personality worship, any form of personal relationship. She always stressed that the teacher is "without a face and without a name," and only the teaching mattered. But it was her presence that inspired us. Whether we were meditating together or having tea and biscuits, she held the same inner affirmation. She knew that the world was an illusion because she experienced the beyond. She experienced the invisible, inner reality that beckoned to us, for which we hungered. *I knew that she knew.* This knowledge had nothing to do with words, spoken or unspoken. Her knowing was stamped in the very core of her being and radiated from every cell. This was the power of her presence and the reason for her authority.

At school I had been a rebel, resenting any imposed authority. Now for the first time in my life I was in the presence of an authority before which there was no question. This was not an authority asserted with rules. Before this authority I unconditionally surrendered, even though the unconditional nature and the degree of this surrender terrified me. Again there was no questioning process; no thinking pattern intruded into this relationship. She is the one person whom I would obey *whatever* she told me. There are no conditions. The absolute nature of this relationship is its greatest security, because it does not involve duality, the dialogue of you and me. It just is. Later I understood that it is a relationship of the soul that is brought from lifetime to lifetime. Belonging neither to time nor to space, it gave my mind no access to question, belief, or disbelief. The relationship and its stamp of surrender belong to an inner commitment to the path.

This commitment comes into consciousness as the knowledge that this is the path that can take one Home. The desire to make this journey is so strong that it overrules any desire to question the authority of the teacher or the teacher's representative. But there is a deeper relationship in which the disciple knows that the authority of the teacher is *one with the path*. On the Sufi path the relationship with the teacher carries the imprint of the inner connection with the path. Mrs. Tweedie would say to us, "Don't trust me here, don't trust the old lady you see sitting in front of you. Trust the part of me that is somewhere else." She meant, "Don't trust my personality with all of its faults. Trust my soul which is merged with the soul of my teacher." The authority of the teacher belongs to this inner relationship, a link of love that runs from teacher to disciple. This link of love is the essence of the path.

The authority of the teacher carries the security born of this link of love, this connection of the soul. But it also carries a quality of fear that is unlike anything else I have experienced. When Mrs. Tweedie was with her teacher she experienced this same fear, for she knew that he would do *anything* for the sake of truth, even kill her.[4] I also knew that she embodied the same ultimate commitment to the path, and to the inner desire of the disciple for Truth. In the Sufi tradition the sheikh is sometimes referred to as "the executioner," and Mrs. Tweedie would refer to Bhai Sahib as her "beloved executioner." The teacher has to take the seeker beyond the ego, help him to "die before death," and the ego knows this. The ego instinctively recoils in fear before the presence of the sheikh. For many years each time I came to my teacher's door I would feel this fear, a sense of trepidation and nervousness. There appeared little external reason for this fear, as most of the time I was treated with great kindness. But inwardly I knew that the sword of love was always present, the power that could cut through all my defenses, my patterns of attachments and desires.

There has been much questioning and misunderstanding about the authority of the teacher and the disciple's need to surrender. In the presence of real spiritual authority, this question did not enter my consciousness. I knew that the personality was not involved, and that there was no personal power dynamic. Real spiritual authority carries the stamp of freedom rather than the subtle or not-so-subtle patterns of co-dependency that are evident in any cult situation. This authority does not come from any desire or egotistic power drive of the teacher, because a real teacher is one who has been made empty. If an individual feels the need to question the teacher's authority, he or she must be free to do so—in the Sufi tradition the seeker is initially allowed to test the teacher. But somewhere, on the level of the soul, the wayfarer instinctively bows down in the presence of a real teacher. If the spiritual being who is present is not one's own teacher, this can be experienced as deep respect, the soul's respect for someone who has been made empty and reflects the divine light. But with one's own teacher the connection to the path carries the stamp of surrender. The deeper the relationship with the teacher, the stronger the link with the path, the more this inner surrender impresses itself upon consciousness. It is this inner impression of the soul that evokes a feeling of both fear and awe in the disciple. In the presence of Mrs. Tweedie I felt both the path and my own need. I knew that she was a doorkeeper of the inner world, and that I would pay any price to go through. However low I needed to bow, even to becoming a speck of dust on the floor, the inner necessity to pass the barrier of the ego would push me down. Her presence, her inner state of surrender, was a living example of the process. The path and the goal had become a tangible reality.

EXHAUSTION

That summer I continued as an architectural student. But studying sacred geometry had lost its meaning. I had found the container I needed, a container without form or structure. I had also realized that I would never become an architect for the simple reason that I lacked any visual imagination. When I had started the course no one had told me the obvious need for an architect to imagine the building he will design. I discovered that I rarely think in pictures, but rather in words, and often my mind is just empty. After two years I left college and also gave away all my spiritual books. I had an instinctual desire to cleanse myself of everything that had belonged to me before I found the path. The books had been an indication, a pointer, but they were no longer necessary and there was a joy in giving them away.

Years later spiritual books were again to accumulate on my shelves; I would no longer seek knowledge in them, though, but only quotations to help me in my writing. When I met my teacher I was very attached to the idea of spiritual knowledge, and I instinctively knew this attachment had to go. It is always easier to get rid of outer attachments than inner attachments, easier to give away books than the desire for knowledge. But in this instance there was no resistance. The Sufi path of the heart gave such substance to my life that I was glad to part with even the desire for knowledge. Initially I gave up reading altogether, and it was many years before I was attracted to reading anything but novels and poetry. During this whole process no one had said anything. Mrs. Tweedie had not suggested that I give up reading—the matter had never been discussed. I was beginning to experience the wonderful alchemy of the path, in which the real teaching, the real guidance, comes from within, from the Higher Self that has become aligned to the path.

I gave up architecture. I gave up books. I found a job in a café. But my physical body and psychological state were still causing me problems. I was highly stressed and could not eat very much. I had a very limited diet at the time and still found it very difficult to digest anything. I tried homeopathy and acupuncture to no effect. I knew the importance of natural methods of healing, I knew that this was the right spiritual approach, but what could I do? One day in despair I asked Mrs. Tweedie. I expected some spiritual advice, but she responded, "Try valium. I often use it and find it very effective." I did what I was told, went to my family doctor, and was given a prescription. The valium calmed down my body, relaxed my tensed nerves. Another concept about spiritual life was thrown away. Just as the chocolate biscuit had dismissed my ascetic ideals, so were my notions of spiritual healing now discarded. I was slowly learning that a real mystical path is not about appearances or external form. It is about responding to the need of the moment and living a balanced, everyday life.

I left the café and found a Christmas job in the department store Harrods. I was in the complaints department. When an order had been misplaced, someone's Christmas hamper had not arrived or someone had received sheets rather than towels, my job was to track down the order and correct it. I remained on this job even after the Christmas period and spent those few months wandering throughout the store. It was an ideally low-stressed job. However, while the valium had calmed my nerves, I was encountering another problem, lack of sleep. For months, however tired I was, I could not sleep more than a few hours. I had left my mother's house and was living alone in a small room that seemed always damp and cold. I would go to bed exhausted at ten or eleven, only to sleep two or three hours. There is nothing more depressing than waking at two in the morning in a cold, damp room, knowing that you cannot go back to sleep, and also knowing that you will be exhausted for the whole next day. Night after night, week after week, this torture continued. I tried taking sleeping pills but they did not work. I would still wake, exhausted, at two in the morning. Lying awake while half-sedated with the effect of a sleeping pill is particularly unpleasant. I limped through each day, always tired, not knowing what to do.

I prayed, I cried, I asked. What was this about? I had always slept so well before. Sleeping had never been a problem. Now the focal point of each day was how I would sleep that night. I was always allowed to sleep just enough to keep me from breaking apart, but no more. Life was truly miserable—it was like being dragged through the mud. Suddenly, one morning in the underground train going to work, I knew what was happening. I was being ground down, being told quite definitely that my life was no longer my own. My Sheikh was in control. I needed to know soon after I met the path that I was in the hands of another. Like a horse in the hands of a horse-trainer, I was being broken in.

The lack of sleep continued for about two years. Often it would be the *kundalini* energy that awoke me, and I found I could only go back to sleep after going for a run. At two or three in the morning, whatever the season or weather, I would jog through the streets. I was once stopped by the police who thought I was running away from a nearby burglary. I became almost used to living a life of tiredness combined with intense energy. Then one day I noticed that it was over, that I had slept through the night, that I could live a "normal" life. But by then I also knew that I belonged to someone else, that my life was not my own.

After I had been with Mrs. Tweedie for about fifteen years she told me that she was not really my teacher. When I first came to the group she had been told by Bhai Sahib to leave me alone and that he would deal with me. I would be in his hands. His training of me began then. When I had been in utmost despair about not sleeping it had been his voice that told me that I was being "trained." I refer to Mrs. Tweedie as my teacher because she has been the person guiding me, helping me along the path. But from the beginning, Bhai Sahib was my Sheikh to whom I totally belonged, although I did not know this on the level of the mind.[5]

A DREAM OF REUNION

My arrogance and sense of independence were being subtly eroded by my inability to fully function in the world. I had always valued my sense of self-sufficiency. But now the inner container of the path allowed my world to fall apart. I had left architectural college, and no longer knew where I was going in the world. I was continually exhausted and suffered acutely from indigestion—eating always seemed an anguish. All my outer identity of living a spiritual life, studying sacred ideas, having a healthy diet had disappeared.

At the same time Beba, whom I had loved since I was fifteen, left me. My heart was torn apart. I was stunned. I didn't understand. When she told me that she wanted to separate because she found the relationship too constricting, I just looked into her eyes and saw such love and closeness on the level of the soul. Devastated, feeling deeply excluded, for months I saw her only at the meditation meetings, sitting across the small, crowded room. I longed to be with her, longed for the security of our love and companionship, but all I had was a damp room in which I would awake at two in the morning.

Yet amid this desolation an inner change was happening, though it was too far beyond the threshold of consciousness for me to appreciate at the time. One night I had a dream in which I was back together with Beba and there was tremendous, unbelievable love. When I awoke I took the dream literally, and waited for her to come back. She never did. She even stopped coming to the meditation meetings and so I rarely saw her. I told the dream to Mrs. Tweedie, who said nothing. Years later I understood the dream, that it had little to do with Beba and my desire to be with her. I realized that the feeling of tremendous love came instead from an inner experience of the Beloved. In the night, on the level of the soul, I had been given an experience of being together with Him whom I loved, with Him for whom my heart really longed. But I had no image for this invisible Beloved, and so I had pictured this meeting in an image which I could identify with love: being back together with my girlfriend.

Real spiritual experiences happen on the inner planes, on the level of the soul. It is on the level of the soul that lover and Beloved meet and merge in the oneness of love. The wonder of the path is that we are made open to this experience and allowed to taste the bliss of real union. The path is the container for such an experience, opening us to the energy of the beyond. On the outer level of the personality I did not even know that a meeting with the Beloved was possible. I had come to the group without having read any Sufi books, and my only concept of love was what was played out in the arena of human relationships. When I had the dream I did not know that the real pain of separation is that of the soul from the Source, the lover from the Beloved.

Entering the path, I had unknowingly stepped into a stream of love, which is the real substance of any Sufi path. This love, flowing directly from the Source, gives the wayfarer a taste of union and awakens him to the pain of separation, the primal pain of the soul. Here is the real teaching of the path, the motivating power that takes the wayfarer Home. The Sufi master Abû Sa'îd ibn Abî'l-Khayr states with his customary directness, "Sufism was at first heartache; only later it became a subject to write about."[6] I had lost my girlfriend, but I was also being awakened to a deeper love and a deeper loss, a more wonderful union, a more painful separation. With whom did I really long to be reunited? Who was the real beloved in my dream?

The drama of love and longing was beginning to be played out. Over the years I would experience unbelievable longing and unimaginable love. But this dream of union also began another process. Sufis value dreams, and at our meditation meetings people would often tell dreams. Group dreamwork had not yet become an integral part of our meetings. Instead, Mrs. Tweedie would respond to the dreams, often directly interpreting them. When I told this dream of reunion she offered no interpretation, and after this rarely interpreted my dreams. I was left alone to work out my own dreams, and gradually discovered that I had an ability to understand not only my own dreams, but also the dreams of others. Dreamwork, which was to become central to my life's work, began with this first dream of union which took me over ten years to understand.

AN ISLAND OF PEACE

After a year the disintegration of my outer life subsided. I left my dark, cold room for a dry attic room. I moved from the complaints department in Harrods to a job in the civil service at the Department of Ancient Monuments. My criteria for a job were quite straightforward: not to make money out of anyone and not to harm anyone. Unfortunately these criteria are also quite limiting in the workplace. I lasted at the civil service for a few months of total boredom. I was in charge of all the ancient monuments in eastern

England, and seemed to have nothing to do all day except write a few memos and a few letters, mainly to elderly ladies about footpaths. I was not allowed to visit the ancient monuments under my administration, and only saw a few black-and-white photos of them in files. They were mainly crumbling stone castles, not the interesting type with battlements and moats, but small, square towers with a few windows, surrounded by an iron fence in the middle of a windswept field.

While writing memos to be stuck in files, I wondered what to do. My life in the last year seemed to have been a simple process of elimination—my ideas and ideals had been lost. There was an unspoken feeling that my spiritual drive was to be quite separate from my external work, which was one of the reasons I had given up architecture and sacred geometry. When I looked into the empty space within me all that I found left was a love of English literature. At school I had loved poetry, both reading poetry and writing my own. I had never studied literature because I felt that it would interfere with my creativity. But sitting at my desk, staring at the files, I realized that this was all that was left. I applied and was accepted for a degree course at a north-London college.

In the summer Mrs. Tweedie would close the group, because her small room became too hot. So during that summer I went to Scotland. If she had not been closed I would have been reluctant to go anywhere, because the meetings had become the outer focus of my life, giving meaning to an otherwise empty time. But she was closed and so with a friend and an old car, I drove north and spent some time camping on Iona. Iona is a small island off the west coast of Scotland, which since the sixth century has had a monastic community. This barren island has a timeless quality which you feel the moment you walk off the ferry. Arriving there is like stepping into a different dimension, and the whole island is filled with a sense of peace and simplicity.

Walking the stone beaches, sitting on the head-lands, attending some of the services at the monastery, I felt the peace, the timeless rhythm of the monks. I have always had a longing for simplicity, for the quality of peace that comes from prayer and meditation. Here the peace was a tangible reality, despite all the inner difficulties that still engulfed me. Maybe the island touched ancient memories of monastic life, a life not troubled by the outer world. I was still caught in a whirlpool of inner emotions, feelings, and psychological disturbance, but sometimes there was a break in the clouds and a glimpse of something deeper, something that I knew but could not yet reach.

Meeting the teacher, meeting the path, had turned my life upside down. A deep need had been answered, an energy unleashed into my life. I did not expect peace or bliss. I did not expect anything. I had no conscious knowledge of what I was seeking, of why a small room in north London had become so important. Yet there were no doubts. Later I discovered that many people have doubts about the path, doubts about the teacher. Mrs. Tweedie's book describing her time with her teacher is full of her doubts.[7] I had many other difficulties, vast problems, but I was never troubled by doubts. The very idea was so foreign to me that I did not even know that I didn't have doubts. It never occurred to me that one might question the path. I had arrived where I belonged.

My outer life had been dissolved, my personal identity fragmented. But I had nowhere else to go. There was no question of "running away" because a drowning man cannot run anywhere. When you are in the vortex of a whirlpool you just take one breath at a time. Somewhere I knew that I was looked after, that He would not desert me. This knowledge, this inner conviction, was always there, though at the time it was mainly hidden behind the chaos and confusion of my own psyche. I was driven by a desperate desire of which I had no understanding; I only knew its intensity, which manifested as impatience, an impatience to reach an invisible, intangible goal. I wanted to find something, desperately, crazily, and I did not care what it cost. I had mistakenly put this intensity onto my physical body, and suffered as a result. But now I had found the path that would take me Home. I could not look back because the past had strangely disappeared. Behind me there was only a life without real substance.

I saw other people having "normal lives" and would have liked some semblance of normality. But my own inner intensity would not allow me. I could not rest and take things easily. From the moment I read the saying about wild geese I had been pushed to live on the edge. Now I know why, I know the purpose of the intensity—then I was struggling with a load that allowed me no rest. I once met a woman at a workshop who was instinctively a mystic, although she tried to ignore it. She shared a dream of flying above a suburban housing estate and longing to go down and live among its ordered streets, where people led ordinary lives. But she knew that she couldn't, for she was drawn to the distant horizon. I know her struggle, her desire to escape the burden of her inner destiny— the fantasy of being a country postman was my escape. But I also know that this inner destiny is more precious than anything in this world.

Gradually over the years I would learn to balance this inborn intensity with the effortlessness of true spiritual unfolding. If there is too much effort it is not spiritual, because it comes too much from the ego, from the seeker. One of the paradoxes of the path is that we need to make every effort and yet our own effort cannot take us to God, as expressed by Abû Saʿîd al-Kharrâz:

> Whoever believes he can reach God by his own efforts toils in vain; whoever believes he can reach God without effort is merely a traveller on the road of intent.[8]

The wayfarer comes to realize that he is taken to God only by God: "Allâh guides to His light whom He will" (Qur'an 24: 35). The work of the wayfarer is to remain attuned, to stay focused on Him whatever the inner or outer situation. The real effort is to hang on whatever the cost, for, in the words of Bhai Sahib, spiritual awareness is "a gift to those who can take it."[9] Bhai Sahib always stressed that there cannot be an effort with divine things. "They are GIVEN, INFUSED.... Divine things can never be forced, however right, however correct is the attitude of the Shishya [disciple]. It is given as a gift."[10]

But initially I had no notion of anything beyond my ego. I did not know that the real process of transformation happens from within, initiated by the teacher and the energy of the path. In my ignorance and arrogance I thought that my spiritual progress depended entirely upon my own effort. Full of desire and impatience, I was still pushing myself too hard. At one time I was aware that I had a lot of fear inside me, and felt that I should go into this fear in order to transform it. Very soon I became swamped by the depth and darkness of this fear. I asked Mrs. Tweedie what I should do, and she told me not to do anything, and that over time the fear would dissolve through meditation and the path. I had to learn patience, to allow the path to change me, and find the balance of effort and grace.

On the island of Iona there was a moment of peace, of picking stones from the sea shore and hearing the monks chant. Over the years the sense of peace that I felt on this island slowly permeated me from within. But then it was just a glimpse of something that seemed unobtainable, separate from the world. I had to return to live my spiritual longing in the city, in the marketplace of human relationships and everyday work. The contradictions between the two worlds would torment me, tear me apart, and help me to realize a oneness that transcends every limitation. Maybe in a previous time and place I would have become a monk and retired from the world. This lifetime it was not allowed. A deeper completion had to take place. I had to accept the world and all of its contradictions; I had to learn to live an everyday life in humility, without the anger or the resentment that arose because I felt abandoned in this world, separate from Him whom I loved.

ALONENESS AND RECOGNITION

Being part of a meditation group, a circle of friends, gave me for the first time in my life real companionship, companionship based upon the inner orientation of the soul rather than personality or social grouping. It is said that souls incarnate in groups in order to help each other; Abû Sa'îd describes how such souls recognize each other by their smell, "like horses." I had found such friends, and felt the inner connection that transcends time and space. But I still felt, and often more strongly than before, a deep, potent aloneness. Often I would wonder why I was here, so isolated, alone. Nature has always been a great healer for me, and there on Iona, walking on the shore, watching the seabirds, or sitting in silence, I felt an inner purpose and strength to this aloneness. But in those difficult years, my aloneness, my inability to really relate to others, was more often an added torment, another way in which I was torn between the two worlds. Even the friends in the group created a particular pain, as I felt that they could relate and be together in a way that was unreachable for me. I knew that the spiritual journey is "from the alone to the Alone," that it demands a quality of aloneness most people would find frightening. But when you are confronted only by separation, both from the Beloved and from feeling a part of the rest of humanity, aloneness can become a terrible loneliness.

One of the wonders of meeting Mrs. Tweedie was feeling that my aloneness, intensity, and other idiosyncrasies were accepted and understood within the spiritual context to which they really belonged. I have met other seekers who also have qualities that create difficulties and confusions in their everyday life because they belong to a mystical orientation. A depth of passion, lack of self-worth, or desire to surrender can become psychological problems until they are seen from a spiritual perspective, when their real value is appreciated.

The teacher is often the first to recognize the true origin and purpose of these qualities. There is a deep recognition that takes place between teacher and disciple that has to do with the destiny of the soul. The teacher recognizes the deepest potential of the disciple, and instinctively understands how aspects of the psyche and character traits belong to this potential, have a spiritual purpose. Then the ugly duckling is recognized as a swan. That was one of the reasons the meetings, the time spent in my teacher's presence, were so wonderful and healing. Without the barriers of personality or the restrictions of personal relationship, she mirrored into me a level of acceptance that was infinitely precious. For those few brief hours each week I could just be myself.

In her presence something within me was recognized for the first time. There were no words in this exchange, just a silent greeting of the heart. Only now do I understand the depth and importance of this recognition, how it allows the wayfarer to place his whole self onto the path. The Sufi path is a "closed circle of love" and the teacher holds this circle in her heart until the wayfarer is able to claim it for himself. The circle of love is the heart's relationship to God, the link between lover and Beloved. Being in the presence of the teacher is stepping into this circle, stepping into the pre-eternal wholeness of the Self. In the words of Rûmî,

Come out of the circle of time
And into the circle of love.[11]

MADNESS AND BLISS

And if He closes before you all the ways and passes,
He will show a hidden way which nobody knows.

Rûmî[1]

HEALING THE *KUNDALINI*

For the next two years some semblance of order returned to my outer life. I was a student studying English literature, immersing myself in the wonders of Shakespeare, T.S. Eliot, and John Donne. I instinctively gravitated to the more mystical writers, but there was also the pure enjoyment of the wonder of words, the beauty of expression. For a number of years literature was to be an important part of my outer life as a student and then as a teacher, until it faded away as a different destiny began to surface.

Although my outer life presented a facade of coherence, inwardly there was often chaos and confusion. The *kundalini* energy was still giving me trouble, keeping me awake, creating unexpected anger and irritation. *Kundalini* is a feminine energy belonging to the earth, and it is necessary for spiritual realization. However, the Naqshbandi Sufi path to which I belong is not a *kundalini* path. In some paths of yoga the *kundalini* energy is consciously awakened from its resting place at the base of the spine, and brought up through the different *chakras*, or energy centers, until finally it reaches the crown *chakra* at the top of the

52

head, where it brings realization. The Sufi path focuses instead on the energy of love and works through the heart *chakra*. The *kundalini* does not need to be awakened until it is experienced through the heart, when it brings states of bliss or cosmic consciousness.

However, there are wayfarers whose *kundalini* becomes partly awakened before it reaches the heart *chakra*. Mrs. Tweedie called these individuals *"kundalini* types," and suggested that the early experience of the *kundalini* is probably the result of having done *kundalini* exercises in a previous lifetime. The way the *kundalini* manifests is slightly different for each person. For example, it can be experienced as a powerful force in the spine, awakening one in the night, or an energy flowing throughout the body that makes one tremble. *Kundalini* can be accompanied by sounds, for instance whirring or purring at the base of the spine or lower stomach. This energy can awaken an unsatisfiable sexual urge, and when it hits the stomach one often feels nauseous. The experience of the *kundalini* can be wonderful, exhilarating, disturbing, frightening. When it comes into the heart there is bliss.

My experience of the *kundalini* was rarely dramatic but just added to the intensity and imbalance of my physical, psychological, and spiritual disposition. I had learned the importance of taking exercise and being barefoot as much as possible. I learned not to eat too much at any one time. And I learned to bear it. This was the message I received from Bhai Sahib when Mrs. Tweedie asked about my condition: "He can bear it."

Then, unexpectedly, the *kundalini* and other energy imbalances in my body were healed. For a short while I went along with some members of our group to another meditation group related to the cosmic

Christ energy. The person leading the group had an inner contact with certain masters who were helping with the evolution of the world. One of these masters had healing powers, and we would often bring names of people who needed healing. One time I mentioned to the person leading the group that I had trouble with energy imbalances, and to my absolute wonder and delight, within two weeks those imbalances were gone.

It was a tremendous relief not to be always on edge with this inner energy. I had suffered for over three years since Hatha Yoga had inadvertently awakened this dormant power. The suffering had been bearable, insignificant compared to what Mrs. Tweedie experienced when Bhai Sahib deliberately awakened her *kundalini* with his psychic powers. But I was very aware of the change when the imbalance was healed, and have been always grateful to the unknown master who helped me.

THE DARK FEMININE

At about the same time that this healing took place, I began to confront certain psychological patterns in myself. I have always felt that we each have a core problem that manifests in different ways during the course of our life. For one person this could be the dynamic of being a victim, while for another the archetypal feeling of being excluded from paradise is central to her psychological life. I was to discover that the dark side of the feminine was at the root of the majority of my psychological problems. I became fully conscious of this a few years later when I was using Shakespeare's play *Hamlet* as the focus for my Ph.D.

thesis. *Hamlet* is a wonderful mirror in which many readers are able to see their own inner patterns. I saw my own relationship with the world in Prince Hamlet's desire to escape "this too, too sullied flesh." Hamlet's confrontation with the dark, feminine depths is imaged in his relationship with his mother, as he accuses her of betraying his spiritual, heroic father for her own sexual desires. Through his mother Hamlet confronts the Great Mother and the terrible, instinctual forces that can overwhelm consciousness.

Soon after I met my teacher I had to confront the depths of my difficulties with my mother, whose drinking and depression were combined with the power of the dark feminine. She could easily drag me into the darkness of her own inner chaos, the pain of her own problems. This was the womb in which I had been conceived, in which my soul had been contained, and I discovered deep feelings of resentment and anger going back before my birth.

I became aware that somewhere I had been free, and then locked into the confines of both her womb and my growing body, feeling the pain and limitations of the physical world. Most people when they are born forget the other world from which they come. The child accepts the state of exile and thinks of the physical world as her real home. One of the blessings and curses of the mystic is that one does not entirely forget. Coming into the world, we know that it is not our true home. The soul helps us to remember, to stay connected even as we appear to forget. The container of the path allowed me to realize deep feelings of anger, resentment, and abandonment that originated in my mother's womb. From a world of light I had fallen into this darkness, in which my mother's pain and my own pain became wedded.

The instinctual feminine had imprisoned me in her darkness. I had deep anger at being conceived and born into a world of forgetfulness, into a physical dimension governed by instinct and not spirit. I felt caught in the coils of physical incarnation, trapped in a world which did not recognize or understand my real nature. This primal shadow dynamic between masculine spirit and the instinctual feminine, which was there in the womb, was further dramatized in my family psychology, which emphasized a split between an idealized father (an English gentleman without a shadow) and an alcoholic, demonized mother. The psychic atmosphere of my childhood was dominated by my mother, of whom my father was justifiably afraid. My mother carried the shadow of both my father and the whole family. In my early twenties I began to become conscious of this collective shadow dynamic, and sought to escape it. I felt a need to redeem the feminine, which meant accepting my mother and her dark side.

Psychology often takes us back to our childhood, so that we can uncover and understand the patterns that have formed us. However, looking back, I have felt deeper and older patterns at play than those of my immediate family. I discovered that the resentment at being in the womb and at being born did not come from a "difficult birth," but from an inborn arrogance at having to accept the limitations of the physical world. I brought with me my own ancient shadow, possibly from previous lifetimes, and this was just reflected in the family shadow dynamic.

From the level of the soul, we attract certain experiences because we need to learn something. I needed to experience the pain that is caused by rejecting the instinctual feminine, see this psychological split played out in front of me. Becoming aware of these patterns made me want to transcend them, which could only be done by accepting the rejected feminine within my family and within myself. The dark side of the feminine and her instinctual cycle of birth and death were both the prison and the key.

This was the baggage with which I had arrived at the teacher's door. I was weighed down so heavily that life had lost its joy; my vitality had become drowned in difficulties, physical and psychological. A deep rejection of the feminine is an awful wound—to begin to become conscious of this rejection creates an even greater load because consciousness carries its own pain. Until I met my teacher I had no notion of transformation, no idea that the darkness was the place of rebirth. I walked always looking down at my feet, my "wings clipped, and life without much meaning," as Mrs. Tweedie told me later. One of the first spiritual practices Mrs. Tweedie ever gave me was to learn to look up, to raise my head as I walked, to bring the dignity of the soul back into my step. She knew the difference between the pride of the ego, which needs to be broken, and the pride of the soul, the knowledge that we are made in the image of God. Learning to walk with my head high reconnected me with this deeper pride which carries the purpose of life. Mrs. Tweedie's presence and the meaning of the path also brought the hidden message of transformation, of something being born from pain.

In *Hamlet* there is a wonderful image of transformation when the split between masculine and feminine, heaven and earth, is redeemed. This image occurs at the graveside of Ophelia, when Gertrude, describing her seemingly mad son, says:

> This is mere madness;
> And thus awhile the fit will work on him.
> Anon, as patient as the female dove
> When that her golden couplets are
>   disclosed,
> His silence will sit drooping.[2]

Prince Hamlet has descended into the depths, has encountered madness. But this passage suggests that through his journey he will transform the dark feminine, his negative mother image, into the "female dove" and her "golden couplets." There is a prayer in *The Acts of Thomas* which uses similar imagery to worship the Holy Ghost in female form:

> Come holy dove,
> Which hast brought forth the twin nest-
>   lings;
> Come secret mother.[3]

Hamlet's "female dove" is the "secret mother" of the Holy Ghost, the Feminine Spirit of God. She is Sophia, the deepest wisdom of the divine feminine. The "golden couplets," the "twin nestlings," are the opposites reconciled, the union of masculine and feminine, spirit and instinct. The split that drew Hamlet into seeming madness has revealed its alchemical potential, the *coincidentia oppositorum* (the mystical union of opposites), that transforms the dark feminine into the divine feminine. She who is an eternal mystery will reveal her highest aspect.

My journey drew me into an encounter with the dark feminine and awoke a need to redeem her. The process which started before birth was coming into consciousness, and bringing with it the terrible pain of the wounded feminine and my own suffering. This process would continue for many years, leading to an awakening of Sophia, the intuitive wisdom of the Higher Self, and taking me, like Hamlet, into the silence that is beyond all words.[4] But becoming aware of these psychological patterns meant confronting the darkness of both my personal and my family shadow. I was about to discover that it would also mean a descent into seeming madness.

PURIFICATION AND REBIRTH

The summer after I had been at college for two years began uneventfully. During those summer months I had no desire to travel. Instead I accepted the offer to flat-sit for some neighbors who were away on holiday. They lived in a basement flat which had a flower-filled garden. I felt the need to be totally alone, to have no one intrude upon this space I had been given. I found six abandoned chairs which had been badly painted, and gave myself the task of stripping and sanding these chairs, restoring them to their natural wood. It was a hot summer, and sitting in the warmth of the garden I enjoyed this simple, meditative work, so different from my academic studies.

But as the days began to unfold I felt an intense introversion of my energy and focus take place. As I quietly sanded the wood in the garden, my attention was drawn more and more inward, deeper and deeper. There was a sense of uncovering a timeless, ancient part of myself, and entering a world far away from that of a college student. As my attention was drawn inward, so energies began to flow around my body, and my consciousness would follow this flow. Then this flow of energy which held my attention started to encounter psychological blocks and hidden pain. What had begun as a simple introversion of energy changed into the most painful and transformative two weeks I have ever known.

I felt a need, an intense drive to stay with the energy as it uncovered these hidden layers of pain. I knew that my consciousness was vital to the process, that I had to willingly go into the agony that was being touched. But the nature of my attention was also important. I discovered that it was not enough just to be with the pain, just to experience the block. Within the pain, within the block, I had to focus on the beyond, and throw my self, my whole being, into the emptiness beyond the mind and beyond myself. As I went deeper and deeper into myself this required intense effort, a greater inner effort than I had ever experienced. Instinctively we avoid pain; but not only did I need to voluntarily experience the pain, I had to stay within the pain and then use every ounce of energy to take it into the beyond, to offer it up to His essential emptiness.

How did I know what to do? In each moment there were two alternatives, avoid the process or focus inwardly on the nothingness which I instinctively knew was Real. A combination of consciousness and an inner commitment drew me into this process and guided me along the maze of agony. There was no desire in me to realize or reach anything, no feeling that I was doing this because it was spiritual. A different process had taken over in which there was only the need of the moment, the call to exert myself more than I had ever believed possible. And as the days progressed the process became more and more intense, more and more painful, more and more demanding. The chairs were soon left behind, unfinished, in the garden. I stayed inside, often lying down for hours. And each hour I thought, I can only manage it for a little bit longer, the end is just around the corner. And then the next hour came, and the next.

The pain I felt was far deeper and more potent than any physical pain I have ever encountered. It seemed to belong to the very nerves of my psyche. This pain was not about something, about being rejected or being abandoned. That would have made it easier. Instead it was the essence of suffering, pure inner psychic pain, pure agony. If I withdrew my consciousness, my inner effort, the pain stopped. I would focus on the beyond, on the inner goal, for as long as I could bear it, maybe thirty seconds or a minute. Then I would retreat, and the whole psyche and also the body would be left quaking. But I *knew* with the knowledge that comes from somewhere, certainly not from the mind or ego, that I had to continue. This process was more important than life itself. I didn't know why. I just felt that the whole dignity of myself demanded this work, this tremendous effort.

I would pause a little to eat and I had a few hours of sleep each night. After about ten days I felt that the process was reaching some point of completion, though what was being completed I did not know. The Sufis talk about the work of "polishing the mirror of the heart," cleansing the impurities of the *nafs* or lower self. Something was being cleansed, cleansed with pain and inner fire. It was the most concentrated, intensely painful time I have ever experienced, in which while I cried out for release there was a deeper and stronger calling to focus on the beyond *whatever it cost.*

I do not remember any comforting presence, any inner reassurance. All that I was aware of was my own ruthless desire, relentless drive, that pushed me through every barrier. It was pain upon pain, not light upon light. There was no warmth of love, no taste of bliss. Just the agony of purification and the timelessness of the inner world. I would think that it couldn't get worse, the pain level could in no way increase, and then the inner pain increased. Sometimes there were moments of inner space, a resting place. But then the drive to the beyond would push me out of this empty oasis, into the desert and the burning.

The process intensified as it reached its culmination. In moments of despair I cried out to my Sheikh; my heart called and called. Every muscle, the whole fabric of my psyche, every cell of my being was stretched. Then there were glimpses of something beyond this process, a peace that belonged to the other world. I began to feel the presence of my Sheikh, him whom I loved and feared. I sensed that he was guiding this process, giving me an opportunity, an opening to something. The ancient spiritual training in which the disciple is pushed beyond every extreme was being lived within me, but only because I was being held by him.

Then he was suddenly in my heart and in a moment of simple wonder he made me conscious that *I am a soul.* This consciousness would stay with me for the rest of my life, the *knowing* that I am not just a physical, mental, or emotional being, bound by time and space, that my ego-identity is just a small part of my whole being. There is a saying of the Prophet, "Be in this world as if you are a traveler, a passerby, for this is not home." Knowing that I am a soul, I know that I belong somewhere else, that I have come to this planet for a purpose, to do a certain work.

Spiritual awakenings are so simple that there is little to say, but the wonder was beyond anything, beyond any pain I may have experienced. Spiritual processes are like childbirth. The agony is often intense, but in the moment of birth the agony vanishes as the mother sees her new child. The intense two weeks of suffering left no trace, no residue. There was no resentment, only the wonder at what had been given, what had been revealed. I felt that I must go to see Mrs. Tweedie and share this wonder with her, for she was the only person who could understand, who could recognize the miracle. I left the house, the womb of my rebirth. I had no idea that the process had only begun.

A WORLD WITHOUT LIGHT

I visited Mrs. Tweedie, whom I had not seen for a while as it was summer and the group was closed. I expected her to know what I had experienced, not realizing that she only knew what she needed to know. The disciple often projects total knowledge onto the teacher, while the essence of the mystical path is to be empty, merged into emptiness. In this state of merging, knowledge comes when it is needed. I told her what I could of my experience, and her recognition of my state confirmed its importance.

After being with Mrs. Tweedie, I went to visit my father for supper. I did not realize that I was in a very altered state of consciousness, very open to the inner and the prompting of the Self. I found myself being prompted to talk and behave very strangely. At another time I would have had inhibitions and resistances to behaving so strangely in front of my father, but for two weeks I had followed the subtle and painful guidance that came from within, *at whatever the cost*, and external, social pressure was not going to stop me now. I don't remember the details of my actions, except that at one point I began taking off my clothes. At the time I knew I was shocking and deeply disturbing him, but I could not stop my words or actions which I knew to be crazy. Many years later I met an elderly woman who had had a similar, although different, experience. When she was in her sixties she felt to invite all her family, friends, and work colleagues to a party. Suddenly in the middle of the party this respectable woman got up and began to dance in the wildest, wildest way. She said it was uncontrollable; something had taken her over. She danced for hours, and her family and friends just sat there shocked, not knowing what to do or say. This experience changed her life; it was an outward expression of a dynamic inner change that had been happening within her. She needed to make some form of outer statement of what was coming to life within her.

Something had come to life within me, but as I later discovered, the need was not to shock my father or family, but to create a container of craziness to allow deeper purification and changes to take place. At first my father thought I might be on drugs, tripping on LSD. But my younger sister, who was living at his flat and had returned after being out for the evening, assured him that I didn't take drugs. I was conscious of my craziness, and bewildered by the whole experience.

But I had an inner hint to say nothing, to offer no reason. Other members of my family then came to try to help, to see what the problem might be. My father's flat was high up on the sixteenth floor in central London, and looking out of the window one could see the lights of the city spread out. I remember this image of the lights in the background as I looked around at the people in the room, the concerned faces, because suddenly I had an experience which was deeply impressed upon me. For an instant the room, the people, the whole world, became grey; the color disappeared, and I knew with the certainty of direct perception that *this is how the world looks if you have no spiritual awareness.* I was shown the greyness of existence of those for whom this world is the only reality, whose spark of spiritual longing has not yet been lit. For the first and only time in my life I reached for a glass of whiskey!

There was no judgment in this experience, no sense that spiritual life is "better," but just a direct perception of life without the luminous energy of spiritual awareness permeating everyday life. Until this moment I did not realize that I always see a quality of light permeating my physical surroundings, dancing around people, sparkling in the air. For me the physical world has never seemed totally solid; sometimes I think I could put my hand through its substance, as if it is a floating holograph. But we are used to our own quality of perception and think that it is the same for everyone. Until that moment I assumed that everyone saw the same dancing light that invisibly sparkles in the air.

I do not remember the vision fading. I only remember the imprint and shock it left behind. I understood that if that grey, unluminous world is one's sole environment, what else is there besides instinctual pleasures and sensations, food, sex, drink, and material possessions? Later I came to realize that spiritual awareness allows the physical world to become slightly transparent, enough for the light to shine through these veils. It is this light that attracts the eye, as we glimpse the wonder of the beyond in what is visible. Our inner awareness opens us to the beyond which is always present but hidden by the limitations of ego-consciousness. The ego can only see this world. The consciousness of the Self, which awakens us to the quest, allows us to see the light.

FAILURE AND SACRIFICE

I must have seemed more reasonable, because the members of my family left and I stayed that night with my father and sister. But that night was to be one of the most terrible in my life. Maybe I slept an hour or two, but when I awoke an intense inner drama began to be played out. This drama began quietly, with an inner voice accusing me of saying things that should not be said. The voice never told me what it was that I had said, but this drama did not involve reason. When the inner self takes over there is no logic, and unconscious forces are far more powerful than reason. The accusations slowly became louder and louder, along with the assertion that I had failed.

Failure is something I have always found very difficult to deal with. I have an ancient memory from a previous lifetime of once having failed, of having misused spiritual power, and of having to pay a terrible price. I remember the price—I was not allowed to be involved in the spiritual path for the rest of that lifetime. I have an image of having to work in the fields as a farmer, planting rice in the ground. The inner world for which I hungered, which alone gave meaning to life, was shut off—that doorway was closed. This memory has always haunted me, has been a powerful inner warning never to misuse spiritual power. Once again now I was encountering spiritual failure, and it threw me deeper and deeper into terror.

The inner voices started to tell me that it was not just a simple matter of having failed, but that my failure had a destructive effect. At first this damaging effect was just to myself; then it slowly escalated and became darker and darker. My failure had allowed darkness to conquer, and this darkness became more and more powerful. As this darkness grew it began to have a greater and greater effect. The archetypal inner world can take us into the whole universe, and the darkness grew until my failure affected not just myself, my environment, but the whole world, the solar system, the cosmos. The darkness spread everywhere, and I was the cause. It is easy to say that I was inflated and crazy, that there was no reason to the terror and guilt. But the inner experience was my reality, and in this state I knew that the only way to save the situation was to sacrifice myself. I had to die. To save the universe from this darkness I had to die. My father's flat was on the sixteenth floor, so I opened the window and prepared to jump.

LIFE'S SWEETNESS

I didn't jump. At the last moment, seeing my sister sleeping in the room, I felt that I would hurt her feelings if I jumped, and I did not want to hurt anyone. My sister awoke in shock, seeing me there at the edge of the open window. The next morning I was taken to a psychiatrist who recommended me to a nursing home. That morning I was still engulfed by my inner situation, still thinking that I had to die. But the terror had gone and I remember stepping outside the apartment block on my way to the car, thinking that I had only a few hours more to live. Suddenly, in the open air I felt the ecstatic sweetness of being alive. Never before or since have I felt the sweetness of life to such a degree, a sweetness that I could feel with every cell. It was a warm summer morning, and the air seemed full of flowers and birds. It sounds like a cliché to say that each moment of life is infinitely precious, but I can still feel the magic of that moment in the open air before I went into the car. Life was present in all of its beauty, softness, and vibrance.

I was driven from the psychiatrist straight to a nursing home in south London, and the next week remains a blank. I don't think that I have much consciousness of that time; maybe I was sedated, maybe I just left my body. I had been through such experiences that the outer world had lost its hold. For an instant life was infinitely sweet, but I had stepped behind the curtain that encloses us in the normal view of reality, and the physical world was no longer my home. Later I was told that this was a time of further purification, in which, like a boil being pierced, my psychological problems were being cleansed of their poison. All the psychological suffering—my primal resentment at being born and caught in the physical world, my experience of the instinctual darkness, and the pain of my mother—was being taken away.

Looking back, I can also see how the stress of my recent experiences had stretched me beyond any limit. First, for two weeks on my own I had been subjected to the most painful and intense time in my life. Out of this suffering I was made conscious that I was a soul, made aware that in my being I was free from the chains of this world. Then I had been made to suffer the knowledge of failure, of the archetypal mistake that threw Adam out of paradise. The experience of failure was also bound with an ancient memory that haunted me with fear, the fear of being denied spiritual life. (Later I also came to realize that failure is the best guard against inflation, against the arrogance of thinking one has reached a spiritual state.)

From the spiritual state of knowing I was a soul, I was reminded I was human, caught in the dualities of good and evil, light and dark. My experience of failure, exaggerated and archetypal, had brought me into the arena of atonement, the ultimate sacrifice of one's own self. This was the drama that had been played out within my crazy consciousness, and it had led to a wonderful taste of the sweetness of life. But afterwards, in the nursing home, for a week or more I was a foreigner to this world. Maybe my consciousness was free elsewhere, in a space where there were no restrictions. I do not know, but the nursing home allowed me this experience, allowed me to step outside the confines of ordinary consciousness.

Gradually, ordinary consciousness began to return. I remember walking the corridors of the nursing home, seeing some of the other occupants through a haze, sensing a strange atmosphere of drugs and depression. I was neither high nor low; I was just not quite here in this world. Most of the time I spent quietly in my room, in a space without thoughts or ideas, without emotions or feelings. I did not feel disturbed or exhilarated. The doctors gave me a few pills and left me alone.

Sometimes I would walk in the gardens. One early afternoon I was walking along the driveway and came to its entrance which opened onto a main road. On the pavement a group of schoolchildren was walking past with their teacher. They were probably on an outing; maybe they had been to the park. I noticed these young children crossing the entrance and suddenly I saw them in a way I have never seen human beings before or since. They were so full of light I could hardly look, and on each child's chest where the heart is, a huge radiance like the sun was shining. Each little child had this dynamic, brilliant light, this radiant sun, in the center of his being. The experience of the light, its brilliance and energy, was beautiful and overwhelming.

The children passed by and I turned to go back, thrown into ecstasy by this experience, energy racing through my body. In such experiences there is no mind that questions, no Why? or What does it mean? Later I came to realize that what I saw is the true nature of human beings—we are dynamic, luminous creatures of light. Within the heart, the light of the Self shines as brilliant as the sun. For an instant my eyes had been opened and I had seen these ordinary schoolchildren as they really are.

As I walked back along the gravel path, the energy exploded more and more within me. I found myself being taken upward somewhere. In that moment I knew that I was free, free of all attachments to this world. I was told that I could die, return to my spiritual home. But then from my depths something in me cried out and I asked to come back to the world in order to help, to work, to be His servant here. This was the moment in which I could have freed myself forever from the physical world. The soul was free. But in that instant a deeper purpose came from the soul into consciousness—the need to serve.

I was so high that I could hardly stand. I returned to my room.

MONTHS OF BLISS

Soon afterwards I left the nursing home. I had had the experiences I needed and my consciousness returned enough for me to come back to the world. During my stay there I had twice been given electric-shock treatment, which had worried me as I knew how damaging this can be. But I also knew that I was under the protection of my Sheikh and no harm could come. The only adverse effect that might be traced to the electric-shock treatment is that since this time my memory does not always function very well. I often forget past incidents, including many things before the treatment. But my poor memory could also come from the change in consciousness. For days my mind was gone from this world and I was in a space of such emptiness that there was no memory. Even after I returned from the nursing home I would sit for hours without thoughts. This was not a drug-induced stupor, but a state in which the mind is not. When the mind is not here, how can the memory function? Even when the mind returns it has a residue of emptiness in which memories do not stick.

The doctors were convinced that the electric-shock treatment had worked and allowed me to leave. I went to live with my mother who was the only person able to take care of me. I was still hardly in this world, and when the new college year began I found that I could not attend the classes. For a while I did try to go to college, to resume a normal life. But I soon realized that this was not possible. Intellectual pursuits demand that the mind be present, and my mind was still on the borders of the beyond. I took a year off college, a year that changed from strangeness into bliss.

My experience had broken many barriers between the conscious and unconscious. Patterns of social conditioning, my middle-class English upbringing, now had little influence. This lack of a normal inner structure of consciousness resulted in strange old patterns surfacing within me. I have always felt that I have had many past lives as an ascetic, and I found myself instinctively fasting, eating as little as I could. I walked about in the middle of winter wearing only a thin shirt and never felt the cold or became ill. I would also spend many nights awake in prayer and meditation, finding that in the morning I was not tired. Only occasionally did I go to the group meetings, which had reconvened at the end of the summer. The friends were very kind, knowing I had had some type of breakdown, but I did not discuss my experiences or try to explain my state to anyone. I was not altogether present in the world of time and outer events.

I spent most of the days in my room, sometimes wandering the streets during the day or the night. When there is no time there is no structure to the days. My mother fussed over me, cooking what she thought I liked, but I ate very little. Sometimes deep sorrows would come to the surface, but mostly neither the outer world nor my own inner self touched me. Empty, I sat in the emptiness. Silent, I sat in the silence.

As December turned into January I found myself more and more in states of bliss. The whole day I would lie on my bed contained in bliss. Day followed day as I lay wrapped in this state of bliss. Bliss is the sheath of the soul, *Anandamayakosha* in Sanskrit, and there I remained. It was a deeply healing period, without any conflicts or problems. For five months or more I remained mostly in this state of bliss, a state softer than ecstasy and more enduring. While ecstasy is a dynamic state that sends currents of energy flashing through the body, bliss is a natural state of being, full of peace.

Early that January I had a dream in which I was shown the Book of the Year. This is the book in which are written the main events that will happen to us during the year. I read that it would be an easy year and that its color would be light blue. I also read that I would have my heart's desire that year. Waking from the dream I knew that my heart's desire was a woman in our group whom I loved, and who was later to become my wife. I was overjoyed to know that this heart's desire would be fulfilled. But this message also had a humorous side as I was to discover. I had to wait almost the full twelve months for my love to be returned!

Winter turned to spring and the bliss and emptiness remained. Gradually, as summer came, my mind began to return. When I was not in meditation I would read, not spiritual books that demanded concentration, but novels. I discovered the works of Charles Dickens whom I had never read, and during four months read all of his books from beginning to end. Along with his social comment, Dickens has a humor and archetypal quality that suited my state. His caricature-like characters do not quite belong to this world; maybe that is why I felt so at home in his stories. Summer came and I finished the last of his books. My mind had regained its "normal function," though it would never be the same—it had tasted too much of the unknown. Before college started I worked as a volunteer in a London hospital, talking to patients and helping with menial chores.

A DREAM OF GURU MAHARAJ

By the end of September I was able to resume college and worked hard that year to complete my degree. I went back to the meditation meetings and fell deeply in love with my "heart's desire." The intense inner process that had turned me upside down and inside out had subsided. I had been purified and healed, seen the radiance of the Self and been wrapped in the bliss of the soul.

On a personal level I had been able to heal my relationship with my mother. Three years earlier I had run away, fleeing her house and her pain. Now circumstances had brought me back. She was able to look after me and I was grateful to her. Over those months of living with her, a deep wound was finally healed. I was able to love her without resentment or bitterness. I helped her to move to a new flat, where I lived with her for a few months before completing this chapter of my life. While I was still living with her I had a dream which pointed to a process that was over, and another process that was beginning:

My problems with my mother were imaged as a motorbike that took me to the bottom of a spiral stone staircase. Leaving the motorbike I climbed the staircase. When I reached the top I was met by Guru Maharaj, the sheikh of my Sheikh, Bhai Sahib. I was invited to a *satsang* (sitting in the presence of the teacher) with Guru Maharaj. He gave me three symbolic articles of jewelry, one of which I remember as being a small flower. Then he showed me a film of himself as a young man flying a kite.

My psychological difficulties and my inner drive to accept and transform them had taken me to a place of spiritual ascent. Jolande Jacobi, a follower of Jung, suggests that individuation, Jung's term for the process of psychological integration, opens us to a world beyond rational consciousness, and thus prepares us for a spiritual encounter. "One might say that in the course of the individuation process a man arrives at the entrance to the house of God."[5]

My psychological work, my descent into the dark feminine and her transformation into Sophia, was far from complete. But an intense period of initiation into the mystery, wonder, and terror of the inner world was over. I had survived the savagery of my personal and family shadow, and like Hamlet's, my experience of madness had taken me beyond duality, beyond right and wrong, into the silence of the Self. The incentive of the psychological work had revealed an inner strength and commitment to the path, and at the same time this work took me beyond the borders of rational consciousness. My previous ego-identity, and many patterns of arrogance that surrounded it, had been demolished. I had learned the humility of failure and the sweetness of life. But more important, the shadow work had taken me into the arena of my own devotion. Journeying into the depths I had found the deepest container of my desire for Truth, a desire to go into the beyond of the beyond. I had also found myself to be forever under the shelter of my Sheikh.

The spiral staircase of ascent had been climbed step by step. Meeting the sheikh of my Sheikh was both a wonderful confirmation and an embrace by the essence of the tradition. I knew where I belonged, a knowing that did not come from the concepts of the mind but from the cells of my body, the substance of my whole being. The consciousness of the soul, the night of terror and craziness, and the experiences that followed made me aware of the tremendous power of the path. I knew that I was in the hands of very great beings, who could do with me whatever was necessary. My Sheikh could turn off my mind, awake horrors in the depths, and reveal the luminous wonder of ordinary people. After such experiences one remains forever in awe, forever bowing before one's master.

In the dream I experienced *satsang* with Guru Maharaj and felt included in this path and tradition as never before. Sitting in the presence of the teacher is the basis of Sufi teaching, which is reflected from heart to heart, from soul to soul. This meeting happens outside of time, on the level of the soul, though it can also appear to take place on the physical plane. Bhai Sahib and Guru Maharaj had left their physical bodies before I came to the path, but the Sufi knows that there is no such thing as death, just a change in consciousness. On the inner planes they are eternally with us as we walk along this path, forming the chain of transmission that takes us back to God.

There are many different Sufi paths, *tariqas*, each with its practices and teachers. Each path is a stream of energy flowing from the inner planes into this world. This energy is held by the sheikh and by the transmission of his spiritual superiors, each merged into the other. I came to know that I belong to the path of the Naqshbandi Sufis, who are also known as the "silent Sufis" because they practice the silent *dhikr*, the silent repetition of the name of God. After my experiences with Bhai Sahib, after he had made me conscious that I was a soul, I became more and more aware of this inner connection, of the invisible presence of my superiors. This connection was to become central to my inner and outer life. The veils of separation had started to be lifted and the work of the soul begun.

In the final image of the dream, Guru Maharaj shows me a film of himself as a young man flying a kite. The film conveyed the simple message, "If you want to fly high you have to have both feet firmly on the ground." A kite flies high only because of the tension between the wind and the person holding the end of the string, a person whose feet are firmly planted on the earth. This was to be a central theme to my whole journey, to learn to have both feet on the ground, to live a balanced, everyday life in the world while at the same time being lifted high by the wind of the spirit. But first I was to experience another madness, the madness of romantic love.

PART 2

*To meet You I look at face after face, appearance after
appearance....
To see Your face I pass by like the morning wind.*

Al-Hallâj

ROMANTIC LOVE

A woman is God shining
through subtle veils.

Rûmî[1]

FALLING IN LOVE

A young man once came to a Sufi sheikh with the
intention of becoming one of his disciples. He had read
many books about the path and begun practicing
austerities. But to his immense surprise the sheikh
asked him, "Have you ever been in love?" The young
man felt quite indignant. He had come to the sheikh to
follow the Sufi path, to realize the truth of *Lâ ilâha illâ
llâh* (There is no god but God). He had read spiritual
books and prayed in the night, but instead of being
questioned about his spiritual aspirations, he was
being asked about something so worldly. No, he had
never been in love. He had no time or interest for such
things. "Go back into the world, fall in love, marry,
suffer, and then come back," was the sheikh's response. Despite his righteous indignation, the aspiring
student followed the sheikh's guidance. He fell in love.
He married. Years later he returned to the sheikh and
was accepted as a disciple. Eventually he became the
sheikh's successor.

I did not need any such incentive to fall in love.
Love had been awakened in my heart and there was an
irresistible desire to project this love on the tangible

form of a woman, to be caught in the mystery and wonder of romantic love. She whom I loved I adored. In the light of my love she became the most beautiful woman I have ever seen. For over a year I waited for my "heart's desire," and once my love began to be returned I was lost, engulfed in this ocean. I had then and have now no resistance and no regrets. Human love is a wonderful way to die.

Since adolescence I had been very romantically inclined, not knowing that the depth of my longing to love and be loved belonged to a different Beloved. I wanted desperately to give myself to the sweetness, intoxication, and deep meaning which I knew to be love. But I never found this quality of love returned, this hunger answered. When I was fifteen I fell in love, and Beba became my closest companion until she left me soon after I came to the group. We had a deep connection of the soul, and at times I was in love with her. Our connection beyond the level of the personality brought with it an intimacy and depth of friendship that neither of us had ever known. But we were not ready for the descent into the bliss and craziness of passion. We were too young, and we each had very difficult home situations, which made our loving friendship too important to be endangered by the tumult of being deeply in love. We needed the security of our relationship more than the danger of intoxication.

After she had left me I had journeyed inward, confronted my family shadow and freed myself of many insecurities. The dark, terrible feminine had become partly transformed, opening me to her beauty and wonder. I was now ready to lose myself without the fear of being torn apart. I could encounter the mystery of the feminine without being engulfed.

Sufism is a path of love in which the energy of love is used to transform the wayfarer and take him or her back to God. Giving ourself to love, we open the door of the heart through which this tremendous power can come into our life in whatever way it will. We gladly become the victim of our loving, knowing that our heart is in the hands of Him for whom we long. Often He will take us into the arena of human love, which is both tangible and elusive. In this arena we can be melted and remade, can come to know the beauty and wonder of being human. Finally we can be taught that we belong only to Him, that no other lover will suffice.

I had longed to be in love and this doorway was open. I could be with a beautiful woman and see in her the face of God. At the beginning of the relationship I thought deeply about whether loving a woman was just falling into the trap of illusion, running away from the inner emptiness which I knew was the only lasting reality. I wrote at the time:

> I put my longing in a woman. Will the beauty of
> our love be a flower that I can offer up to You?
> Or am I just putting Your eternal jewel in
> another vessel so that neither You nor I can see
> it in its fullness?

But I wonder if any philosophical speculations could have held me back—I wanted so much to feel, to touch, to taste the loving.

Writing this now, returning to those feelings, I see that I had little awareness of who she was. I can see my own feelings, the depth of my need and awakening love, but little knowing of the actual person of my beloved. The loving was enough—it swamped all sight. She had come to our group, and for many months I had seen her across the room. I felt that we shared the same deepest longing. Her English was not very good as she had recently arrived from Israel. Her name is Anat and she is an artist. But these outer realities were just on the surface. Far more potent than the desire to know her was the call to enter into the mystery of human loving, into the sacred space where man and woman meet. Invited into this space, a man can taste the eternal quality of the feminine, of the Goddess herself. Love had invited me and this was enough.

Since then I have read many psychology books. I know about projection, how a man or woman projects his or her inner partner onto another human being. This projection creates the magic and danger of the relationship, as we see our own inner divinity in the eyes and body of another. She whom we love becomes a goddess, he whom we adore a god. Falling in love, we feel we have known our lover forever, not realizing that we only see our hidden self, our archetypal inner partner whom in truth we *have* known forever. Then there comes the crash, when the ordinary person whom we think we love cannot live up to our projection, when we are confronted by the human and not the divine. Lost in the magic of our projection, we cannot and do not want to see the ordinary nature of our partner, his or her faults and character traits. But then the realities of life break through the wall of our projection, and mystery topples into the mundane.

But would it make any difference if we knew about projection, about the psychological process of falling in love? This inner archetypal happening is so potent that in the moment of its awakening it would throw off any theory. There is a need in the human psyche to engage in this psychological ritual, a need which is almost as strong as the sex drive itself. In our culture the desire for romance and sexuality appear to arrive together, as my adolescent daughter hinted when I asked her if she believed in romantic love. She replied, "Of course, I'm a teenager."

We need to find ourself in another and taste the archetypal fruits of this inner embrace. Later, after our initial encounters, it can be helpful to understand what is happening, and how romantic love can lead beyond sex into the inner union of masculine and feminine. When my daughter was four she one day stood up in the bath and surprised us with an understanding of this deeper truth, stating, "When a boy grows up he becomes a girl, and when a girl grows up she becomes a boy. And that means sorted out."

THE BEAUTY OF GOD'S PHYSICAL FORM

I have always had a deep conditioning to seek God only in the emptiness, beyond form or image. I have never been attracted by the idea of a personalized God, especially not the heavenly father figure of Christianity. Although I went to church every Sunday of my childhood, there was no internal resonance and in my early adolescence I became an atheist. Then, at sixteen, awakened by a Zen saying, I found tremendous meaning in the formless void of this tradition. "Enlightenment" in Zen does not involve any relationship to a personalized deity, but a state of inner awareness that is often symbolized by an empty circle. This emptiness of Zen is not just an abstract idea, but a dynamic reality which I had experienced in meditation, and also found in nature. Only through the empty mind of the watcher can the haiku-like moment be realized. The pure experience of the moon on the water evokes a quality of life that just is. The simplicity and formlessness of Zen evoked a deep echo within me, a formlessness which is also a state of being.

However, although I had experienced moments of pure being in nature, I was more attracted to the inner emptiness beyond creation. For me the created world carried the shadow of the feminine, the limitations of time and space, which I longed to escape. I was more drawn to His transcendence than His immanence, looking inward in meditation rather than outward into life. After I had been with Mrs. Tweedie for about a year she gave me a practice in which I had to try to see God in everything. Wherever I walked, whatever I did, I had to feel His presence. At the same time she gave me an invaluable little book, *The Practice of the Presence of God* by Brother Lawrence. This seventeenth-century Carmelite lay brother, whose only concern was to live in the presence of God, describes his simple spiritual practice of living "as if there were no one in the world but Him and me."[2] Working in the kitchen, washing the potatoes, whatever his daily activity, he felt himself in the living presence of God.

I had found that this little book opened a door into a new way of living in which I no longer had to escape this world in order to find Him. He was not only in the intangible emptiness, but could also be found in this world, alive within His creation. But after a while it was no longer enough to try to feel His presence. I needed to love Him in a tangible, created form. Ibn Arabî writes that "Woman is the highest form of earthly beauty, but earthly beauty is nothing unless it is a manifestation of Divine Qualities."[3] Through this beauty I could come nearer to Him, feel Him in the closeness of His creation.

I found something wonderful and unexpected about being able to love God in a woman. A deep, passionate need was being met, the need to feel the beauty, the softness, the warmth of His feminine form. I found an intimacy I never believed possible. Sometimes just being near to Anat I would experience a bliss that I now know comes from feeling the embodiment of the divine, the numinosity of the eternal feminine. Anat carries this quality, the sacred nourishment of life, which is a part of the essence of a woman because a woman gives birth out of her own body. There was also the continual sense of mystery, of the unknown and unknowable, which belongs to the feminine, to the veils of the Goddess. At the time I was just caught and often confused in this encounter. I was bewildered, but blissfully, knowing I had fallen into love's trap, as is echoed in a Sufi poem:

> Her tress is a trap,
> Her mole is a bait;
> I, by such ruse,
> Hopeful-hearted fell
> Into the Beloved's snare.[4]

My heart's desire was full of the contradictions of the feminine. I was a victim, turned this way and that, accepted and then rejected. But deep within me I did not care. I felt like a winter-worn ascetic unexpectedly encountering a warm and wonderful spring. I had recently read a story by Tagore, which I found hauntingly appropriate to my own state:

In the depths of the forest the ascetic practiced penance with fast-closed eyes; he intended to deserve Paradise.

But the girl who gathered twigs brought him fruits in her skirt, and water from the stream in cups made of leaves.

The days went on, and his penance grew harsher till the fruits remained untasted, the water untouched: and the girl who gathered twigs was sad.

The Lord of Paradise heard that a man had dared to aspire to be as the Gods...and he planned a temptation to decoy this creature of dust away from his adventure.

A breath from Paradise kissed the limbs of the girl who gathered twigs, and her youth ached with a sudden rapture of beauty, and her thoughts hummed like the bees of a rifled hive.

The time came when the ascetic should leave the forest for a mountain cave, to complete the rigor of his penance.

When he opened his eyes in order to start on this journey, the girl appeared to him like a verse familiar, yet forgotten, and which an added melody made strange. But the ascetic rose from his seat and told her that it was time he left the forest.

...For years he sat alone till his penance was complete.

The Lord of the Immortals came down to tell him that he had won Paradise.

"I no longer need it," said he.

The God asked him what greater reward he desired.

"I want the girl who gathers twigs."[5]

ALONENESS AND LONELINESS

Love was bringing me back into the world, a world not of alienation and rejection, but a place where I wanted to be. Anat seemed to be a part of life, to have a natural connection to people and life itself. Relating for her seemed natural, not something to be learned. Through her I sensed that I too could connect to life and to people.

For a long time I had felt deeply isolated, unable to relate to others. At times I felt like the wanderer in the cold, desolate street who, looking in through a window, sees people together, talking, laughing, in the light and warmth. My only real companionship was with friends from the meditation group, fellow wayfarers. But here I still felt separate. At our meditation meetings we meditate in silence, and then drink tea and talk, before discussing dreams or other spiritual questions. For many years I did not understand the need for people to be together and talk of ordinary things. I came to the meetings to meditate, to reach an inner goal, something beyond the outer world. Years later I came to understand the importance of just being together, fellow wayfarers on a path of infinite aloneness. But then I found it very difficult to relate to anyone; only meditation held the promise I desired.

How long this deep loneliness had haunted me I don't know. I became consciously aware of my inner self only when I was about fifteen, and have few memories of how I felt as a child. Probably I repressed many feelings. I remember as a teenager at boarding school feeling very separate, unable to join in. After I came to the group these feelings were again surfacing, along with the impression that those around me in the group had an ability to relate, to be together in friendship, that was somehow denied to me.

There were two sides to these feelings. One was a deep inner aloneness in which I was quite content with my own company. I have always liked myself, and later in life was astonished to discover that many people do not like themselves. I have since wondered how someone can live with herself if she does not like herself. Because we see only through our own eyes, conditioned by our own character, other people's problems are often a mystery. But my own aloneness also carried an arrogance, a feeling of superiority to those around me. This arrogance was not just compensation for feeling separate, but egotistic pride. My first years on the path, when I was unable to sleep, unable to eat ordinary food, unable to join in with others, were a time of painfully grinding down this arrogance, teaching me the wisdom of humility and being ordinary.

But there was another aspect to this aloneness which I remember surfacing with my teenage years. I felt unable to participate in superficial social interaction. This was partly an adolescent rebellion against my middle-class background with its codes of superficial talk and social politeness, in which, according to English custom, no feelings are ever expressed. But there was also a hunger for a real inner connection with something deeply meaningful. I could not accept the emptiness and superficiality I felt around me, and the only path was inward into aloneness.

I hungered for meaning, for relating from the depths, and at times I found this in individual relationships. My first girlfriend, Beba, was partly Greek and did not have the English inhibitions about expressing feelings. Also, our deep inner connection allowed a depth of relating beyond the level of personality. After she left me I was in deep despair and terribly alone. Then within my meditation group I again found the intimacy of real friendship. However, even in the midst of this deeply nourishing friendship, I still carried a sense of being cut off, isolated. Often this isolation evoked a sense of despair, and I would think of going out and relating, being with people in order to fill the emptiness within me. But at the same time I instinctively knew that this door was closed—there was no point in picking up the phone. Even when I was with friends whom I loved, after a time I would find myself exhausted and would withdraw.

Now I understand why I carry such a strong imprint of aloneness, how I need to be alone in order to live out my destiny. The mystical path is a one-to-one relationship with God, and as such demands a degree of aloneness that most people would find frightening. Ultimately the mystic needs to be free from any attachment; the lover must look only to the Beloved. The instinctual aloneness imprinted into the soul forbade me to become attached to the outer world. It had the effect of making empty any relationship that did not help bring me nearer to God. The ninth-century Sufi Dhû-l-Nûn tells a story which has always touched me:

> I was wandering in the mountains when I observed a party of afflicted folk gathered together.
> "What befell you?" I asked.
> "There is a devotee living in a cell here," they answered. "Once every year he comes out and

breathes on these people and they are all healed. Then he returns to his cell, and does not emerge again until the following year."

I waited patiently until he came out. I beheld a man pale of cheek, wasted and with sunken eyes. The awe of him caused me to tremble. He looked on the multitude with compassion. Then he raised his eyes to heaven, and breathed several times over the afflicted ones. All were healed.

As he was about to retire to his cell, I seized his skirt.

"For the love of God," I cried. "You have healed the outward sickness; pray heal the inward sickness."

"Dhû-l-Nûn." he said, gazing at me, "take your hand from me. The Friend is watching from the zenith of might and majesty. If He sees you clutching at another than He, He will abandon you to that person, and that person to you, and you will perish each at the other's hand."

So saying, he withdrew into his cell.[6]

INFINITE LONGING AND THE FEMININE

The path of love takes us from our own aloneness into an embrace which fulfills our deepest need. In my aloneness I have felt unbelievable nearness, such intimacy, love, and belonging that any sense of separation dissolves—walking, feeling His companionship, going to bed to know that He is waiting to take me to Him. I have felt almost guilty, wondering why I am being given so much. I know that the Friend wants me for Himself, could never allow another to come between us. But I also remember the times in the desert, the agony of isolation, the desolation of loneliness. Even when I was deeply in love, entranced by Her beauty, the soul's hunger was also present, underlying every physical embrace. Reading through a book of old poems, I discovered a few lines that I wrote at the time, words that speak of the painful solitariness of a wayfarer seeking what cannot be found, knowing that the journey is infinite and the real Beloved beyond reach:

> It was not really because he was lonely,
> but just
> there seemed to be an ocean
> without end.

Longing is the mark of the lover, the soul's song of separation. Deeper than any worldly loneliness is the sense of separation that haunts the mystic, the separation of the soul from the Source, the lover from the Beloved. Looking back, I know the journey is worthwhile because I now know what awaits the traveler. But then there was no such knowledge and the path seemed to stretch forever, the goal just a distant dream beyond the horizon. All I knew was my need and the sense that no one person could answer it. I wanted what the world could not give, and this evoked a quality of aloneness beyond imagining.

Yet I was also in love and at times deeply happy. There is no contradiction, because just as there are different degrees of closeness, so are there different qualities of aloneness. On a human level, as a man, as a lover, I had found my heart's desire. I had found the one woman whom I would love for the rest of my life, the one person with whom a certain closeness and intimacy would be allowed. But if I looked closely I also knew that this was not enough, that I longed for a deeper and more complete union than could ever be reached with another person. And I came to know that Anat shares this stamp of the mystic, that she can never give herself completely to anyone but the Beloved. For both of us something pointed beyond what was given, towards the innermost chamber of the heart that belongs only to God.

In every human relationship, however close and loving, there are always two. The mystic is born with a memory of a different love in which there is only oneness, in which lover and Beloved are united forever. In a human love affair we sense this possibility. In the deepest human relationship there can be a meeting of souls, a sense of intimacy that is beyond the physical. To experience this for the first time is intoxicating. Making love is more than physical orgasm, for one merges into the beyond, into the infinite inner space which feels like the cosmos itself. Physical closeness becomes a doorway to the inner worlds, to mysteries which have always belonged to the feminine. These were part of the mysteries taught in the temples of the Goddess, whose priestesses were trained to initiate a man into the sacred spaces of the feminine. In the moments of merging, of being taken beyond oneself, it seems as if an ancient promise is being fulfilled, that we are being touched by the finger of our Beloved. There is also a sense of real wonder that a human lover, a physical embrace, can take us into this inner ecstasy.

But there is also a danger for the wayfarer, and I think in particular for a man. The world of the Great Goddess is in essence a world of unconsciousness, the instinctual round symbolized by Ouroboros, the serpent eating its tail. Every man has a primal pull to return to this unconscious oneness, the archetypal world of the mother from which he feels banished. There is a reason why, in primitive cultures, at puberty the boy has to leave the women's hut or the home of his mother, never to return. The feminine mysteries hold the instinctual attraction of returning to the unconscious oneness which allows us to lose the burden of consciousness. I found this pull almost irresistible. To lose myself in a woman whom I loved was like a doorway to eternal childhood, to be forever in the arms of the Great Mother. There I could receive the nurturing and warmth I had always desired, the mothering I had never received, and then every instinct would be fulfilled.

I do not know how many others have consciously experienced this test. I have always been very open to the archetypal world, and the drama of the inner feminine has been central to my life. Projecting the anima, my inner goddess, onto Anat took me deeper into the inner world than I knew possible. I felt the bliss of her seduction. But luckily Anat was very aware of the moment I changed from a man into a child. She in no way would play the mother—an instinctual taboo forbade it. Thus the pull of the inner also evoked a rejection—I was allowed to taste but not become lost in Her embrace. I could sense the eternal beauty of the feminine, but I was always to remain outside. At times this evoked anger and a feeling of betrayal. She who was so close was also forbidden. Now I am grateful because I know a more enduring love affair, and how the embrace of the feminine can carry the curse of forgetfulness.

A human love affair gives us a taste of together-ness, a hint of union. The heart can be opened to a depth of passion that transcends reason. But finally, however close we become, we are always two separate individuals with different needs. A human love affair can remind us of love's touch, can make us realize that love needs to include all of ourself—that it is not a cerebral affair. (There is a real reason why mystic love poetry is so full of erotic imagery.) But what the soul hungers for is a union in which duality does not belong on any level, in which there are a merging and a quality of completeness dependent only upon Him. Another human being can never give us what we want. I knew this and yet I was also caught in the wonder of what was given through a woman.

This struggle was central to my years of romantic love, and was a way of fully incarnating my own love and devotion. I have found that in many relationships there are a lover and a beloved, one who loves and one who is loved. I was the lover. I needed to love, to adore. There was an inner certainty that this was the one woman I would love. Early in our relationship I had a powerful experience when sitting with her one evening. I suddenly found myself out of my body on the inner plane of the soul. In that space I was with her soul and I knew that I could trust her on the level of the soul. Whatever the difficulties and differences on the level of the personality, I could give myself to my loving of her with the totality of commitment that is my only way to live.

COOKED IN THE POT

In a human love affair the inner wonder and taste of bliss are caught in all the complications of personal psychology and character differences. The opposites of the soul and the personality can tear a relationship apart and bring immense suffering. Here lies the danger of projection, in which we expect our partner to carry our idealized soul-image, and we give little consideration to the difficulties of personal relationship. For this reason the Jungian Robert Johnson advises against marrying someone with whom you are in love, saying that after a few weeks of bliss come years of suffering. Yet, acknowledging the power of romantic love in our culture, he likens it to a Zen teaching that inner growth always involves an experience of "a red hot coal stuck in the throat." "We can't live with it, and we can't live without it—we can't swallow it and we can't cough it up!"[7]

Romantic love throws us into the primal contradiction that we are human and divine. Seeking our divinity in our partner, we are only too often confronted by human failings. Combined with this are the very real difficulties of communication between men and women. The English mystical painter Cecil Collins was known to remark that men and women are so different, it is astonishing that they can even talk to each other! Yet romantic love can be an alchemical vessel of inner transformation, a vessel in which the opposites are melted down and reformed. The "red hot coal" can take us beyond duality into the paradoxical realm of a deeper truth. I once asked a wise old man, Werner Engel, who had been a friend of Jung, what was the way to resolve the seemingly impossible contradictions of being in love. He replied with two words, unconditional love. Unconditional love has no reason or limit to its loving.

Romantic love was a deeply painful place of my own transformation. The power of my projection, my idealized inner feminine, was balanced by deep differences in character between my beloved and me. For example, Anat is a feeling type; feelings are her primary mode of experience and expression, which is combined for her with a great sensitivity. I was brought up in a family and collective atmosphere in which feelings are strictly taboo—I never so much as heard my parents disagree until one weekend when I was fourteen and they announced to all six children that they were getting a divorce. I was also sent off to boarding school at the age of seven. A collective masculine environment with cold baths first thing in the morning is hardly conducive to developing feelings or sensitivity! Added to the alchemical pot of our relationship were ancient masculine and feminine wounds and shadow patterns. These and other personal and archetypal dynamics were bound together with love, a deep connection on the level of the soul, and a shared commitment to the path. I often felt like the chickpea in Rûmî's story, in which the chickpea tries to escape the boiling pot, only to be knocked back down with the cook's ladle:

> A chickpea leaps almost over the rim of the pot
> where it's being boiled.
>
> "Why are you doing this to me?"
>
> The cook knocks him down with the ladle.
>
> "Don't you try to jump out.
> You think I'm torturing you.
> I'm giving you flavor,
> so you can mix with spices and rice
> and be the lovely vitality of a human being.

Remember when you drank rain in the garden.
That was for this."

Grace first. Sexual pleasure,
then a boiling new life begins,
and the Friend has something good to eat.[8]

Every wayfarer has to be cooked, boiled to perfection.
We each have our own vessel, the container of our
transformation. On the deepest level this container is
the relationship with the Beloved, reflected in the
relationship with the teacher and the path. But for
many seekers a human relationship can also be a
powerful and potent pot, for which passion, feelings,
and love are the fire.

How many nights have I cried silently, caught in
the opposites of the human and the divine which form
the cross of every lover's crucifixion. I felt like an
ancient ascetic, a monk of many lifetimes, bewildered
by the contradictions of the feminine, unable to reconcile the power of my projection with the human
differences that confronted me. There is love, devotion, a deep connection of the soul. Why cannot one
live forever within that sacred circle, that intense,
luminous loving? Why do the personality, the differences of character, intrude, bringing one back to earth
from worship and wonder?

The wayfarer is always thrown between the opposites, the more potent the loving the more powerful the
oscillation. Meditation and the energy of the path add
to this effect, dramatically energizing outer situations
and relationships, stirring the pot, bringing aspects of
the psyche into consciousness. Mrs. Tweedie calls it
the "yo-yo syndrome" in which we go up and down,
from nearness to separation. In my loving this was

played out to every extreme. Divine nearness was followed by two egos breaking apart, leaving me in the anguish of separation. In this despair and isolation I would turn inward into the emptiness, cry out for help, and then the love and nearness would return. Divinity would again be in front of my eyes.

I was being cooked in the pot of my own loving, tenderized by the impossible opposites of masculine and feminine, human and divine. I once had a dream in which I was told that I had been "made soft by a very hard system." The Sufi system is hard because it takes you to the extremes within yourself, pushes you seemingly beyond endurance. Sometimes this is just an inner drama; sometimes it is dramatized on an outer stage. A human love affair can combine the inner and outer, the secrets of the soul and the visible dynamics of two human beings. When the deepest contradictions of your own nature are continually thrown in your face, there is no alternative but to surrender, to give up the pretensions of the ego, the desire for power or the demand to be right, and leave everything to be burnt away.

Arrogance and independence, anger and alienation, vulnerability and defensiveness, all these aspects of my character were cooked in the cauldron. They were brought to the surface, into the drama of the relationship and the light of consciousness. I remember that it was particularly painful to be vulnerable in front of another person, to allow my defenses to dissolve, and to stand naked. Often in these moments I would react in anger—the anger covering my wounds and vulnerability. Within myself everything was exposed and stripped of pretensions. The opposites of our characters constellated aspects of myself that might otherwise have remained hidden, and Anat has a penetrating sensitivity and insight that could see through my defenses. Finally I had to accept my own failings, my own inadequacies, my own ordinariness. I was just another human being, nothing special, just a soul walking home. Longing to see the divine in another, I was forced to accept my own humanness. With humility these opposites were brought together.

THE WOUNDED FEMININE

Romantic love awakens the anima in a man, the inner feminine or soul figure. She is not only a goddess, but also his muse and guide in the underworld. As my own journey into the inner world continued, leading me into the personal and archetypal world, I found aspects of my shadow, my cruelty and carelessness, as well as my own feminine self. The intimacy of a relationship allows many aspects of the psyche to surface, many dynamics of projection to be played out. The energy of love is the container for a whole psychic story to be brought into consciousness and then accepted, allowed to live in the sunlight.

My inner feminine was experienced projected onto my partner, but my anima also appeared in different forms in dreams. Sometimes she was an artist, a therapist, or an unknown lover. I also remember her wounded, in a wheelchair. This image of the wounded feminine returned many times, and I responded with active imagination, Jung's technique of going back into the feeling quality of the dream. There I would ask her about her pain and try to heal her. Our masculine culture easily wounds the feminine, and we thus lose our sensitivity, our openness to feelings and emotions. But a wound can also take us deeper within ourself, as the desire to heal and understand draws us inward.

I wandered through the maze of my inner self for many years, guided by both the wisdom and the wounds of the anima. Deeper and deeper I went into my own treatment of the feminine, my rejection of her and my need to redeem this wound. Again I had to encounter the dark, terrible power of the feminine of which men are most afraid. I had experienced this fear in my childhood and adolescence in the psychic darkness surrounding my mother. Now, at another level of the spiral, she reappeared, powerful, but no longer so demonic. I found her both acted out in my partner and alive within myself. In the entanglement of a relationship it is often difficult to know what is a projection and what belongs to the other.

She, who is described in the Song of Solomon as "fair as the moon, clear as the sun and terrible as an army with banners,"[9] is the primal energy of the feminine. She carries the instinctual wisdom that belongs to nature and to the unconscious wholeness of life. Ignorant of her wisdom, and frightened of a power so different from the visible world of masculine consciousness, men have projected their fear and burnt her as a witch. Finding this archetypal fear within myself, I was relieved to discover that Jung towards the end of his life also acknowledged it: "Woman is a very very strong being, magical. That is why I am afraid of women."[10]

Romantic love had taken me into the arena of the feminine, into her passion, power, and beauty. It was easy to follow the collective pattern and idealize her, like Hamlet calling Ophelia his "soul's idol." I projected this image, the purity, warmth, and nurturing care, that has become symbolized by the Virgin Mary. But her dark sister is always present and cannot be ignored. Encountering her passion and power, her terrible beauty, I uncovered a personal and archetypal wound. I tried to close the door, to keep my love celestial and soulful, but I had chosen a woman who would not allow such rejection, who would not play this collective denial. She is too natural a human being. Finally, one night I had a dream in which I heard the most pitiable and sorrowful sound I have ever heard, the cry of a wounded tiger. Until then I never realized how I had hurt the feminine, and how my fear of her power was a cause of this hurt:

> I am left to look after a house while the owner of the house goes out for the evening. A fire breaks out in the house and I go in to rescue a couple who are living there. They represent the idealized anima relationship. I suddenly see that there are three tigers in the house, and realize that they will be made very nervous by the fire and could be dangerous. I rescue the couple but close the door so that the tigers cannot come out and attack us.
>
> The owner comes back and telephones the fire brigade, which is in fact already on its way. He rescues the tigers who are his pets. They are very badly burnt and as they come out one makes such a sound of pain and distress that it is awful to hear. I have never heard such a whimpering and sorrowful sound before and it deeply moves me. Two tigers are taken off to the hospital and one is left with me. Because of its pain I am not afraid of it.

Within the house of my psyche there is a fire, a conflict. From this conflict I try to rescue my idealized anima relationship, my fantasy of how a man and a woman might be together. However, I find that this couple are not the only inhabitants of the house; there are also three tigers. The tigers image the primal power of the feminine—traditionally the Goddess rides on the back of a tiger. A conflict was burning within me, a split between the idealized feminine and her darker, more powerful nature.

But I am frightened of the tigers, and so shut the door of the house and leave them to burn. How often through fear do we close the door on our shadow, unaware of the pain that this inflicts on these wounded and neglected figures? These figures of the unconscious are real, and the pain that they felt was my own inner suffering. Possibly these tigers could be dangerous; such primal energies will always have a dangerous element. But out of my fear I leave them to burn. I leave them caught in the conflict.

Eventually the tigers come out of the house and their pained moaning is one of the most distressing sounds I have ever heard. To see such beautiful and powerful animals limping from the house, moaning in distress, touched me deeply for days. Later, in active imagination, I asked one of the tigers, "Why did this happen?" To which the tiger simply answered, "It had to be that way." Possibly the only way I could realize this inner energy and treat it with love and not fear was to see it so wounded, so pitifully hurt.

When the owner of the house comes back he knows exactly what to do. The fire brigade is already on its way. The owner rescues the tigers who are his pets. The owner is the Higher Self, the master of all the energies of the unconscious. The Self, the true owner of the house of my psyche, let my ego experience the conflict and the pain caused by my idealization of the feminine. Only through seeing the pain of the tiger would I cease to fear her, and thus be able to live the power of my primal feminine self. The day after the dream, synchronicity reinforced its significance when I saw a film on television about a "wild boy" from Africa, whose pet was a tiger.

After this dream I embraced the wounded tiger, took her to my heart and, with the energy of active imagination, nurtured her with love. Months later this dream had a sequel which imaged a deeper integration of the feminine:

> I am with my teacher beside a clump of tiger lilies which have to be cut down. I cut them with a bush knife. In the next sequence I have woven a meditation mat from these lilies and am shown a diagram which describes how their energy is integrated.

The image of the tiger lilies beautifully embraces the two sides of the feminine. The lily is sacred to all virgin goddesses, and in Christian symbolism is associated with purity, innocence, and the Virgin Mary. The tiger lily thus images the natural flowering of the feminine, in both her purity and her passion, her innocence and her instinctual wisdom. Yet this flower has to be cut down; only then can the dual nature of the feminine be integrated and its energy put to creative use. The tiger lilies are woven into a meditation mat, suggesting that this energy now has a spiritual dynamic. The feminine no longer holds me in the embrace of an idealized lover, but has the potential to reveal the secret hidden within creation.

The cutting of the natural flowers points to the alchemical mystery of the *opus contra naturam*. On one hand the alchemical *opus* is the most natural process. The birth of the Self follows the deepest rhythms of the psyche, and dreams often use the images of nature—of giving birth and the opening of flowers—to express this mystery. Yet, in the realm of the Great Mother, there is no such transformation. In the rhythms of nature everything that is born decays and dies; nothing can escape this closed circle. The Great Mother is the spider-mother eating her children, resisting the birth of individual consciousness. She resists even more the inner birth that takes us beyond the duality of opposites, beyond life and death. It is the flowering of the Self that finally frees us from her power, and this is experienced as a violation of nature, as in the cutting of the flowers.[11]

My relationship, my human loving, had taken me deep into the realm of the Great Goddess. There I found both the power and the wounds of the feminine and was able to nurture her pain. The transformation of the feminine took me out of the captive wonder of her embrace, beyond the opposites of masculine and feminine, into the mysterious union that belongs to the birth of the Self. Soon I began to have dreams of babies, children born with stars in their eyes.

LEARNING THE FLOW OF LOVE

Romance was a loving and painful way to be cooked. There were different ingredients, different herbs and spices. On the deepest human level there was a soul-link, a relationship and love that belong to a different dimension, that we brought with us from before. I always knew that Anat was the one woman I would really love; about this there was never a question or doubt. I also sensed that we had come together for a certain work, a purpose beyond our own individual life. Years later, when we came to California to start a Sufi Center, this purpose became clearer.

But in those early years there was just the intensity of loving, and the soul-link was combined with a powerful projection. She was my goddess, and embodied the beauty and mystery of the feminine world. I was held fascinated, enthralled. One day, some years later, I was shown the simple power of this projection, and how it can turn an ordinary woman into a mysterious goddess. By this time I had realized the real inner wonder of the anima and no longer needed to project her. But in the short space of an hour I saw this projection fall onto a woman and transform her. It happened after meditation one day in Mrs. Tweedie's flat, as I visibly experienced a woman suddenly become mysterious, profoundly beautiful, and alluring. For fifteen minutes she carried the irresistible attraction of the Goddess, and my eyes and my whole inner attention were drawn to her. Then something in me withdrew the projection, and to my astonishment she was suddenly just an ordinary woman. There was no mystery, no allure. She was just another woman in the room. Again my projection fell on her, and in that moment she changed back, once again carrying the magic of a goddess. Then finally the projection was again withdrawn, the curtain that caught the light of my own soul was lifted, and the woman in front of me was again dressed in the clothes of this world. I had been allowed to witness the wondrous power of the anima projection.

For about seven years I was lost in the magical whirlpool of romantic love. I had found my soul's idol and worshiped her. I tasted the honeyed nectar of the Goddess and also encountered her terrifying power. I was torn between the opposites of the divine and the ordinary, between the projection and the personality, between the heart's desire and the difficulties of two strong individuals living together. Through prayer and pain I tried to reconcile these impossible opposites, and was taken inward, along the maze of the psyche, forced to confront and accept many difficult aspects of myself.

I began to learn about the nature of human loving, the mysterious ebb and flow of love that happens between two people. Like everything in this world, love has masculine and feminine qualities. The masculine aspect of love is "I love you," and it carries a commitment to stay true to this statement of the heart. For me this was easy, to be steadfast in loving whatever the difficulties, for it carries the quality of a challenge and the drive to persevere. Whatever the difficulties, the love remained, and I knew that love was the only lasting reality. Once, when the relationship seemed to be swamped by psychological difficulties, I inwardly asked my Sheikh, and in a dream he just told me, "Love is the wine."

I found the feminine nature of love more difficult. Mrs. Tweedie often quoted the lines of an Italian love song, "to hold love with light hands," and I had to learn this wisdom. While the masculine holds firm in loving, the feminine nature of love is its eternal flow and change, the fluctuations of the heart. The currents of love would carry me back and forth, sometimes deeply in love, sometimes withdrawing. I began to understand the sacredness of the *space* between two people, and how that space holds the real magic of the relationship, its invisible quality. At the beginning I wanted to always hold her, for the wonderful closeness to be always there. But gradually I became aware that this limits a relationship, limits the ability of love to flow. When we were married, Mrs. Tweedie quoted to us the passage from *The Prophet* by Kahlil Gibran:

> Love one another, but make not a bond of
>   love:
> Let it rather be a moving sea between the
>   shores of your souls.
>
> ...Give your hearts, but not into each
>   other's keeping.
> For only the hand of Life can contain your
>   hearts.
> And stand together yet not too near to-
>   gether:
> For the pillars of the temple stand apart,
> And the oak tree and the cypress grow not
>   in each other's shadow.

Learning to give space to another's loving and another's life is not easy. I wanted to hold, to possess, to feel the security of ownership. Soon after I was married I felt a primitive instinct to take my wife off to a cave of my own, where she would belong only to me!

SPIRIT AND MATTER

The Sufis say that the only real relationship, the only real loving, is with the Beloved. But through human relationships we can learn to love Him, just as a little girl plays with dolls, because one day she will become a mother. Through the power of projection I was drawn into the arena of human loving, into the touch and taste of lips meeting. I began to understand my own human nature, as well as the ways of love. I finally put aside the cloak of the ascetic, my desire to renounce the world. I had found love not on the remote mountain top or in the desert, but in a physical embrace, in the magic of the feminine.

I came to realize that the particular power of the anima and the potency of being in love come from the combination of spirit and matter. The eternal beauty of a woman combines the two worlds, the Creator and the creation—as Rûmî says, "A woman is God shining through subtle veils." In the face and body of her whom I loved I experienced the inner and outer worlds dancing together, the magic at the core of creation. One night I was told in a dream that the essence of the anima is "spirit impregnated with matter." The anima belongs to the soul, to the spiritual center of ourself, but she carries the seed of matter, the wonder of the created world. The anima rises from the unconscious through the alchemy of love in which there is the need of the soul to be known, to be experienced here, in this world. Pure desire, solely physical attraction, will never constellate the anima. Love alone can combine the two worlds, and the deeper the love, the more unconditional its nature, the more these worlds, the human and the divine, can be brought together. From this union of love, the qualities of the soul can become conscious.

But love drew me further, and I was not allowed to remain forever with my eyes and heart turned towards a woman. The very captivating quality of love, that it combines the human and divine, was also the crucifix that freed me. In the impossible moments, when the conflicts and the difficulties of human loving seemed just torture and betrayal, I cried to God, to the one Beloved who I knew could never desert me. I asked why I was made to love in this world of contradictions and imperfections, why I was caught in the web of loving a woman. In these nights of despair and soul-searching, when the opposites seemed irreconcilable, an alchemical inner process was spinning straw into gold, transmuting my romantic nature into devotion. The inner feminine began to return to my own heart, to reveal the qualities of Sophia who opens us to the deepest meaning of life. She is the divine feminine who leads us into the presence of Truth.

One day I suddenly knew that I could never be in love again. I knew that this phase of my life was over; the clothing of the romantic had been put aside. I felt tremendous sadness at the time, as if a door to a human experience had been closed. Since adolescence I had felt the attraction of romantic love and the desire to worship a woman. The inner process of the path had freed me from this attachment, but I also regretted its passing. Once again I felt separate from the normal patterns of human life. I felt the inner aloneness of the mystic. But since then I have found a love that is far beyond anything that can be experienced between people, however much they are in love. I see the frailty of human love affairs, and how much of an illusion is romantic love. With my Beloved there are no psychological problems nor differences of character. There are not two people, but a merging and melting into oneness, and a presence that is always within the heart.

Recently I sat next to a young woman on a plane and we began to talk. I told her that I lectured on dreams and she shared a near-death experience she had had. I knew from the experience that she was an old soul who was destined to see beneath the veils of illusion. The young woman was just out of college, and was telling me about a man she loved, who did not seem to be in love with her. I asked her what she wanted from life and she replied, "To love and be loved." In my heart I knew the truth of what she said, and how a man could never answer the depth of her need. However, as she talked about her boyfriend I saw that she had, as yet, no other concept of love. I said nothing, but felt the sadness of an old traveler who knows the length and suffering of the journey that awaits someone just starting out.

SHAPER OF BEAUTY

There was another ingredient to my romantic loving which I begin only now to appreciate. I realize that what I saw in Anat was not just the numinosity of my projection, the beauty of the soul. There was another light dancing around her form, caught in the curl of her hair, in the curves of her body. Through the veils of form the beauty of the real Beloved was shining; a luminous epiphany permeated her being. Inwardly my eyes were open to this light. Seeing but unknowing, I was caught, entranced.

Over the centuries we have separated the sensual and the spiritual. But lovers have left hints of the secret hidden within the physical world, reflected in its beauty. Sufi poetry uses the symbolism of a woman's beauty to describe aspects of the divine: her curl signifies "the Divine Selfhood, unto which no one can penetrate,"[12] her beauty spot the "Divine Essence itself." More explicit is the poetry of Mirabai, who knew of the soul's rapture with her Dark Lord, Krishna, and speaks of the body's "hidden treasures":

O friend, understand: the body
is like the ocean,
rich with hidden treasures.

Open your innermost chamber and light its
   lamp.

Within the body are gardens,
rare flowers, the inner Music;
within the body a lake of bliss,
on it the white soul-swans take their joy.

And in the body, a vast market—
go there, trade,
sell yourself for a profit you can't spend.

Mira says, her Lord is beyond praising.
Allow her to dwell near your feet.[13]

The body of a woman beckons to a man with the secret hidden within creation, the beauty of the Beloved's face. The feminine holds this secret, which for the Sufi is symbolized in the very word of creation, *Kun* (Be!).

In the beauty permeating my beloved I felt for the first time this quality of divine immanence rather than transcendence. Before, I had always loved Him as beyond form, sought Him in the emptiness. Now I felt Her, saw Her, could even touch this divine quality. In this way the Beloved drew me nearer, revealed more of His secret. In Himself He is unknowable, but through His qualities, His names and attributes, we can come to know Him. I found Him as *Al-Musawwir*, the shaper of beauty.

The danger in feeling the sensuous beauty of the divine is that we may try to possess It. With my invisible Beloved I am always the victim, waiting for Him to come. In my longing I cry to Him, but I never know when I will feel Him in my heart. Sometimes He has been absent for months. But the physical world is a tangible presence. She whom I adore can be held in my arms. Reaching out I can feel her softness, sense the nourishment of the divine. To experience the beauty of the Beloved in a woman can be a dangerous addiction, in which physical desire can be confused with longing. Longing for God, feeling the pain of the heart, I would also know that there was a woman, a physical presence, with whom I could taste a bliss that was not just sexual. Whose scent did I really smell when the perfume of the Beloved was mingled with that of a woman?

Longing and pain, confusion and bliss, the different realities interpenetrated. But through the ebb and flow of our relationship I have never been allowed to feel any sense of possession. I also knew deep down that no external beloved would be enough, no human loving fulfill me. Inwardly I was always looking elsewhere, crying out in my heart to be taken by God to God. The passion of my soul was only partly contained in a woman, long enough to know Her presence, to no longer reject this world as empty of love.

Finding the Beloved here, in the beauty of a woman, opened my heart. When the heart is opened it knows the source of its longing and turns towards this One Light. The power of the heart's deepest desire helped drag me through the maze of the psyche, and also pull back the projection of my own soul. The light of the Beloved was a catalyst in this process, drawing me into the physical embrace, but not then allowing the divine to be limited to a single person. Finally I found this light all around me, saw His beauty wherever I looked.

Abi'l Khayr says that "love is God's trap." I was trapped long ago, my soul caught in His embrace. But I needed to put aside the limitations of the renunciate and bring this love into the world. For the imprint of His presence to be made real I was caught in the beauty of a woman, in the wonder that is hidden within creation. Slowly this wonder crept into consciousness. I was no longer alienated from this world, but began to feel the magic that is life itself.

LIFE AS A HOUSEHOLDER

*Correctly combined, the secrets and the most ordinary
things in this life
may make it possible to achieve the Longest Journey.*[1]

MARRIAGE, A CHILD, AND A HOUSE

After finishing college I trained as a teacher, and was
soon thrown into the chaos of the classroom, the noise
and confusion of teenagers. I worked in a south-
London public girls' school, trying to make myself
heard and understood. There is a tradition in such
schools that the newest teachers are given the most
difficult classes, full of the most unruly children, where
the sole desire of the new teacher is to keep some kind
of order and survive. Each day I would return home
exhausted, rest, try to meditate for an hour, and then
prepare my work for the next day before going to
sleep. This was a painful initiation into the "real world"
of the classroom.

Here was a very different world from the ordered,
disciplined life of my boarding-school years. I remember one particularly disruptive girl who would never
keep in her seat and was often talking and shouting,
making it impossible to teach the class. I found her so
difficult until one day I heard her story, how she and
her younger sister never had a hot, cooked meal,
always coming home to either a drunken parent or a
cold, empty flat. She became a lesson in compassion as

I glimpsed the environment that had formed her. Then, even when she was most disruptive, I felt that I could no longer judge her or inwardly complain.

At this time I was living in a small room in the same house as Anat. My room looked out over a rose garden, and the house was full of peace, a complete contrast to the classroom! This was the same house in which Mrs. Tweedie used to live—a year earlier she had moved to a nearby flat as the group had grown too big for her small room. It was wonderful to live in a house singing with the energy of meditation, with the heart's praising of God. There was a silence and a song in the very walls of the building, permeated by years of meditation and love. I was happy there, despite the exhaustion of teaching. Anat had a room across the corridor, facing the street and the same trains that had rattled the house when I had come to Mrs. Tweedie's for meditation.

We were married from that house, with a reception in the garden. Mrs. Tweedie and all of the friends from the group were there. I cooked the food for the reception and my mother made the cake. We were one of the first couples in the group to marry, and also the first to have children. Our son, Emmanuel, was conceived in that house, and came back from being born in the hospital to the small room with a gas fire, a cooker, a sink, and a bed. I was so happy when he was born, seeing this soul come into the world. I remember walking down the street full of utmost joy. Sufis believe that we choose our parents, and the miracle of birth was combined with the wonder that a soul would want to come to live with me.

Life was simple, contained, and exhausting. Anat was exhausted from a son who needed to be fed every few hours. I was exhausted from teaching, from the demands of unruly children. On Fridays Anat would go to the meditation for an hour and then come back so that I could also go. This was to be a routine for many years, as one of us would look after the children so that the other could meditate. It was very rare that we could both go to the meditation meetings together.

We could not live forever in the two small rooms, which were not at all suitable for a child. The moment he started to crawl, everything would be dangerous—the cooker, the fire, the pots and pans. I had inherited some money from a family trust, and we were able to look for a house. I knew with a deep conviction that I needed a house rather than a flat, a piece of space between earth and sky that belonged to nobody else. We found a house nearby that seemed perfect. The house had been built in the nineteen-thirties, when the tube train extension made the area accessible for people working in central London. Then, in the sixties, the house was converted into two flats, one on the ground level and one upstairs. We had been looking for a house for our family and to my astonishment we found a home for the whole group: we asked Mrs. Tweedie if she would like to live in the ground-floor flat and she accepted.

Mrs. Tweedie had been unhappy for some time in her other flat, which had become increasingly unsafe for an elderly woman living alone. I had no idea of this as I only saw her at the weekly group meetings, and she was for me still an impersonal teacher-figure. However, Anat has a far more intimate relationship with Mrs. Tweedie and before Emmanuel was born would spend time with her. Anat was aware of how difficult it was for Mrs. Tweedie to live alone in her flat, with squatters next door, a dog always barking, and drunken soccer fans sometimes climbing into the garden from the railway line that ran at the end of the garden. Once she was assaulted and almost strangled by a man who robbed her of her small pension. She had opened the door to him, thinking it was one of the group she was expecting. So when we found our house, Anat suggested what I would never otherwise have considered, that we offer Mrs. Tweedie somewhere to live. I was totally shaken by even the idea of living in the same house as my teacher. But we were to live in the same house for eleven years, and the imprint of that experience will last with us forever.

A SENSE OF FULFILLMENT

We spent the summer decorating and remodeling. The house had been neglected for years, and the previous occupants had removed everything, from light fittings to door handles. We first moved in upstairs and then prepared the downstairs flat for Mrs. Tweedie. My external relationship with Mrs. Tweedie began to change as I found myself more often in her presence. One day I had to drive her to a store to choose door-handles, and in the midst of the morning traffic she told me, "Remember, we are all dispensable." I did not know it then, but a different part of my training was beginning. I had many lessons to learn.

Mrs. Tweedie moved into the house in September and the energy of the path and the power of her presence permeated everything. For a while it was very difficult to even begin to have an ordinary life upstairs. Before, I had only visited her for meditation and was grateful for the energy of her presence that stilled the mind and awakened the heart. Once, when we were still living in our bed-sit, she had asked Anat and me to look after her flat when she went away for a week. The energy in her room was so powerful that the only way I could go to sleep was to put a mattress on the kitchen floor! Now I was living with this energy constantly flooding up through the floorboards. I would sit at my desk to work and my mind would become still and empty. Finally Mrs. Tweedie put an inner barrier between the two flats, allowing us to have an almost normal life.

But having a house was wonderful. For weeks I would wander from room to room just feeling the space. For almost two years we had lived in two small rooms without a separate kitchen and with a shared bathroom down the hall that in winter was intensely cold. Now, for the first time in my life, I had my own place. I could have a bath and leave the door open. I marveled at having a whole kitchen, and for a few weeks delighted in stocking the shelves and the refrigerator with the foods I liked most. There is something immensely satisfying in seeing a row of jars filled with different grains and pulses. A primitive longing in me was being satisfied.

For many years I had sensed that I had three primary desires: for a wife, a child, and a house. These desires had rested at the threshold of consciousness, occasionally appearing. I remember at school when we were discussing our ambitions, what we wanted in life, I had surprised myself by saying that I just wanted a wife and children. Now I was unexpectedly fulfilled, feeling that I had everything I wanted from life. This sense of fulfillment was so deep that I felt that life could give me nothing more. Why were these natural desires so important? The full shelves in the larder also evoked a satisfaction beyond what seemed normal or rational.

Maybe many lifetimes as an ascetic or monk had left their traces in a longing for what was denied, a home of my own, a woman, and a child. Now I had what I wanted, what I had denied myself for so long. The spiritual path was taking me full circle, completing something within me.

LEARNING ABOUT MONEY

The traveler on the journey is never allowed to rest for too long. States of fulfillment or completion give way to the next turn of the spiral, the next test. I had to learn a painful lesson about the responsibility of being a householder, a husband, and a father. This inner drama began to unfold with the feeling that the rest of my inheritance should be put to use to help others. Some friends in the group were looking for small self-contained flats, which were difficult to find in our area. One man who came to the group was a builder, and he had helped in the remodeling of my house. We came up with a plan that if I bought a nearby house, he would convert it into flats for our friends. I would supply the capital for the house, and he would sell a houseboat which he owned to finance the construction work. In exchange for his work and financial input, he could have a flat in the converted house. This was our arrangement, but nothing was written down, because I felt that this was unnecessary between spiritual friends.

We found an appropriate house and I agreed to buy it. I remember asking inwardly if I should do this, and received the answer, "Trust." Maybe I did not hear the first part of a well-known *hadith*, "First tie the knee of your camel, then trust in God." Possibly I just heard what I wanted to hear; certainly I needed to learn a lesson. I signed the papers and my "friend" then told me that he wasn't going to sell his boat. He had thought that I was going to pay for both the house and the conversion. I was left with an empty house on my hands without even the money to pay for it because at that time the family bank which held the remainder of the trust would not release any funds due to some legal complication. I was unemployed—my first teaching contract had been for only a year—and so I could not get a mortgage. I talked to my father, but he wisely refused to help me. Bank interest rates had just reached a high of nineteen percent, which was what I had to pay when I finally found a banker willing to lend me the money on the security of both houses.

Mrs. Tweedie was furious and Anat, who was then pregnant again, was very upset. Mrs. Tweedie said that she could not live in a house with the aura of money worries. The worry in the atmosphere disturbed her work. One morning I came down to her flat to find that she had gone, leaving just a typed note on the kitchen table. "This flat is not to be used. If I am not back in three months consider me dead."

My so-called spiritual friend had let me down, and I learned never to trust appearances, especially when they appear to be spiritual. I felt guilty, a fool, and a total failure. Maybe there was a hidden wisdom in this failure as it destroyed any sense of inflation I might have had about having Mrs. Tweedie living in my house. She was gone and the group was closed on my account. During the day I walked the streets, dejected and depressed. How could I have let down myself and my family, allowed myself to be caught so naively? This was a bitter and painful lesson.

Added to this situation I felt the collective depression and guilt at being unemployed. For a year I had been a teacher, had a position and an identity. Now I was one of the unemployed, and there are few places more depressing than the "dole queue" at a social security office. Walking the streets during the day, or just going to the shops, I felt that people were looking at me, thinking, "Why isn't that young man at work?" I felt the power of the collective and its imprint of worthlessness on those who are not working. I came to realize the strength of the collective identity of being "part of the working humanity," and the sense of guilt and failure if you are not employed. On a personal level there was no real reason for me to feel this way. My inheritance provided enough money to live simply, and I was only a year out of college. But an individual has to be very strong to dismiss the influence of the collective.

During this time I learned that my responsibility was first and foremost to my family, and that my inheritance was for this purpose. Sufis say that the family comes first, that this is the wayfarer's first responsibility. I had to look after my money. It had been given to me for a purpose. In later years Mrs. Tweedie often spoke to me about money and the importance of being responsible. Bhai Sahib told her that when we die someone will ask us first if we have left any debts, and then how we have used our money. Money is energy and should be respected as such.

Half a year before I was married I had been given a lesson that also pointed out my irresponsibility. At the time I cycled to college, and the quickest route involved cycling the wrong way down some one-way streets. Being carefree, I thought nothing of this, until one morning, as I was cycling down a one-way street, I was suddenly hit by a car. I remember nothing except waking in a nearby hospital with a hairline fracture in my skull. I discovered that I had been hit by the local minister who was taking his children to school. Fortunately a nurse was walking nearby, and she looked after me while the minister, who was very distraught, phoned for an ambulance. When a policeman came to see me in the hospital he said there would be no charges brought against me as obviously I had "learned my lesson." Even in the hospital I knew the message: I could no longer afford to be reckless. If I was going to be married and have children, others would be dependent upon me.

What I had learned about physical carelessness was repeated on the level of money. I tried to sell the house I had inadvisably bought, but with interest rates so high it was a bad market. I waited all winter, until one night I had a dream in which Mrs. Tweedie told me, "You have learned your lesson." The next week there was a buyer, and I was glad to be free of the property, even though I lost some money. Mrs. Tweedie also suddenly reappeared, just before the three months had passed. She had been in India, traveling in the foothills of the Himalayas and meditating in Nepal. For a while after she returned she was in silence. But the group soon reopened, and then, unexpectedly, I found a job.

LEARNING FROM CHILDREN

My next and last job as a schoolteacher was in a small, private girls' school in central London, near to Hyde Park. An English teacher had had to leave in the middle of the school year because she was pregnant, and I was

offered her job, mainly because my younger sister had
been a student at the school a few years before. On the
first day of my new job I was delightfully shocked. The
girls sat quietly at their desks; there was no shouting,
no chaos, no disturbance. Before, I had taught classes
of over thirty students. These classes had fifteen to
twenty students and it was like paradise. I could teach,
not just attempt to keep order.

I worked there as a part-time English teacher for
over five years and it was very enjoyable. As in any job
there were difficulties and periods of boredom, but
teaching adolescent girls was always full of fun. The
principal soon wisely moved me from teaching gram-
mar and spelling—I have never been able to spell—
and I focused on Shakespeare and other literature,
trying to awaken their interest in the deep meaning of
these classics. As a part-time teacher, and also one of
the few men in an all-girls school, I managed to avoid
the politics of the staff-room; I always felt more at
home with my students than with the other teachers.
Teaching teenagers, I was also able to relive my own
adolescence, which I had never fully lived, as at the
time I was too serious and weighed down with problems.

The main interests of my students were naturally
parties, boyfriends, and clothes, which provided a
good balance to the seriousness of my inner life. The
school was not overly academic or disciplined. I
remember one girl arriving late to class and giving the
excuse that she had been taking her dog to the
hairdresser! I tried to prepare these girls for their
exams, and at the time I thought that I would continue
to be a teacher for many years—it was my chosen
profession. But my students knew better. They saw
that I was very different from their other teachers, and

would ask me how long I was going to teach at their school. I lived in the moment. I gave myself fully to my work, but I had no ambition, no desire for worldly success.

I taught three days a week and spent the other days with my family. My daughter Hannah was born the May after I started work, and I helped at home, cooking, cleaning, changing diapers. I was not able to be present at Hannah's birth, as I had to look after Emmanuel, who was only sixteen months old when his sister was born. Hannah was a baby in bliss—for many months she radiated the peace and bliss of a soul that is still in heaven. Emmanuel in contrast resented the birth of his sister and felt betrayed by his mother. When I was at home I spent much time with Emmanuel, and a deep masculine bonding began. We would go for long walks in the park, and I would look after him while Anat was with Hannah. It was wonderful and strange to find myself having such a friendship with this soul in a child's body—a friendship that has often been stronger than any father-son dynamic. At times I would have to remind myself to play the role of the father.

I have always felt very solitary, and it was a tremendous joy to unexpectedly find myself with this young but ancient companion. There was always a strong sense of a link from the past, that we had been together before, wayfarers traveling the same path. Maybe this welcome companionship made me over-possessive at times. But what amazed me was the way a child comes so open, unprotected by personality or the barriers of conditioning. With every other relationship you have to get to know the person, to slowly peel away the layers of personality in order to reach any degree of intimacy, any real knowing of the person underneath. A child comes with the soul singing, with the light of the Self in his eyes. We met without the coverings of the ego, with just the joy of life and of friendship refound.

Everyday life had opened its door and my children became my teachers. I had to learn patience because children live in a timeless world. A walk to the local shops could last an hour as every leaf was to be inspected, every puddle explored. I rediscovered the wonder of the moment, and also found the depth of my own anger. I had always thought myself to be a peaceful person, but my son evoked in me an anger that had been well hidden. He was always very strong-willed, protesting his sister's birth with a brown-rice fast which he instinctively knew would upset his mother. He pitted his will against mine with the issues which can engage a child, such as his refusal to wear a coat when going outside in winter. It was as if he was inside my own skin, and I had no defenses against my own anger, which would erupt with shouting against this small child. Our wills raged against each other, he as defiant as I was angry.

Later I came to realize that my anger was not just the result of a masculine power struggle between son and father. His freedom to express his will touched an unconscious wound: the hurt that the conditioning and rules of my childhood had never allowed me such freedom. His instinctual freedom evoked in me a desire to repress and restrict him with the bonds of my own childhood, for I had been born into a world in which young children were supposed to be "seen and not heard." The shadowlands of my own wounds evoked feelings and responses so different from the love I felt.

In despair I asked Mrs. Tweedie what I should do, knowing that she had heard these arguments through the floorboards of our flat. "Nothing," she said. "Just watch your anger." Then she gave me a very wise piece of advice. "Try to get angry consciously. Find an issue which you feel is important, and make yourself get angry." The danger of anger is that because it has been forbidden and repressed, it explodes through the shadow. Thus the anger can carry an intensity and destructiveness that belong to the unconscious. Until this time I had never expressed my anger, and now, when it was evoked by someone so close to me, the anger had me in its grip. I was caught in the darkness of my own shadow and repressed feelings. Learning to consciously become angry broke this shadow dynamic, broke the destructive potency of its force.

Anger is at times necessary, as every parent knows. Mrs. Tweedie told us an incident in which she saw Bhai Sahib shouting in anger at a servant whom he had caught stealing. She was horrified at the force of his shouting, until a friend told her to look at his eyes, and she saw they were full of compassion. He needed to teach a lesson to the servant, but he was master of the situation and in no way in the grip of his anger.

MEDITATION AND THE GROUP

When Mrs. Tweedie moved into the downstairs flat she changed the routine of the meetings, opening her flat during the week, Monday to Thursday, from two in the afternoon until eight. We continued to have the main meetings on Friday evenings, when everyone would try to be present, but the rest of the week was open to anyone who could come. During those first two or three years ten or twelve people would come in the afternoon, meditate, and then sit around the kitchen table while Mrs. Tweedie talked and served tea. Her book, *The Chasm of Fire*, had just been published; she had appeared once on television and was beginning to become known. The group was no longer secret and anyone was welcome to come to the meditations. All that was necessary was a desire for Truth. But compared to later years when almost a hundred people crowded into her flat, the group was very small and intimate, and it is amusing to think how she would say, "We had so many people today—at least ten people came."

Although she was open every afternoon, I rarely went downstairs those first years. On the days when I was not teaching I would spend the afternoon looking after the children, giving Anat time to go downstairs for a couple of hours to meditate and sit with Mrs. Tweedie. For myself I was happier meditating alone, and I still found the talking and cups of tea unnecessary. My meditation was going well and I had regular experiences of *dhyana*, when the mind merges somewhere and one is left in a state of unconsciousness which can seem similar to sleep. For an hour or so in the afternoon I would close my door and leave this world behind, dissolving consciousness within the heart and the energy of love that is the central power on the path.

The experience of *dhyana*, being lost to the world, became like a necessary intoxicant, a drug that held me somewhere. I would wait for that precious time when I could let my mind sink into my heart and feel it drift away. For about a year, at the beginning of my meditation I experienced a few moments of fear as my mind would feel itself about to become lost in the emptiness, but then this deeper state would overtake consciousness. Some time later I would return, carrying the sense of having been somewhere where I really belonged, and feeling deeply nourished by the beyond. My mind could not know or grasp this other dimension, this inner plane of pure being. Gradually over the years it would become refined enough to finally awaken there, beyond the world of forms. But in the state of *dhyana* there were the peace and fulfillment of being elsewhere, and of returning to this world with a secret sense of the infinite emptiness. This nourishment and hidden knowing carried me through the day, helping me to live in a world I knew to be an illusion.

Sometimes I would ask Mrs. Tweedie if I should go downstairs more often, not just to the general Friday meeting which I regularly attended. But she always dissuaded me, giving one reason or another. Then one night I had a dream after which I went downstairs more frequently during the week. In this dream it was made clear that I could not go downstairs just for myself; it had to be also to help others. I was made to realize that if I went into that atmosphere of contained love just for my own needs, it would create a dependency on something other than my inner connection to the path. I was only ever allowed to rely upon what was within my own heart. At times I was almost jealous of those who could sit immersed in the love that filled Mrs. Tweedie's flat and unconditionally flowed from her. Friends would come and unload their weary self, to be held and nourished by the stream of her giving. But for myself, although Mrs. Tweedie was a tremendous support, I was never allowed to become dependent upon her. Anat once had a dream in which I told her that the only way to possess Mrs. Tweedie was "when she turned into a basket of bread and wine." Only the inner teachings are real; the outer teacher is just another illusion.

FAMILY LIFE

During those first years, although we lived above Mrs. Tweedie, I did not see her very often. I would come to the meetings on Friday evenings and early Saturday mornings help to clean her flat. Sometimes, on those Saturday mornings, I would ask her about experiences, dreams, or inner questions. I was tremendously in awe of her and could not relate in any normal human way. Anat spent more time with her, sometimes helping her with shopping, but Mrs. Tweedie was very independent. We were a young couple with the intensity of young children in the house, and Mrs. Tweedie led a very different life, spending much time in meditation. She also loved to garden, and occasionally I would be called upon to dig, to prepare the soil for a new plant. Mrs. Tweedie did not believe in talking to her flowers, but feeding them compost and manure until they gulped with satisfaction. The roses in front of the house were always beautiful.

Strangely, those first years living above Mrs. Tweedie we were quite isolated from the group. We were the only couple in the group in London with children, and that is a very different lifestyle from being single. Friends who came hoping for deep, meaningful conversation would be surrounded by the noise and activity of pre-schoolers. In the evening, after suppertime and bath-time, Anat would often be so tired that she would fall asleep while giving a final hug to Hannah. I would read Emmanuel a story and then meditate when the house was quiet. Maybe I would watch television or read for a short while before going to bed, when I would feel the joy of my heart going Home, going to my Sheikh whom I loved; then I would be awakened in the early morning by my son creeping between the covers for a cuddle.

Weekends we would go to the park, and on Sunday mornings I would visit my mother. During the summer I followed the English custom of keeping the lawn closely mowed and teaching my son the rituals of cricket. Hannah was often happy to be left alone; remaining within the sacred circle of her own self, she could play undisturbed for hours. Sometimes we would talk to Mrs. Tweedie in the garden, enjoy the beauty of the flowers she had planted, and try not to let our games go into the flower-beds. Whenever there was a spare hour I would relish the chance to close the door of my room and meditate, to be absorbed somewhere.

I bought a secondhand Volkswagen camper-van, and for holidays we would go camping, in the south of England and once to Switzerland, for we all loved the mountains. Sufis say that life is the greatest teacher, and in the midst of these ordinary activities were many teachings. One lesson I had to learn was not to project any sense of happiness or perfection onto material objects. The lesson would be quite simple: if there was something I really wanted, a new stereo or a new bicycle, once I bought this object it would break. The stereo would fuse; the gears on my new bike would snap. The camper-van was a most obvious example. I loved the idea of a camper-van with its sense of taking one's home wherever one went. It imaged a freedom and self-containment that felt wonderful. Soon after I bought the van, we prepared for a camping holiday. On a beautiful summer morning we left the city early to escape the traffic. Five hours later we were driving up a hill close to our campsite near the sea, when the engine exploded in a cloud of smoke. At midnight we were home again in London on the back of a tow truck. A week later the engine was fixed and we were camping on the hillside, but the van no longer held the same feeling—it was just a vehicle with a cooker and a bed. Once again I had been taught that what I sought does not exist here, in the world of material objects. Nothing could be trusted except Him.

Material possessions can be an object of desire and an obstacle on the path. But having a family dragged me into the material world. When we moved into our house we put all of our possessions into the back of a station wagon. Within three years we would have needed a large truck to move. In our culture children and family life demand "worldly goods," everything from washing machines to children's toys. I often found it difficult to be surrounded by all these possessions, and liked to give things away. I also like order, and for a while I was constantly tidying after the children, until I had a dream in which Bhai Sahib told me not to bother!

With young children everything is emphasized, the joys and constrictions of life. Everything is brought to the surface, tested, exposed. As a parent I tried so hard to be different from my own parents, to give my children what I felt was missing from my own childhood, a sense of freedom, a quality of feeling. Yet only too often I found myself trapped in my own conditioning, echoing the attitudes of my father. And in the midst of this, life was swirling in its wonder, both the unexpected and the familiar. My children took me by

the hand and reintroduced me to life, to their unconditional openness, desire for experience, and joy in
what is simple. Within all of these everyday moments,
the tears and triumphs, riding a bike for the first time,
learning to swim, I felt myself an onlooker caught in
the experience, involved and yet also separate. Although I spent much time with my children, having a
family remained slightly strange, a ritual I would never
completely learn. And always my attention was partly
elsewhere. My daughter in particular felt this inner
absence, my lack of total involvement in everyday life.
Now she teases me about it, calling me an "absent
father." However hard I tried to be a parent, I was
always somehow a stranger, a wayfarer never quite
convinced by the reality of the world.

INNER GUIDANCE

Life was opening its doors, revealing its kaleidoscope
of colors. And in the midst of this I began to develop
an inner guidance which is the mystic's way of walking
the thoroughfare of the world. Inner guidance comes
to each of us in its own way. For some it is a still small
voice, for others a prompting within the heart. My
guidance began to come as an input of energy at the
top of my head. Suddenly I would feel energy hitting
the top of my skull, which would awaken me, turn my
attention elsewhere. Sometimes this energy would be
accompanied by a thought form, a hint I needed to
follow. On other occasions the energy would just point
me in a direction. As in all instances of inner guidance
I learned to follow it mainly through making mistakes,
through ignoring its prompting and then suffering the
consequences.

This guidance could be about both inner and outer circumstances. I might be prompted to inwardly explore an attitude or work on a shadow projection. If I did not follow this hint I could be unnecessarily caught in a situation, or act out a shadow dynamic. In the outer world the guidance could prompt me to talk to someone, share a dream, or keep quiet. What I found most astonishing was that this outer guidance was not limited to spiritual matters, but functioned in everyday affairs. For example, if I was about to go to a shop to buy a particular item, and I felt this energy gently knocking in my head, it would be a message not to go. Initially I would dismiss this guidance, only to find that the shop did not have the item I wanted, or even that the shop was closed. So many times I dismissed these promptings concerning outer, worldly things, often because I was caught in the desire for what I wanted. But they were always accurate, and I would cycle or drive to the shop only to find it a useless journey.

Eventually this guidance became an invaluable way to live, and I learned to always listen inwardly, whatever I was doing. As I learned to listen, to become inwardly attuned, so the prompting became subtler, less of a knocking on the skull and more a flowing of energy. I began to live with a conscious awareness of the flow of energy, feeling the discord in this flow if I was going in the wrong direction. For years, since the *kundalini* energy had become awakened, I had been aware of energy flowing through my body. Now my attunement to this energy became a way to live, to harmoniously flow with the river of life. Through this flow I felt the interaction of the inner and outer and was guided through the marketplace of life. And because this inner guidance covered all aspects of life, even the most mundane, I came to know the oneness that includes everything. In this oneness nothing is either spiritual or worldly, because everything belongs to Him. In the words of Abû Sa'id, "Sufism consists of keeping the heart from anything that is not He. But there is not anything not He."

Before I came to experience this everyday guidance, I had often found it very difficult to make mundane decisions. In our contemporary world of infinite choices it is difficult to know what to choose. If you have no real worldly desires it can be almost impossible. If you know that it does not matter and you don't care, how do you decide? In the important matters of life, for example relationships, jobs, even deciding where to live, I have never felt any choice. There never appeared to be an alternative, and I have always had a strong sense of personal destiny. But, for example, if I wanted to see a movie yet I didn't really care, it was almost impossible to decide which movie to see. For many years I never went to the movies for this reason, and I still hate going to a video store. Yet we have to live in this world; we have to make many decisions. My inner guidance enables me to walk through the marketplace of this world without having to focus on the ego to make mundane decisions. I don't have to try to think what I want, because all I really want is to go Home and be of service to Him.

As my inner guidance developed, it became stronger and stronger and I trusted it more and more. Of course I still made many mistakes, particularly when a desire or psychological block stopped me from being attuned, or made me dismiss the guidance. Even the desire to please others can be a limitation. For example, one summer after we had all been at a Sufi retreat in Switzerland, we thought of driving back through Paris. I had a feeling not to visit Paris, but the children were very keen on climbing the Eiffel Tower and seeing the Mona Lisa. The first night we spent at a Paris hotel our car was broken into. The remainder of our stay was expensive and unhappy.

THE *DHIKR*

The Sufi path teaches the wayfarer to become one-pointed, to always look towards Him, whatever our circumstances. Learning to follow His guidance, we seek His face in our daily activities. Repeating His name, we remember Him in our heart and mind. The *dhikr*, the constant repetition of a name of God, is an important Sufi technique for remembrance. When I first came to the group, Mrs. Tweedie gave a *dhikr* to individuals only upon instructions from her teacher. (Now the instructions have changed and everyone who comes to the group is given the *dhikr*.) I was given a *dhikr* practice soon after I was married, a few days before my first trip to Israel to visit Anat's parents, which was a wonderful time to work on the *dhikr* and imprint it into consciousness. In Israel, while everyone was talking in Hebrew, which I don't understand, I would be silently repeating His name with each breath. After three weeks of this intense inner focus the *dhikr* became a part of me.

The beauty of the Naqshbandi practice of the silent *dhikr* is that wherever you are, whatever you are doing, you can look to the Beloved and repeat His name. There is the sense that no moment is ever wasted. Standing in line for a bus, lying awake at night—each breath is an opportunity to say His name. I have always carried an intensity that rarely allows me to rest, an inner drive that pushes me onward. I have felt the preciousness of the moment, the feeling that here, in this world, there is something to be achieved. The *dhikr* became a welcome tool to help me in this work, to help me to focus my mind, my whole self, towards the object of my longing.

I discovered that the *dhikr* also helps with inner work. In the intense two weeks before Bhai Sahib made me conscious I was a soul, I learned to work with my inner blocks and problems through the flow of energy. Since then, when a problem comes to the surface in life or in a dream, I focus on the problem with the energy of my devotion, with my longing for God. Holding the problem in this energy helps to dissolve or transform it, and then a block can be released and the energy flow through. I discovered that the *dhikr* helps to keep an inner focus on this work, helps my consciousness to stay with the problem. Many times the problem included pain, for problems often constellate around a wound. The *dhikr* helps to contain the pain with the power of His presence, with my longing to be with Him. Through the *dhikr* I can offer it up to Him, helping Him to heal me.

I do this work often in meditation, with my entire consciousness focusing inward. But sometimes an attitude of meditation takes me beyond the mind and psyche, and I lose contact with the problem. Then it is more helpful to walk. Walking enables me to keep my feet on the ground while focusing on an inner problem. How many difficulties I have resolved on the streets of north London, repeating His name with all of my inner concentration. The rhythm of my footsteps, the rhythm of my breath, and the light of my longing singing His name all combine in the process of purification, the ancient work of polishing the mirror of the heart.

Through my own efforts, through the intensity of my desire, I polished and polished, the slow work of clearing away the debris of the ego and the psyche. I tried to face myself with honesty, see through my defenses and patterns of conditioning. But all the while a deeper process of purification and transformation was taking place, the effortless work of His love which is usually hidden from consciousness. Love's martyr, al-Hallâj, describes the simple wonder of this work:

> Now the Lord is with them in every alteration,
> Performing an unimaginable work in them
>   hour after hour.
> If they only knew! they would not withdraw
>   from Him even for the space of a wink.
> For He does not withdraw from them at any
>   time.[2]

Surrendering to the path, the wayfarer gives himself into the arms of love, which alone can take him Home. In the secret places of the heart we are remade, a lump of clay turned on the wheel of His love. Sometimes we are allowed just a glimpse of this wonder, of the deepest work within the heart. One day, during meditation, I was given a powerful vision in which I saw my chest opened from behind with a knife. My heart was taken out, breathed on, and dust was blown off. Then the heart was spun. When I told Mrs. Tweedie this vision she just said that it was very auspicious. Years later I began to understand its significance, how breath purifies and brings to life. The spinning of the heart is the activation of this inner organ of divine perception. The spinning heart of the lover takes him Home, back to the Beloved. One of our

superiors, the teacher of Bhai Sahib's teacher, describes the potency of this spiritual system: "We are
simple people. But we can turn the heart of a human
being so that the human being will go on and on,
where nobody can even imagine it."[3]

THE TWO WORLDS

Daily life, relationships, meditation, *dhikr*, and the
energy of the path brought light and darkness to the
surface. Each day was another adventure, sometimes
sweet and sometimes bitter. But gradually my feet were
learning to walk on the surface of the earth, as my heart
looked towards Him. Sometimes there were days of
great peace, a peace that belongs to the Self. Inexplicably this peace would descend, tangible and soft. The
"peace that passeth understanding" cannot be disturbed by outer events; even in the midst of the
classroom, surrounded by adolescent girls, it remained
undimmed. This sense of peace would come and go
according to its own invisible laws and reasons. Once
it remained a whole week or more, until it silently
slipped away. It would return, and then disappear,
until it remained always, just under the surface—the
peace of the soul which is with God.

Longing was also there, fluctuating with the inner
states of the heart. The pain of longing is the most
potent pain in the world, and it cannot be healed by
any remedy. Often my physical heart would hurt,
echoing this inner pain. The heart can be so heavy, its
sting so bitter. For hours, days, weeks, the longing
would continue, sometimes intensely penetrating, sometimes just a dull ache always present. When the longing

seemed almost unbearable, love would come, sweet as honey. The states are always changing, and the lover is always caught unprepared. Sometimes I was left in a feeling of separation more desolate than anything I could have imagined. There was an anguish of emptiness which tore into me; or, even more difficult, the separation left me without sensation or feeling, without even the desire for God. I love a challenge, and even the pain of separation was preferable to this desert, when only will power took me through endless, meaningless days.

Pushed to the limit of inner endurance, I held on, to find the state suddenly, inexplicably changing. In the place of desolation came a sense of closeness, a tenderness melting in the heart. Always what was given was more than anything I believed possible, the sense of fulfillment deeper, richer, more complete than ever I might have expected. When times of great happiness first came, I was worried, wondering how long it could last until I would be thrown again into the pit of my own despair and longing. But gradually I learned not to care, to enjoy the bliss when it is given and thank Him for the gift, to drink the cup of wine and not to think of tomorrow. Beneath the mundane outer events, being a father, visiting the zoo, playing board games, or vacuuming the flat, these inner states would change and evolve: sunshine, clouds, cool breezes, harsh winds.

I also noticed that the intensity with which I had come to the group had changed. At first I was worried that the burning, crazy, heedless rush for Truth seemed to have subsided. Had I lost my desire, my longing become buried? Had my outer life distracted me from the goal? But then I became aware that a shift had taken place; my relationship to the path had changed. I had a dream in which Mrs. Tweedie was leading the group away from a school, and then leading us round and round in circles. In the dream I felt both anger and disappointment that we were not going anywhere! When I awoke I realized my ignorance, that one does not "go anywhere" on the spiritual journey, and walking round and round in circles images a path towards wholeness.

When I first arrived at the meditation group, I thought of the spiritual journey in the only concepts available to me: a linear path towards a distant goal. Gradually I came to realize that the spiritual journey is a closed circle of love in which we slowly come closer to the center of ourself, which is always present. In this journey there is no "progress" but a shifting of consciousness that unveils our own essential nature, "the face we had before we were born." As this spiral path unfolds, so our concepts of both ourself and the journey change, and we come to realize the deeper truth: that the traveler, the journey, and the goal are all one.

The Sufi says that the real pilgrim is not the ego or personality, but a substance within the heart of hearts. This divine substance is activated by the energy of love and devotion, and infuses its presence into consciousness. But when I began the journey I had no concept of anything apart from my own ego. My ego carried the stamp of my spiritual desire, the intensity of my longing. I was a spiritual seeker, and this identity helped to drag me through my early difficulties, endure the physical and psychological problems with which I was so burdened. But as the real nature of the path unfolded I began to realize the limitations of any ego identity, spiritual or otherwise. On the journey towards nothingness, everything has to go. One day I spoke about this spiritual identity to Mrs. Tweedie, who just responded, "It was a necessary crutch." Soon afterwards I had a vision in which I saw a gravestone on which was carved, "Spiritual aspirant."

From the moment I came to the group and Mrs. Tweedie offered me a chocolate biscuit, saying, "Sugar is good for you," my ideas about spiritual life were slowly eroded. The Sufi Dhû-l-Nûn said, "Whatever you think, God is the opposite of that," because every concept is a limitation. I had brought with me many concepts about what it means to be spiritual and where the journey is leading. Everyday life and the energy of the path softened me, revealing something I could never have imagined: spiritual life as something very ordinary. This was reflected in a dream I had in which I was told that Bhai Sahib was "buried in brass at the foot of the mountain." The image of my Sheikh being buried not on some high mountain top, remote from the world, but at its foot, together with the symbolism of brass, which contains impurities, suggests an involvement in ordinary life. Sufis are "in the world, but not of the world," serving Him and going Home amidst the noise and problems of family life and the workplace. The impurities of life give us an opportunity to look for Him everywhere and find His oneness wherever we look.

LIVING ABOVE OUR TEACHER

These inner states and stages of the path unfolded amidst the daily routine of children and work, and at the same time Mrs. Tweedie was living underneath our family. Our kitchen was over the room where she meditated, and in the evenings, when she was in deep meditation, the peace spread through the floorboards. Just as my attention was drawn inward, so was there a hidden focus that pulled me downstairs. There the path of love was being lived to its fullest, in both surrender and intoxication, the wonder of an old woman in love with God. The depth of her commitment sang through the house, inspiring Anat and me. Here was a woman who had given herself totally to God, to a depth and degree that left hardly a trace behind.

Living in the same house as such totality of surrender and dedication imprinted into me many qualities of the path. For Mrs. Tweedie, duty was everything; whatever would help someone to take one step nearer to the Truth was given unconditionally. The energy of this devotion was so strong that everyone in the house was a part of it—one could not live in the same house without allowing this dedication to the path and the work of her Sheikh to overshadow all other activities.

I soon realized that the house did not belong to me but to the work, to the energy of the lineage. Everything was focused towards this one purpose, and I learned to live with this focus, to know that nothing for myself really mattered. Initially I would be glad when Mrs. Tweedie left to lecture or for a retreat, for suddenly the house and garden would be ours—the people and the power of her presence would be gone, and I could sit in the garden like an ordinary householder. Interestingly, when she left and we went into her flat to clean, there would be no residue of her presence. Normally when you visit someone's house or flat in her absence, you still feel her presence; the quality of her personality hangs in the air. With Mrs.

Tweedie there was nothing left but an impersonal energy. She had been made empty and lived in the emptiness.

But gradually I gave up any desire for my own life, my own house. I no longer resented the depth of surrender that was required in living with her. Her work became an invisible part of my own being, and we were always there for her. Sometimes she would ring on the door at seven in the morning to discuss some issue, some concern to do with people or the path. Any time of the day or night she would have our undivided attention, our complete commitment. Because she is so totally focused on the work of the path, we had to honor this in our response, in our being with her. We had to unconditionally respond to the need of the moment. This was the only way to live in the same house with her. At times this created tremendous pressure, and conflicted with family life. But we were always held by the power of love, even in the most demanding moments.

Learning to live with the energy of the path was a tremendous teaching, evoking both love and awe. Sometimes I would see her in the morning if I had to give her a message (she had no telephone of her own), when she was just out of meditation, her eyes still frighteningly distant. I would be inwardly trembling at the intensity of eyes that looked far beyond this world. Then gradually she would come back into her self and the terrifying gaze would be gone.

But Mrs. Tweedie was also an elderly lady with her own idiosyncrasies, her fiery temperament and dramatic nature—she was of Cossack descent. Learning to live with one's spiritual teacher on a human level, changing her typewriter ribbon, explaining a tax form, was another teaching. So often we idealize our teacher, denying her human needs and fallibilities. Mrs. Tweedie was full of inconsistencies which were only emphasized by her function as a spiritual guide, as the dynamic energy of the inner world affected all aspects of her outer life. And although the path embraced every aspect of her life, not everything she said or did was a teaching. She could be irritated or angry like anyone else—sometimes it held a deeper meaning and many times it did not.

But the only way to live with her was to forget distinctions and put aside the judgments of the mind. From the moment I first met her my mind stepped aside, as if I instinctively knew that the path could only be traveled in its unadulterated wholeness. Somewhere deeper than the mind I was held by the knowledge that I needed to surrender and accept all aspects of an often confusing situation, in which an elderly Russian lady and a spiritual teacher were united and also quite separate. I learned about the ordinariness and failings that can remain in a human being who has given herself totally to God. This was to give me a great sense of freedom—the freedom of knowing that only He is perfect.

A DREAM ABOUT MY WORK

Our family life was a strange combination of these worlds, of light, love, and everyday life. Mrs. Tweedie also said that for her it was a new experience to be almost part of a family, as she had never had children. She would see the children playing in the garden, hear their laughter and fights. Although she lived quite separate, the house sang with one song of life being lived and held within the heart of our Sheikh. His love, his presence, and his work were an integral part of our life. Gradually my own part in this became more visible, more conscious. In the afternoons when I was not at school I would go downstairs to sit in the presence of the teaching. In the evenings we would try to put the children to sleep before seven so that we could both be downstairs for an hour.

Slowly more people came to the group and our involvement increased. We answered the telephone, found accommodation for people who wanted to stay nearby. We cleaned the drains when they became blocked (when we began to have over thirty people a day, one toilet proved to have its limitations!), and helped in what little ways we could. Sometimes we smelled burning coming up through the floorboards, and would realize that once again Mrs. Tweedie had left something cooking and then gone off in meditation. My job was to scrub the pot clean!

When Mrs. Tweedie was away in India I had an important dream, intense and powerful. In this dream Mrs. Tweedie is about to vanish completely and my work is to bring people to her and also to protect her. For the eleven years we lived in the same house this was the secret core of my work, although I hardly knew it. The wonder of the Sufi path is that most of our work is hidden even from ourselves, so that the ego and the mind can neither identify nor interfere. On the inner planes we meet and help each other, while in the world we wear ordinary clothes and do our daily job. But in that house the two worlds came together, and the path permeated more and more of my whole self. Everything was included, from diapers to dreams. Mrs.

Tweedie lived immersed in her Sheikh, gradually merging deeper and deeper in that ocean of oneness. Our family stood on the shore, learning the currents of this ocean, the ways of love, and helping with the work of the path.

THE ARCHETYPAL WORLD

All ages before us have believed in gods in some form or
other. Only an unparalleled impoverishment of symbolism
could enable us to rediscover the gods as psychic factors,
that is, as archetypes of the unconscious.... It is the
archetypes that decide the fate of man.

Carl Jung[1]

JUNGIAN PSYCHOLOGY

Three years after I moved into our house I had a dream
in which I was told to read the works of Carl Jung. Over
the next two years I read his *Collected Works* from
Volume Five, *Symbols of Transformation*, to Volume
Fourteen, *Mysterium Coniunctionis*. Reading Jung
formed a foundation for an understanding of spiritual
psychology that became an integral part of my work.

Before Mrs. Tweedie went to India for the first time
and met her teacher, she had worked as a librarian at
the Theosophical Society, where she studied the works
of Jung. During the time she was with Bhai Sahib she
was amazed to discover that although he knew nothing
of Western psychology, his process of spiritual training
had similarities to the Jungian process of individuation.
Coming to him, she had hoped for spiritual teachings,
but instead he forced her to face the darkness within
herself, the rejected shadow. Many other elements of
Jungian psychology, such as the danger of inflation,
were present in his training. After his death, when she

149

returned to London and started her group, she integrated a Jungian approach into Sufi teachings, particularly in dream interpretation. For ten years I had been learning about Jungian psychology through the group meetings, experiencing my own shadow and the projection of the anima. But I had not read any of Jung's books. When I came to the group I put aside all spiritual books, and it was not until I had this dream that I again picked up a book to find knowledge.

Reading Jung, I immediately appreciated the greatness of his work, that of giving us a model of the Western psyche in its archetypal depth. One knows, reading his work, that he speaks with the authority of someone who has made this inner journey himself. He is not describing merely psychological concepts, but an inner landscape he has explored as fully as possible. In his autobiography, *Memories, Dreams, Reflections*, Jung states that it was his own descent into the unconscious, which lasted for a period of four years, which formed the basis, the *prima materia*, for his lifetime's work:

> This was the primal stuff which compelled me to work upon it, and my works are a more or less successful endeavour to incorporate this incandescent matter into the contemporary picture of the world.[2]

Jung's own experience of the unconscious has a profoundly spiritual quality, and his work reflects the awe of one who has been touched by the divine within himself.

In Jung's writings I found a language and framework that helped me to understand much of the psychological process that I had been experiencing over the previous ten years. Of particular significance was *Mysterium Coniunctionis*, which Jung regarded as his most important work. *Mysterium Coniunctionis* is full of alchemical symbolism, and was initially difficult to read. But I found it an invaluable map of the way the psyche is transformed on the spiritual path, the way the opposites are separated and then united within the Self. Jung rediscovered the significance of alchemy: that the *opus* of turning lead into gold is fundamentally symbolic, and refers to the purification and transformation of the psyche. The importance of his discovery is that the alchemical tradition provides an understanding of the Western psyche and its symbolic processes, which are in some ways different from those of people from the East.[3] For example, Westerners live farther from the collective than people living in India do.

For ten years I had been immersed in a process of inner work, confronting the shadow and looking to the Self. Yet I had little conscious understanding of what was happening. Sufism is an ancient system that activates the unconscious and through the energy of love reveals the light hidden in darkness. I dedicated myself to this work that came up within me, to the pain and darkness as well as the joy and light that arose. With love and devotion I looked inwardly towards Him, following this invisible path. When I met Mrs. Tweedie I left books behind, trusting only the presence of my teacher and my desire for Truth. My container was the knowledge of her link with her Sheikh, and my connection to this system. Mrs. Tweedie always stressed that we needed nothing else. Her teacher had taught her nothing, just given her experiences and opened her heart.

Chasm of Fire was published after I had been with Mrs. Tweedie for six years, and I avidly read this diary of her training with Bhai Sahib. Suddenly here was a written description of the path and the teachings of our superiors. In *Chasm of Fire*, and its unedited version, *Daughter of Fire*, this particular ancient system is written down for the first time, and its words sang in my heart. I have always found it easier to put my faith in a system than a person. A spiritual system is an impersonal energy structure that for centuries has been taking wayfarers Home. Following in their footsteps, we walk this ancient path, which is beyond the limitations or fallibility of any one person. Seeing this system made conscious, written in words, was a tangible support, even though I knew the deeper truths were left unsaid. When Mrs. Tweedie was with Bhai Sahib he explained very little. Often in response to a dream or a question he would say, "You will know by and by." Much of the time unknowing is helpful, as in the image of the lotus that grows underwater before finally pushing through the surface to flower in the sunlight. Although *Daughter of Fire* describes what is fundamental to this Sufi system, there was also a need in me to understand some of the psychological processes which had been developing within me. Jung's writing helped to make this internal process a part of my conscious self, and it also helped to bring together the wisdom of the heart with the understanding of modern psychology.

SYMBOLS AND OUR COLLECTIVE HUNGER

Immediately on reading Jung I began to have a series of archetypal dreams and visions. I dreamt of a wedding, and a woman wearing a garment with a rose mandala embroidered over her heart. I had a vision of my body in a diamond, out of which flowed four rivers of golden light. I saw a golden cup into which a dove entered. I dreamt about the number four, symbolizing wholeness, and had a vision of unicorns. All these images pointed towards the Self, which was emerging within me. Reading Jung gave me a context to see the way the psyche constellates around the Self, and to grasp the wonder and wisdom of this process.

As I read Jung's descriptions of archetypal symbols, I learned about the ancient language of the psyche, a language of images which is older than words. I began to consciously attune myself with this inner world, become familiar with its rhythms and flow. Reading Jung and listening to my own dreams, I ceased to be a stranger in this inner world. My consciousness now had a tool with which it could uncover more of the majesty and beauty that lie under the surface of humanity, and that for millennia have been expressed in powerful images. I also felt the poverty of our own time which has forgotten this language and lost touch with its numinosity. I came to realize that these symbols are not just images, but actually transformers of psychic energy which enable mankind to be nourished rather than overwhelmed by the undifferentiated psychic energy of the depths. Since the beginning of time they have helped to connect us with the deeper wisdom of life, with the energy and meaning hidden in the unconscious.

Then I had a powerful dream which imaged the horror of our collective plight, how we are starving ourselves:

> I am walking down a street and on the right-hand side there is a magnificent new hospital, gleaming white, with doctors walking in. But on the left-hand side of the street is a totally different picture. There are cattle trucks, full of men and women, reminiscent of those that took the Jews to concentration camps. The people there are unwashed, undernourished, and standing in their own feces. For a long time nobody has cleaned out these trucks, but most tragic of all is the fact that the men and women there have got so used to this situation that they no longer care or expect anything else.

The right-hand side in a dream symbolizes consciousness. The dream images how we idealize the healing powers of our masculine consciousness, "the magnificent new hospital gleaming white." Our hospitals and our lives are full of the results of this approach, the technological wizardry in which we place so much value. Each time I fly in an airplane I marvel at the science that can lift so much machinery and so many people above the clouds and fly them around the world. Such wonders are not to be despised, but they have been bought at a price. In our fascination with the world of science and its tangible results, we have starved and neglected the inner feminine world of the unconscious. Feces symbolize creativity, for they are produced from within. But what do we do with our inner creativity? Unused, it pollutes us. And most tragic, we have even got used to this situation. The figures in the cattle trucks no longer expect anything else. We are starving and our hunger is all the more desperate because we do not even recognize it.[4]

Jung writes, "The world today hangs by a thin thread, and that thread is the psyche of man."[5] This dream of the cattle trucks haunted me with the dangerous imbalance of our culture. I felt both our need for inner nourishment and our culture's inability to access the archetypal world from which meaning can come. I saw how we have been caught by the success of technology and only look outward. Jung's work took me not only within my own psyche, but also into the collective where the wound and the hunger are horrifying. A need within me was awakened to work to restore this imbalance—in what little way I could, to redeem the collective. As the Self rises into consciousness it brings a hint of the purpose of the soul. I saw a part of my own deeper destiny beginning to take shape: a need to contribute to our awareness of the importance of the symbolic inner world.

JUNG AND SHAKESPEARE

Family life, school, the study of Jung, meditation, and the group filled my days. Then one February morning the principal of my school unexpectedly announced that, because the intake of pupils had fallen, they could no longer afford a part-time English teacher. My contract would expire that summer. I was stunned. I had been there for five years and knew that I was a good teacher. I never felt that I fitted in, but then I have never felt that I fitted in anywhere. I actually found it quite reassuring to lead two separate lives, as a high-school teacher and as a spiritual seeker. None of my colleagues had any idea of the passion and path that possessed me. I never spoke about my spiritual interests. Keeping these two worlds separate was a protection that I needed, but what I did not realize was that I could no longer live in this way. I could no longer afford to separate my inner and outer life. The Self was pushing from within, needing to fully live out its own destiny on the stage of life.

For the next few months I looked for other jobs, but received no response when I sent out my curriculum vitae. I didn't understand why I was not even asked to any interviews, until a friend laughingly explained that fate had thrown me a strange card, one that made me almost unemployable. I had a good degree and good teaching experience, but my education history read very strangely. I had attended one of the most prestigious private schools in the country, Eton College, where the pupils wear tail suits and bow ties to class. But I had not followed the normal pattern of going on to Oxford or Cambridge. Instead, I studied for my degree at a "polytechnic," the English equivalent of a community college. I had decided to return to college very late in the year, and I did not want to wait another year in order to go to a prestigious university. The polytechnic accepted me at the last moment, and I enjoyed being a student there. Image or worldly identity meant nothing to me. However, what I did not realize at the time was that this polytechnic was renowned for being the most left-wing, radical college in the country. The political students were always heading demonstrations, sit-ins, and strikes. So my curriculum vitae made a very peculiar impression, and any employer would think that something was wrong. Furthermore, a right-wing school principal would not want me because I had obviously become a radical, while my prestigious high school made me unacceptable to a left-wing employer. Fate had played a joke that stressed that I could never belong to the world. As I failed to find another job I actually became happier and happier, sensing that another door was opening. What came into consciousness was the thought of studying for a Ph.D. When I was at college I had originally intended to continue with postgraduate work, but by the time I graduated the idea of spending three or four more years staring at books was suffocating. I wanted to be out in the world interacting with people. But now there was a different need. One afternoon, sitting on Mrs. Tweedie's porch in the early-summer sunshine, I had a vision in which I saw a diamond on my index finger. I knew from this vision that it was time to bring the Self into consciousness, to live what was deepest within me. Writing a Ph.D. thesis on Jungian psychology and Shakespeare was to be the vehicle. I had loved Shakespeare for years, finding him both human and profound. For the last three years I had taught *Hamlet*, and the idea of exploring an archetypal approach to *Hamlet* began to take shape.

First I needed a tutor, someone to supervise me in this work, but the gods had everything well planned. A few months previously a lecturer whom I knew from college had arrived at the group. I asked Alan if he would supervise my thesis and he kindly agreed. Alan is a playwright as well as a college lecturer, and what I did not know at the time was that one of his principal tasks would be to teach me how to write. Alan intuitively grasped this fact, but when he suggested it to me I exploded and said that I had no wish to be a writer! On the surface I thought I was studying for a Ph.D. in order to continue my teaching career. But my Higher Self had other plans, and was again about to take me into the unconscious. However, this time the suffering would come not from any inner wound, but from the struggle to make conscious and describe the meaning and music of what I would find. A hidden agenda to my doctoral work was to create a link between the inner archetypal world and the outer world of consciousness.

WORKING WITH THE ARCHETYPES

In England a doctoral degree is not taught; it only requires a written thesis which is "an original contribution to the field." I began my work in the reading room of the British Library, and each day I would look through twenty or more books, exploring what had already been written in my subject area. There have been more books and articles written on *Hamlet* than on any other book besides the Bible, but luckily only a few on Jungian psychology and Shakespeare. For three months I worked my way through innumerable books and articles, occasionally finding an interesting piece of research. This is the established way to conduct academic research, immersing oneself in existing, pertinent work.

But one morning in early fall, when I opened the first book on my pile, my mind would not register the words. Sitting in that magnificent room where so much research has been conducted, I stared up at the great dome stretching above me and then looked back at the book. But nothing went from the pages to my brain. I knew that there was no point in fighting, so I cycled home and closed the door of my room. In moments of unsureness or transition I always look inward in meditation to find the next step or discover the reason for a block. Lying down on my bed, I went deep inside and waited. Something seemed to be calling me, pulling me into the unconscious.

I allowed myself to be drawn into the unconscious, and there began a strange and transformative period of study. Each day for over a year I would spend an hour or more in the depths of the unconscious. But this was not my personal unconscious inhabited by repressed pain or unacknowledged feelings. This was the collective unconscious, deeper and more ancient, which has a very different feeling quality; it resonates on a deeper level. In this inner dimension I began to make a relationship with its primordial inhabitants, the archetypes. They taught me about their world, which is as real as our physical world, only it is a world of images rather than three-dimensional objects. The archetypes taught me how to go there, and how to travel freely in a dimension in which dragons are real.

This work in the collective unconscious is not easy to verbalize. It was an intense and often demanding process, involving working with the energies in the depths in a similar way to how I work in my own personal psyche: allowing the flow of energy to take my consciousness on a journey. At times there would be interactions with other energies, and sometimes images were evoked, which I recorded in a diary. For example, the very first image I encountered on that first day depicts the awakening of the "world tree," the primordial energy which stands at the axis of the world and lies within each of us:

> I see a great tree with roots going out above a pond. It is the tree of all nations, but is almost asleep, unconscious. That is the way it has always been. People have to go through the

forest to get there. I become the tree and the
spirit comes through me from above. It wakes
the tree up. There is such love and kindness in
the tree. It is happy. I feel a great smile in the
tree.

In this experience I identify with the tree, because
the archetypal world is a part of our own being, but in
our culture we have forgotten this. Our rational culture
has divorced us from these gods, and as a result life has
lost much of its meaning. One of Jung's important
realizations was that meaning in life comes from the
archetypes, that they are the "determinants of meaning." Jung also rediscovered the alchemical technique
of "active imagination," which uses the imagination as
a way of consciously exploring the inner world. Using
"active imagination" I was able to reconnect with the
archetypal world. Becoming the tree, I related to my
own roots in the unconscious, and then a transformation happened: "the spirit comes through me from
above." The masculine spirit of consciousness, which
is a divine gift, entered into the feminine depths of the
unconscious and the tree woke up.

This inner dimension has the reality of fairy tales
and numinous dreams. Shamans of all ages and cultures have had access to this world and worked in its
depths. One of the qualities of the archetypal world is
that alone it cannot transform itself. This is one of the
tasks of individual consciousness, which brings its
divine spark into the depths. In these inner experiences I was guided here and there, healing and
transforming. I knew that this guidance was the Higher
Self, without whose help one can easily become lost or
overpowered. The gods are real psychic forces and can

be dangerous to individual consciousness.[6] But the Higher Self, that "boundless power, source of every power...maker of past and future, the same today and tomorrow,"[7] contains within it the entire archetypal world, and is the master, king of this world. It is only safe to enter into the archetypal world under the guidance of the Self, protected by its power.

Many strange and wonderful experiences followed. I experienced the archetypes as being within my physical body, with the sun in my heart. I felt myself holding a shining sword, with which I cut open a large fish; out came a space child, who is the cosmic child, the light shining in darkness. One day in the bottom of the sea I found a pearl and became the pearl.

Another time I found myself walking up stairs to a white door. I wanted to go through it, but I couldn't make the last few steps. Then I surrendered, and a hand opened the door for me, and helped me up. Inside the room was a yellow sun-mandala. I went to the center of the mandala, and became a three-dimensional mandala. The lower half of my body then became a black cobra's body, which came up behind me, its hood over the top of my head. I thought, can it harm me? No, because I am already surrendered, dead. The cobra put out its tongue and I touched it with my tongue. We communicated through this.

As these images evolved, and the inner process deepened, one imaginal theme continued: that of building a bridge between the archetypal world and the world of consciousness. At the beginning it was just a thin rope-bridge which was difficult to cross. But as the months passed a stronger bridge of girders was slowly built. After six months the first half of the bridge was of blue metal, with a red walkway on top, the second half remaining a rope bridge. Then after a year, the second half of the bridge was a steel girder structure, beyond which a path went into the forest. Through this work I was building an inner, imaginal bridge between the two worlds, a bridge which I later discovered was not just for myself but also for others. Bringing consciousness into the depths enables the ancient, alchemical work of transformation to take place. Consciousness transforms the unconscious, so that we can be nourished rather than threatened by its primal energies. Another theme that repeated itself in this year was using the sword of consciousness. I experienced the great snake of the unconscious and was prompted to cut it with the shining sword I held. At first I was reluctant to cut up this beautiful and powerful snake, and resisted. But when I was "awake" I knew that I had made a mistake, and the next day I went back into the depths and cut the snake with my sword. Then I was able to cook the snake over an open fire and so digest the contents of the unconscious.

During this time I became familiar with the archetypal world and learned of its importance not just from books but from real experience. I realized that the archetypes are not just concepts, but dynamic, living energies that are a part of our psyche, and at the same time are autonomous powers that used to be worshiped as gods and need to be respected. I also discovered that the archetypal world is very sad and wounded because it has been neglected. It needs to be transformed; it needs to be woken up. Sunlight and the laughter of children need to return to this inner, symbolic world. But the archetypal world cannot transform itself; it needs our own individual consciousness to help unfold its future.

After a year this process came to an end with a number of images of union, of masculine and feminine uniting, the sun and moon coming together and merging. Then there was an experience with a dragon in which I put a golden collar around his neck. I locked the collar with a golden key and swallowed the key. I had tamed the power of the unconscious and had access to its energy. Finally I closed a book, locked it with a golden clasp, and offered the book to the fire. The wisdom of the inner world was for the moment closed, offered to the fire of spiritual transformation.

WORKING WITH WORDS

While this process was happening in the depths, I was struggling, writing an outline for my thesis, trying to express my ideas about the archetypal world in words not images. This was to become my crucifixion as I was torn apart by the difficulty of expressing the fluid, amorphous nature of the unconscious in a rational, sequential form that was academically acceptable. The unconscious does not like to be contained or ordered, and is the opposite of intellectual coherence. Yet I had chosen the form of an academic thesis and I had to follow its rules.

Each time I thought that I had expressed myself coherently, my supervisor Alan would kindly, but straightforwardly, disillusion me. I would complain, feeling unfairly attacked, my work falling to pieces around me. But despite my inner anger and sometimes fiery outbursts, I respected his role as teacher and mine as student. Often I returned from these meetings almost in tears, feeling painfully rejected and sensing the impossibility of my task. My work had also been increased in that I had to learn a whole language of literary criticism that had changed since I was at college. I discovered that it was not enough to offer a Jungian response to *Hamlet*, but I had to integrate this idea within a theory of criticism called "reader response," which suggests that it is the stance of consciousness of the reader that determines what is experienced in reading. Just as we see and experience life through our subjective patterns and conditioning, so is reading highly subjective. "Reader response" is concerned with the interrelationship of a text and its reader—with what a text does, how it affects the reader—and is thus concerned with the reading process: how we read a text.

"Reader response" is a perfect partner for archetypal work, as one of the primary qualities of an archetype is that it only has meaning through its subjective effect. One cannot study archetypes with intellectual objectivity—Jung equates this to reading about an illness as compared to having an illness. One has to become aware of the feelings that are evoked by an archetypal image, and discover in what way the image is personally meaningful. My descent into the archetypal world was giving me direct, fully-felt experience, and "reader response" was a good academic vehicle for expressing archetypal theory within the field of literary studies. But it meant that I had to study and learn a whole new field of academic theory and incorporate this into my work. I loved reading Jung, but I found most literary criticism very intellectual and difficult to assimilate. My mind, used to the fluid nature of symbolic imagery, found the dryness and rigidity of purely mental concepts hard to grasp. I rebelled, but was forced back into the academic harness. Now I see that this was a very good training: to learn how to contain and express feelings and concepts about the unconscious, to discipline the mind so that it could be used for the purpose of uniting the inner and outer world. At the time I just felt the agony of the restriction.

I also felt that I was not understood, that my ideas were not appreciated. My thesis was not just an intellectual exercise, it was a part of me; my own depths were being expressed. This constellated the powerful projection of the father-figure. My own father had never understood me, and the longing to be understood by an older man was thrown onto Alan, who wisely declined to accept the projection! Unconscious patterns combined with the difficulty of accepting the academic constraints, and I felt deeply rejected. This dynamic continued for over a year, during which time I continually looked for someone to understand my work and felt that I found no one.

Gradually I became aware of my pattern of trying to find a father-figure outside of myself. Each time I felt the pain and rejection, the pattern came slowly closer to consciousness. Then an older man, a therapist who was a friend of Mrs. Tweedie's, offered to read part of my thesis. I was excited, but as I went to meet him at a London hotel I felt this old pattern again resurfacing, and saw that I was projecting far more into this meeting than it warranted. I became so fed up that I consciously withdrew the projection. I had an enjoyable meeting without any of the unconscious expectations or disappointments. When I returned home I found everyone asleep, but the television had been left on and it was showing a late-night nature program about the life of a stag. I walked in just at the point in the young stag's life when he returns to the herd to challenge and defeat the ruling stag. Only when I awoke the next morning did I realize the synchronistic implications of the program. Within myself a natural cycle had been completed in which I had claimed back a part of my own masculine identity from the unconscious. I had owned my own inner father.

About a year later there was a sequel to this experience, one that finally confirmed my own masculine identity in the deepest sense. At the time I still sensed a need for a masculine mentor or role model. Living with Mrs. Tweedie powerfully constellated the archetypal feminine, but as a man I felt the lack of a masculine spiritual identity. In my family and environment there was no model for such a role. About this time, on a few occasions, walking in the streets I saw an Indian man dressed in white who for an instant each time reminded me of Bhai Sahib. I realized from this that a masculine image in the unconscious was coming to the surface, reflected in my projection.

Then one day a friend asked me to collect a personal physician of the Dalai Lama from the airport and drive him to a London train station, where he was to take a train to the west of England to attend a conference on healing. This Tibetan doctor had been imprisoned and tortured by the Chinese for many years, and only recently been given his freedom. I collected him from the airport, along with his translator, a young Tibetan woman, and spent an hour in an Indian tea shop while we waited for his train. He spoke little, just a few words of greeting, but his silence conveyed an inner stillness. However, it was not until I awoke the next morning that I glimpsed the significance of the meeting. I had been with a man who was just himself. Despite his years of imprisonment he projected no feelings of anger or bitterness, he just *was*. Real spiritual teaching is never with words, but reflected from being to being. His presence impressed upon me the simple but powerful statement that it was all right as a man in the world to just *be*.

CREATING AN EMPTY SPACE

Intellectual study, trying to write, working with the archetypal world, and an unrecognized father projection dramatized the first two years of my thesis. At the beginning of this time I also had an important dream that pointed me in the direction I needed to take:

> I am together with Bhai Sahib, who asks me to go to the town and get him a chocolate Easter egg. As I leave him I meet Mrs. Tweedie who is walking towards him. I search all over the town but cannot find an Easter egg. I go back to where I left him, where I find Mrs. Tweedie who tells me that he couldn't wait.

When I awoke from the dream I felt very upset. The one time that my Sheikh asked me to find something for him I couldn't find it; and not only that, but he couldn't wait for me. But as I thought about the dream I suddenly understood. A chocolate Easter egg is made of a thin chocolate shell surrounding an empty space. What he wanted was not the chocolate, but the empty space in the middle. My work was to create an empty space within which something could be born.

Working on my thesis, I learned to be always attentive to keeping an empty space. There were so many books that I could have read, offering different avenues of research, but I had to stay true to the inner feeling of the thesis and use this as a guidance as to what to read. Learning what *not* to read, what avenues of study *not* to follow, was an important discipline. I had to allow the thesis to unfold in its own way, follow its own strange course, attracting the inner and outer material it needed. I began to grasp the wisdom of Lao Tsu when he says, "Less and less is done until nothing is done. When nothing is done, nothing is left undone."

My mind had to become attuned to the inner rhythms of the unconscious, in both writing and reading. Slowly I learned to let the unconscious express itself coherently while at the same time staying true to its amorphous nature. My mind began to work in harmony with my inner self, allowing a deeper meaning than consciousness to express itself in words. Through my work the two worlds began to come together within me, to be no longer antagonistic strangers but a couple working together creating the *coniunctio*, the union of opposites that is an aspect of the Self.

I had known from the beginning that my thesis was about the manifestation of the Self—this was the vision of the diamond ring on my finger. What I did not realize was that the Self is a state of being, a state in which the opposites of masculine and feminine, conscious and unconscious, are united in harmony. This mystic marriage was happening within me through the vehicle of my thesis. The need to express the archetypal nature of Shakespeare's *Hamlet* forced me to bring these opposites together. I experienced this inwardly in the images of the union of sun and moon, and outwardly in an ability to put words on paper. The outward process was the more painful because there was always a longing to keep things hidden: I knew how easily the mystery and numinosity of the archetypal world can be lost in the clear light of consciousness.

There were times when I almost despaired of this process, when I felt that I couldn't go on. Writing a Ph.D. thesis is an exercise in solitary perseverance with little external echo. There was a period after about two years when I felt exhausted, without the strength to continue. Then I had an experience of dropping deep into the unconscious, where I met a powerful bear. Contacting this primal energy, making friends with the bear, gave me the energy to continue. After this, whenever I felt that I needed more energy, I would go inward and reconnect with this bear, which a shaman would call my power animal. He became both a friend and a source of energy.

Slowly the pages were written. For over two years my children awoke to the sound of my typewriter, for I always like to start in the early morning when my mind is clear of the thought forms of the day. This was before the time of the blissful silence of the laptop computer I now use; then I only had an electric typewriter. As I corrected and rewrote, I would have to retype each page many times over. Once, towards the end of this time, I almost bought a word-processor, an early model with green writing on the screen. I had spent a whole day with Mrs. Tweedie, whom I had accompanied to a wedding. This was the first time I had ever spent a whole day with Mrs. Tweedie, and just sitting beside her was like sitting beside a vast, empty space of nothingness. My mind and ego were quite terrified by this experience, and as soon as I had taken her home I rushed off to the store to buy a computer. When I brought it home Anat asked me if I really needed it, and I saw that I was just trying to give my mind something to hold onto, to fill that intense and terrifying emptiness. I was able to return the word-processor to the store before even taking it out of the box. I think that I would have found its flickering green screen and complicated commands a difficult distraction.

The thesis was alive within me and gave me many different experiences. I gained a deep theoretical understanding of the unconscious and in particular of the archetypal world. I learned to listen within, to follow the images of the psyche, and to write about this flow. My mind and my psyche learned to work together, creating a relationship that has since been the basis for all of my writing. Something infinitely precious was being born in a sacred empty space, a way of living in the world true to my deepest nature.

My thesis even took me to America. There came a point when I needed an external supervisor. Alan was a lecturer in English literature, and the college required that my archetypal work be validated by an accredited lecturer in psychology. At the time no one taught archetypal studies in any English university, so I wrote to a number of different people in America. A lecturer at the Institute of Transpersonal Psychology in California kindly agreed to read my work, and in February of 1987 I flew over to San Francisco for a two-hour tutorial!

During that first visit to America I spent two weeks in Berkeley, staying in a house with a view of the Bay, in a bare room normally used by visiting Tibetan monks. I liked this college city, its unpainted shingle houses, the early spring flowers, and the smell of eucalyptus in the hills. One afternoon I drove through San Francisco, across the Golden Gate Bridge, and sat on a rocky headland overlooking the bridge and the

Pacific Ocean. I felt the space and brightness of the light on the ocean, the warmth of the sunshine. Suddenly, and to my total astonishment, in the depths of my very being I knew that I belonged here, in California—that this was where my life's work would be. In this moment there was a quality of joy that belonged to life, to the earth, and to my spiritual destiny. All were combined together in a moment both in and out of time. A different quality of consciousness permeated my whole being, a sense of connection and purpose I had never before experienced. Important experiences always take you by surprise: I never thought that I would belong to a physical place, but believed I would always be a stranger in this world. Now it was suddenly different. The experience lasted for just an instant but it left an imprint forever. The inner and outer worlds had come together in a way that I never could have expected.

DISSECTING A RAT

My life's work and my thesis were intimately con-nected, though not in a way that I then understood. I still thought that I would become a university lecturer. After this experience of belonging, I wanted to move immediately to California. I even wandered the streets of Berkeley looking for a suitable house. But as it turned out I would have to wait five years. I had to return to England and finish my thesis, and it still had much to teach me. One was a lesson in detachment.

My thesis had become my baby, my inner and outer child. I felt a need to explain and to honor the archetypes, these misunderstood and half-forgotten gods. I was also exploring ways of using active imagination, which both the alchemists and Sufis have practiced as a means of entering and experiencing the archetypal world.[8] Weaving together images, experiences, and theory, I tried to create a texture through which the reader could feel and understand the numinosity and significance of these primal energies. I felt that the archetypes themselves were speaking through the pages, communicating their meaning, reestablishing their function. As the pages unfolded I experienced a deep fulfillment, but also a trepidation: how would this child be received by the world? And more immediately, how would my supervisor respond?

I was devastated when Alan's initial response was that the four hundred pages or more were not academic enough. If this work was going to be accepted for a Ph.D., certain intellectual arguments needed to be included. He was right, but I felt betrayed. I felt that the world needed to accept my child as it was, whole, unchanged. In describing the archetypal world, the feeling quality is all-important; otherwise, as Jung says, "Those who do not realize the special feeling tone of the archetype end with nothing more than a jumble of mythological concepts."[9] Adding more intellectual arguments would destroy the feeling quality I had so carefully conveyed. The numinosity would be lost, the archetypes become just concepts.

How could I do this to my child? How could I betray the archetypes, allow them to be lost in games of the intellect? I realized the futility of academic work: that the mind could not grasp the significance of the inner world. I knew that what I wanted to say could not be understood within an academic format. This was a moment of profound despair, when it seemed that three years of struggle would yield little visible fruit. I asked Mrs. Tweedie what I should do, and she said that she would meditate and ask Bhai Sahib. The next morning she told me the story of the rat. A friend of hers was studying to be a doctor. A final part of the training involved dissecting a live rat. She protested and refused. How could she, a committed vegetarian, cut up a live rat? It was against all of her values. Finally she had a meeting with the college principal. He explained quite simply that in order to graduate she needed to dissect the rat, and it had to be a live rat. He could not change the rules, and she had to either give up all of her studies, everything that she had done so far, or dissect the rat. Mrs. Tweedie left me with this quandary. She added that spiritually it would not make any difference whether my thesis was accepted.

I knew what had to be done. With the knife of the intellect I dissected my thesis, killing the child that I felt it embodied. Mrs. Tweedie gave me another suggestion: just do this work like a nine-to-five job, as if you were doing it for someone else. It was a painful process, but finally I didn't care. The thesis was no longer my child and I learned to be detached. I withdrew the projection carried in those pages, and in two months had rewritten them. For over three years this had been my child, the baby I was bringing into the world. Now it was just a piece of writing that no longer belonged to me.

Finally I had to rewrite the thesis again, as my examiner wanted me to include certain ideas. But I no longer cared. Dissecting the rat had forced me to become detached, to not identify with what I was writing. My child was alive within me, and those pages were just pieces of paper. When it was finished and I was awarded a Ph.D., I had already moved on and knew I would never be a lecturer. Eventually the only person apart from my supervisor and examiner to read the thesis was my mother, who was just starting a philosophy degree herself! But learning to be detached from my writing was an invaluable lesson that has stayed with me, allowing me to write with total involvement and yet not identify with my work.

Many times on the path you think that you know what you are doing, only to discover that your actions have a very different purpose. I needed to think that my thesis was an important document while I was writing it. But I now know that it was what I learned during those four years that mattered. I was taught to write in harmony with the unconscious, expressing feelings as well as psychological and spiritual ideas. I received a solid grounding in Jungian theory that was to be invaluable in working with people. Also, and most unexpected, I was taken deep into the archetypal world, becoming fully aware of the reality of this dimension. I made a conscious relationship with this symbolic world of images and its primordial inhabitants. An archetypal integration took place, a marriage of opposites, and a bridge was made between the two worlds. This bridge was the most important element of the work, because it was not only for myself but also for others.

ARCHETYPAL JOURNEYS

I had made my descent into the archetypal world, and placed a golden collar around my dragon. Then one day, a friend in the group told me a dream in which I had said to her, "If you want to go into the depths, I know of a way." She asked me if I had any idea what the dream might mean. I thought that it might possibly refer to going with her into the unconscious. We met, and I asked her to close her eyes, keep her mind empty, and be receptive to any images that might come. I emptied my mind and waited. Slowly images came to me, and then particular images that carried a stronger feeling. I described these images to her and they unfolded into a journey. This journey was both personal and archetypal, and explored certain issues that were important to her. We talked with the archetypal figures that we met and worked with them, helping to heal and unblock certain deep problems. She confronted a powerful monster which she cut in two with a shining sword. She was given a cloak of protection and traveled to an island where she took off a mask she had been wearing. The experience gave her an imaginal insight into her own inner world, at the same time as it worked to rebalance certain archetypal dynamics. What was fascinating was that we worked *with the archetypal energies*, consciously interacting with these forces, helping them to change their patterns.

People in the group came to know of this journey, and I led a number of other friends into the depths. Each journey was quite unpremeditated; I had no idea what to expect. We would meet different archetypal figures, travel through different lands. I knew that these were real archetypal experiences from the feeling quality, the numinosity of the interaction. Journeying with an individual, I actually entered his or her psyche, and I had to be invited. Often the person would open a door with a key that belonged only to her. Then we would work at the interface between the personal and the archetypal world. I discovered that although the archetypes are tremendously powerful, ancient beings, they need the participation of individual consciousness to change their patterns. Alone, they remain stuck in their rhythms, in patterns forged over time. Through our talking with them, loving them, guiding them, these patterns could be changed, the dynamics of the unconscious subtly shifted. If our motives are pure we can travel freely in the inner world. We can find a mother her lost child, or a poisoned king a healing herb.

I had told Mrs. Tweedie about these journeys, and suddenly during one afternoon group meeting she suggested I try making a journey with the whole group. I was taken aback because I had never thought of taking a group of people on a journey. But that afternoon I tried and it worked. I emptied my mind and waited for the images to arise. We shared a powerful and deep experience. After this meeting I worked with groups rather than individuals, and followed a course of seven journeys over seven weeks. The number seven was suggested by the unconscious, and it relates to the fact that seven is the number of the collective unconscious—there are seven major archetypes.

Over the next six years I made this series of journeys two or three times a year.[10] Each journey lasted about an hour. The nearest equivalent I have found to these journeys is in the Shamanic tradition. In this tradition the shaman will often begin with the image of a tunnel or hole, and through this the shaman goes into the unconscious, where he may meet a power animal, which is considered very important for the individual. Like shamanic journeys, these archetypal experiences are real ventures into the archetypal world, and are never preplanned. They are spontaneous ventures in which both the individual and the archetypes benefit. These group journeys entered the shared collective of the group and went deep into the archetypal world, even to the book in which the story of creation and the seeds of the future are held.

I could only travel into the archetypal world when I took others on a journey. I could no longer go there for myself. But during these journeys I learned more about psychology and the archetypes than from any books, for they were direct living encounters with the energies of the inner world. I discovered that the archetypes need to talk to us. For so long they have been locked deep in the unconscious, and many people only experience them through phobias, addictions, or physical symptoms like backaches. The archetypes have so much to give, and yet their gifts do not fit into the external purposes of our conscious lives. They speak of an ancient journey begun long ago. They speak of the destiny of the soul rather than the fleeting fantasies of our everyday desires. But until we acknowledge their existence and invite them into our lives there can be no creative interrelationship; they cannot share with us the deeper direction of our lives of which they are the custodians.

There is a psychological rule that states one should never go into the unconscious for the purposes of the ego. Many fairy tales warn us of the danger.[11] The best attitude is to go into the unconscious to work, to help. These journeys confronted us with the wounds of the archetypal world, and we worked to heal them. Often the first figure we encountered was the wounded feminine, who cannot see through her tears. The depth of her pain was a powerful reminder that our masculine culture has caused a deep inner wound. We saw the damage that our Western world has caused through its rejection and denial of the ancient world of the gods, how not only have we cut ourself off from our inner psychic foundations, but the archetypes themselves have become wounded and sorrowful through isolation and neglect.

We found that our coming had been expected, waited for. In their pain and sorrow the archetypes had called us, and each journey was an answer. Working with the power of the imagination and the strength of consciousness, we helped to heal these wounds. We brought the seventh fruit from the tree of life to the sorrowing woman and freed her from her tears. We confronted the shadow of disbelief, the shadow in the inner world created by our belief in rationalism and our rejection of the symbolic. Then magic could return to this realm and we could hear again the laughter of children who live in harmony with the ancient rhythms of life. We reconnected time to eternity, bringing meaning back to an endless succession of minutes, hours, and days. We faced the dark power of the feminine and danced with her deepest magic, so that the purpose of life's illusions could be understood.

Often these journeys involved reconnecting parts of the inner world that have become isolated from each other. We took a purple flower from the primal fire of creation, and placed it on the eyes of a king, who then awoke. We took a necklace of pearls to heal a queen, and the seed of a grape of joy to a garden so that it could blossom into laughter. Sometimes we took understanding, which is the greatest gift. To the wounded woman we brought the primal picture of light entering the dark waters of the feminine like a sword, and showed her why this light is needed.

In performing this imaginative work we discovered that the archetypes are not healed by some mysterious, symbolic substance, but by ourselves. When we gave the sorrowing woman the seventh fruit of the tree of life, in that moment we realized that *we are the fruit*. Just as our collective rejection of the archetypal world has created its wounds, so it is our individual relationship to these gods that effects its healing. Through journeying into the inner world, relating to its inhabitants and working with them, we formed within our individual psyches a bridge into the archetypal world.

Alone, in my own individual inner process, I had worked to help form this bridge. Now, as we continued this work in a group, I came to understand its deeper significance, as one archetypal figure explained:

> Each time you come from your world to this inner world, and you come with understanding, not greed, then a grain of sand crosses the great divide. However small it may be, that grain of sand has immense meaning, for it comes with love. It forms part of an immense pattern like a mandala, and when this pattern is complete then there will be a healing beyond all healing as the outer returns to the inner and the Self reveals itself. Then a new life will be upon your earth and upon my earth, and there will be a flowering as there has not been for thousands of years.

THE CHILD OF THE FUTURE

Working in the archetypal world, we received many gifts. The greatest gift was to experience this inner reality and meet its inhabitants. As we interacted with the archetypes, they shared their numinosity and their wisdom. Individually and as a group we felt the reality of this rejected dimension, and would emerge from the journeys full of wonder and deep nourishment. The split within our psyches was slowly being healed. But the archetypes also gave us symbolic gifts of infinite worth. One journey gave us a seed from the tree of life, a seed which belongs neither to yesterday nor to tomorrow, but to the moment in which all life is. Another journey gave us a flower of hope which became a serpent ring, and the eyes of the serpent were diamonds which carried the wisdom of the Self. Once a child came to us, the child of the future, who belongs to the new age, and gave us a harp with seven strings that plays the prayer of the heart. In another journey this same child gave us a kiss on the heart. This kiss is the prayer of the future, a prayer which carries the deepest meaning of the soul, of our own soul and the world's soul. Through this kiss our heart can touch the hearts of others. Our heart can sing to their heart and our song awaken them to their song.

The archetypal figures taught us about the inner world, the wonder as well as the pain. They shared with us the transitions that are taking place in the depths, the changes that will shape our world. This time of transition can be seen as a time of danger, but from within the unconscious we could also glimpse the tremendous possibilities that can unfold. We saw how the pain of the archetypes is a part of this transition, and how even the wounding of the earth belongs to its process of transformation.

The child of the future who came to us shared a life lived in the eternal now. This child is the emerging archetype, the symbol of the coming age. Yet unlike the other archetypes, the essence of the child is a space rather than a form, a sacred space in which we can be our true selves and experience the joy which belongs to life itself. In one journey this space is imaged as "a stage":

> Slowly a curtain rises on a new stage. Your own life is this stage. Yet even the idea of a stage is a limitation because it belongs to the world of forms. The stage of the future is not a structure. It is a quality of closeness, a quality of intimacy, a quality of being touched and of allowing yourself to be touched. It is a quality of sharing something most secret always, of being shown something most secret always. It is a quality of togetherness, of being together with yourself, of becoming familiar with yourself, of not forcing yourself into corners or pushing yourself back against a wall. It has to do with freeing yourself of so many restrictions that are totally irrelevant for they belong to another time.

The deepest meaning of the inner world can only unfold into our life when we are true to ourself, when we live our own life, singing our own song. We each have our own destiny, our own unique way of living what is most precious. For some it can be baking bread with love, for others, painting a picture. Jung says, "Find the meaning and make the meaning your goal." The archetype of the future holds a sacred space, "a temple without walls in which everything is holy," in which this deep meaning can be lived, the sacred moment be now. In this moment we are open to life, to the miracle of being human and the wonder of being divine.

The secrets of the archetypal world are the simple secrets of life being lived in harmony with the soul. In these journeys we tasted this truth, felt its wonder and joy. Each of us in our own way was opened by these journeys, and through this opening could hear our own song and know it as a part of the song of all life. In this way we came to realize the value of our individual song. The archetypes are the powerful, eternal parts of our own being, but we are in tune with them only when we live our own story. The child of the future is a space that gives us the inner freedom to catch the thread of our story and allow it to unfold into our life. There we feel the oneness that belongs to the depths, hidden under the surface multiplicity. We know ourself to be a part of this oneness, and that our own life carries a seed of purpose beyond our comprehension.

WE ARE THE GIFT TO BE GIVEN

Over the six years as the journeys progressed, this archetype of a sacred space evolved and became more and more central. At the beginning the journeys focused on the individual archetypes which were often personified into figures, like the image of time as an old man with silver hair and silver beard who sits alone in a cave, counting the minutes as they stretch into eternity. This figure of the ancient of days taught us about the patterns of time, how the seasons relate to the ebb and flow of galaxies. But sadly he had lost contact with happiness and the laughter of children, and our task was to reconnect him with the woman from whom he had been separated, the feminine flow of time. In another journey we met the abundant energy of creation as a man made of living things, of the harvest, the song of birds, and the music of waterfalls. But in all of this abundance there was no joy and we were guided to dance with this man. We danced with all our heart and soul as the day became night and on till the dawn appeared. Through this dance joy returned and the water of life became rainbow-colored.

As we gave ourselves to this inner work, the archetypes were transformed, and the seven came together to reveal the eighth, the child who forms a magic circle. This circle includes all the seven, and yet is a new unfolding. As the journeys progressed it became clear that we are the new unfolding, for just as the archetypes are a part of us, so is this circle our own wholeness. Our own story, our own song, is the seed of the future. Gradually the forms of the past, the figures of the wounded archetypes, were healed and then merged together into the new, and the journeys focused more and more on the journeyer. Traveling into the archetypal world, we found our own dance beating in tune with the stone at the foundation of the world. Through a window we smelled the sweet perfume of our own soul. We became a part of what we had forgotten, silence pulsating with the heartbeat of joy.

Finally, in what I knew was to be the last series of journeys, all images disappeared, and there was no traveling, for there was nowhere to go. We learned to hold hands with silence and watch the thread of our own destiny. We were told not to expect any miracle because a miracle has already happened: the future has been born. We hardly notice this miracle because we have been conditioned to see only forms, and the new unfolding is a sacred space, an emptiness full of potential and the essence of life. We felt the tentativeness of this new beginning, and how it is not born from the past but from the eternal present. We experienced how the future that is now "is a moment to be grasped, not something that will happen. It is not a place for problems to be solved or wishes to be granted. It is only a place to be alive." Finally, at the end of the last journey we were told of the importance of our individual story, and how our own self is the gift to be given:

> Wait till you feel your own story like a dream, like a possibility, and then give it to the earth as an offering. Give your own story to the earth as an offering, full of meaning, full of possibilities, and full of the song of the soul, that ancient song, so ancient it was born before the beginning and yet also knows the meaning of time. The earth has been so much cut up that it needs again to know wholeness, to be given wholeness as a gift. What you can offer is your own story which is your own wholeness, the essence of your becoming, to give that as a seed to the heart of the world. It has been given to you and so you give it, you pass it on, your own story, the essence of your own unfolding.
>
> Each moment we expect something to happen and so we do not give ourselves, not realizing that this gift is the happening. When we give ourselves to life, life is impregnated with the future. Life is longing to be opened, to be made holy, to be redeemed from so much materialism. And remember this is only the beginning, this opening to a different dimension of being.
>
> You have arrived. There is nowhere else to go. You are where you ought to be. There is no future and no past in this moment. But you make

it holy through giving yourself. Just give the seed of your own story to life; open it with love and life will respond. Life will take your seed and place it in the heart of the world, where it will keep alive the fire that burns there, that burns in the heart of the heart of the world. That is your offering. That is all that you can ever give. Slowly the world will start to spin on a new axis of love.

PART 3

―――

We are never given for ourself.
It is always for others.

Bhai Sahib

DREAMWORK AND THE GROUP

Ours is the way of group discussion. In solitude there is renown and in renown there is danger.

Bahâ ad-dîn Naqshband

OPENING THE DOORS TO THE WORLD

The years that I was working on my thesis coincided with the period when Mrs. Tweedie's work expanded most visibly. The afternoons when ten or twelve of us sat around the table or on the floor of her kitchen became only a memory. More and more seekers came to her flat, until we were so tightly squashed that people were standing in the hallway.

This transition in the group happened at about the same time that I finished my role as an English teacher. Following the publication of *Chasm of Fire* in German, Mrs. Tweedie had started lecturing in Europe. When I first came to the group she occasionally lectured at the Theosophical Society in London, but the European lectures introduced a very different stage for the work, as I experienced when she was invited to The Rainbow Festival at Interlaken in Switzerland. Instead of the Theosophical Society lecture followed by tea and polite talk, this was an international spiritual conference with representatives from many different traditions, Zen Buddhist, Christian, American Indian,

Shamanic. The Dalai Lama was also there. Mrs. Tweedie was representing the Sufi path, and a number of us from the group went to Interlaken for the week.

This was my first week away from my children since they had been born, and my last week at school had just passed. I felt like a teenager let out of school. The sense of freedom was blissful. I awoke in the morning knowing that nobody needed me, that I could come and go in my own time with no demands. The hotel where I was staying was a twenty-minute walk along the lakeside to Interlaken, to the nineteenth-century casino where the conference was being held. In the morning I would walk with the hills reflected in the lake, sometimes glimpsing the snow on the distant mountain tops. There were sunshine, spiritual friends, mountains, meditation, and freedom. I was beaming with happiness.

But more significant was the effect of seeing Mrs. Tweedie lecture in public. At first I was profoundly shocked seeing her on stage, representing Sufism to the world. Her sitting there in front of hundreds of people, dressed in black, representing our tradition, shattered some deeply held conditioning of mine that the path should never be made public, but always remain hidden, almost invisible. The experience was like seeing someone naked, exposed, beautiful, and powerful.

Since I had met Mrs. Tweedie the group had slowly grown, but it was still a very small, intimate gathering. There was no sign on the door—it was just open to those who found their way there. I remember one friend's story of how, on reading *Chasm of Fire*, she wondered if Mrs. Tweedie was still alive, and if so, where, in what part of the world she lived. She asked the person who had given her Mrs. Tweedie's book, and received the reply, "Just go down to the traffic lights, cross over, and take the second turning to the right. Her house is halfway down on the left and she is open every afternoon, from two till eight. " Another friend walked on a pilgrimage all the way from Switzerland. People gradually arrived at our home in north London, to drink from the inner emptiness that was always there. But now things were changing as Mrs. Tweedie became a visible presence, known in the world.

At the Rainbow Festival I glimpsed a wider view of her work, how it needed to go out into the world and touch many more hearts. Years later, when for the first time I sat in front of an audience in Germany, continuing her work, I was amazed and deeply moved to see how many hearts she had touched, how many people had her face imprinted into their psyche. As she became more visible and well known, the door of her flat seemed to open wider. The small group of friends swelled as people came from all over the world, particularly from Germany, Switzerland, and then America.

Yet as the numbers increased a strange chemistry took place; the group became both more intimate and more impersonal at the same time. Even when she was on a stage lecturing to hundreds of people, Mrs. Tweedie could evoke an atmosphere of intimacy, in which individuals thought she was talking just to them. Someone described her as having the ability to make love to an audience, and when I first saw her in the old casino in Interlaken I knew it was true. She told her favorite story of the fishes who went on a quest to find what water is, and everybody's heart and eyes expanded as the story unfolded. Finally, when the few remaining fish found the answer, that "where they were was water," we all felt intimately included in this mystery, as if we too were the fish realizing our true nature for the first time.

What I had seen in Switzerland continued in Mrs. Tweedie's flat. People came, bringing their troubles and their longing. One of the qualities of the English is their reserve: they leave their neighbors alone. One can live for twenty years next door to someone and never exchange more than a polite "hello." In all the eleven years of our meetings, the neighbors neither questioned nor complained about what was happening in our house. For the last years of Mrs. Tweedie's meetings, every afternoon over forty people would gather on the pavement before she opened, and then disappear into an ordinary-looking suburban house. More people would arrive during the afternoon, and then, in the evening as the meeting ended, all would spill out on the street, talking and hugging before they dispersed. No noise came from behind the door, and the neighbors must have been curious. Once a woman who lived next door asked Anat what class the old lady gave, thinking maybe she taught a language or something. At the time Anat's English was still not very good, and, thinking that the neighbor was asking if she took upper- or middle-class people, she replied, "She takes all classes." The neighbor, understandably confused, never asked again. Another lady across the street had heard that there was meditation, and thought it might be good for her husband. She asked Anat, "How much does it cost?" But when Anat said that it doesn't cost anything, she replied, "Then I understand nothing," and never asked again.

We meditated in the afternoon, usually from half past three to four. People liked to lie down for the meditation, and so during that half hour Mrs. Tweedie's flat was full of bodies lying on the floor, even in the hallway. On the warm summer days there would also be people lying in the garden. One afternoon during meditation the doorbell rang. As I was sitting nearby I opened the door to find a neighbor outside. He owned the house at the rear of ours, and we had had some discussion about who owned a fence that had been blown down in a recent storm. There was astonishment on his face as, standing on the doorstep, looking past me, he saw the flat full of people lying all over the floor. I quickly closed the door behind me and we discussed the matter of the fence. He never asked what was happening, but he must have been very curious to know what was going on in the house of the old lady whom he saw pottering in her garden.

We were left alone, undisturbed. For a while there was even a local policeman who would come to the meetings on his big black policeman's bicycle. He had started coming to the group with his wife, and then fate had transferred him to be our community policeman, and he made the most of the opportunity. To anyone watching it must have been strange to see him cycle up wearing his uniform and policeman's helmet, park his bicycle, and vanish inside with all the other people, to appear a few hours later, put on his helmet, and ride away. Every country has its characteristics, and the English custom that neighbors "keep themselves to themselves" was very beneficial to our group.

DREAMWORK AND THE PATH

The summer Mrs. Tweedie attended the Rainbow Festival she also lectured in America for the first time, both in New York and on the West Coast. In California she found a publisher for the complete version of her diary. She had never been happy with *Chasm of Fire* because the editing that reduced the eight hundred pages to two hundred took away the real message of the book. The story of the slow grinding down she had experienced with her beloved Bhai Sahib had been lost, and none of her dreams had been included. She always felt that her book, *Daughter of Fire*, was her lifetime's work, and it was now the right time for the complete story to be known.

Her work as the representative of her teacher was to bring his lineage of Sufism to the West. This was the work that was unfolding through her lectures and through the daily meetings. Unknowingly I was a part of this work; my destiny was tied up with hers and with the path in a way I did not realize. But for the years of my thesis I followed the routine of studying in the morning and attending the group meetings in the afternoon. These two elements of my life moved hand in hand. At the time I thought them separate; I now see how they belonged together. My studies of Jungian psychology gave me an invaluable understanding of the way the psyche changes and develops, and provided a language to help describe this unfolding. In the group I would see this process at work, and through dreamwork help to make it conscious.

When I first came to the group, Mrs. Tweedie would occasionally interpret people's dreams. But mainly she spoke about her teacher, whom she lovingly called *Guruji*. With fire and passion she talked about her time with him, inspiring us with the wonder of the path, inciting us to work harder upon ourselves, make more effort, and look only to the goal. But gradually the intensity shifted. She became softer and gentler. She also gave more and more time to dreamwork, encouraging the group to participate in telling and discussing dreams. By the time I began my thesis, dreamwork had become central to the format of our afternoon meetings. As people arrived she would talk for a while, about spiritual or everyday matters, about the Beloved or the weather. Then we would meditate for half an hour, after which we would have tea and talk. But the final hours of the afternoon were given to dreamwork, interspersed with teaching or discussion. Mrs. Tweedie had the wonderful ability to keep everyone entranced with whatever she was saying, telling stories, talking about the garden and the problems of old age. She always used to advise us not to grow old, but in the same breath would say, "But you will never listen to this advice." The dreamwork was held within the flow of her presence, which followed an invisible course that kept one's attention always alert. Sometimes a dream would receive the simple response, "That is a good dream. Next." Sometimes a dream would be seemingly ignored, as what appeared to be a different topic was discussed. On occasion she would give a direct interpretation, but more often the group would be asked to offer interpretations, and the dreamer was left alone to feel which interpretation was right, which one(s) resonated with his or her dream. During this process Mrs. Tweedie's attention was sometimes present and sometimes absent, "listening to something else."

What was fundamental was the invisible container, and the real work that was being reflected from heart to heart. This was the energy that held us all, the quality of love that kept everyone's inner attention. The group was an alchemical vessel of many ingredients, and the conscious and unconscious were blended together, different worlds spinning around a hidden center. I loved to just sit in the enveloping energy, watching with wonder the way she held the flow. Mrs. Tweedie never called herself a teacher, just "the caretaker of her flat." People didn't believe it and liked to attribute to her all sorts of powers, but it was essentially true. She liked to quote Bhai Sahib, "This is a house of drunkards, and this is a house of change."

In her flat the destiny of the soul was given precedence, and dreams and dreamwork became a central theme. She told us that dreams were guidance. In her presence we could hear their hidden message more clearly. She had discovered that I have a particular talent for dream interpretation, and began to have me sit near to her and help with the dreamwork. Over the years I had heard many dreams, and learned to listen to and try to interpret my own. Now I combined this experience with my studies of Jungian psychology and a developing intuition.

At first, when I heard a dream I would try to interpret it, associating its images with my knowledge of symbolism. But I quickly discovered that a better approach was to keep my mind as empty as possible when a dream was told. Sometimes the meaning of the dream would then fall like a seed into the empty space. From this seed I could use my understanding of symbolism, psychology, and the dynamics of the path to explain its meaning. Often a sentence would come into my mind that pointed towards the dream's essence, sometimes in the form of a question to the dreamer. At the beginning it was quite miraculous to find a dream's meaning revealed so clearly, and the sense of wonder has stayed with me, even after listening to thousands of dreams. I know that it is not me, because I do not "interpret" the dream—its meaning just appears in the empty space of my mind. But to be a part of this mysterious unfolding is very precious, like being the guardian of a temple.

I found that often I could see to the core of a dream, and my study of Jungian psychology gave me the language to express its meaning. For example, when someone dreamed of a boat floating down a river which was full of stinking, decaying corpses, I knew that the dream was imaging the process in which the contents of the psyche are broken down, a necessary part of the process of transformation. Jung's reading of alchemy describes this as the stage of *"putrefactio,"* or putrification, which can be accompanied by the smell of decomposition. Identifying her dream as a part of this alchemical process allowed the dreamer to be reassured rather than horrified; she could realize the transformative nature of her own disintegration.

Sometimes the whole meaning of the dream would be instantly present, but more often the meaning would evolve as I offered my interpretation. I discovered that my psyche could speak through me, revealing the more complete meaning of a dream both to the dreamer and to myself. As I spoke I would see the dream more clearly, and at the same time realize its implications for the dreamer. As this work continued I began to see that when I was interpreting someone's dream I was interacting with her psyche. My dreamwork was not a detached observation, but a dynamic interaction with the psyche of the dreamer. Talking to the dreamer, I could enter her psyche and reveal more of the dream's implications. Yet this was never at my own will, and happened only if the dreamer wanted the dream to be interpreted. Sometimes a dreamer does not really want her dream to be interpreted. She thinks that she knows what it means, and tells the dream just for confirmation or even self-gratification. On these occasions I feel the wall of her resistance, and do not bother to offer any response to the dream, other than a polite comment.

Archetypal journeys had taught me to enter the collective unconscious of a group. Practicing dreamwork in our group, I found that at times there would be an open door within the dreamer inviting me to explore a dream more fully. Talking to the dreamer would become both a conscious and an unconscious interaction, and this would take place within a group situation. All the while Mrs. Tweedie was there, the caretaker of the space, creating the deep sense of security that enabled the inner work to take place. She would be listening inwardly and outwardly, though the main focus of her attention was always inward.

WATCHING THE SPACE OF THE GROUP

But interpreting a dream was only a part of the work. When a dream was told I did not immediately offer a response, even when I knew its meaning. Other people would suggest interpretations and I would watch the flow, being particularly attentive to Mrs. Tweedie and any response she might have. Initially I did this so as not to dominate the dreamwork, giving others an opportunity. I was aware of the danger of my ego's putting itself forward. But I also felt a deeper reason. Just as I had to put aside myself to create a space to hear the dream, I felt the importance of the group space and the need in group discussion also to put my ego to one side. Listening to the flow of the dreamwork, and being attentive to the inner space, I would wait for the right moment to offer any interpretation.

Within this flow the inner and outer dynamics of the group took place. Mrs. Tweedie steered a path both with her presence and with words, though more and more she stepped back, giving the group itself precedence. I learned to focus on the inner space and watch it move both in silence and in words. Sometimes there was a feeling that a dream should not be interpreted, and I learned to respect this, despite any initial feelings that I knew what the dream meant. I learned when to allow a wrong interpretation to remain, to allow the ego of a dreamer to be gratified while a problem was overlooked. And I also learned when to hit a dreamer with a response that would not be consciously appreciated. From the dreamer's response one could feel his or her real openness to the dream, and how deep the interpretation should go. Throughout this work, the living, dynamic space of the group was the real teacher, the real guide.

On a number of occasions Mrs. Tweedie told me that it did not really matter if a dream was correctly interpreted. At first I was shocked, as I was consciously working on dream interpretation within the group. But gradually I began to see that a deeper process was taking place. Just in the sharing of a dream within the sacred space of the group, something of great importance within the individual was valued, listened to. This work of listening to and valuing the dream helped not only the dreamer, but all those present. A deep, alchemical sharing was happening, in which the consciousness of the dreamer played only a small part. The story of the soul was being told and heard, contained in acceptance and love.

Mrs. Tweedie also gave me the freedom not to have to know. At first when she pushed me forward as being "an expert in dreams," I felt the need to be able to interpret a dream, to know what the dream meant. But often she herself would freely say, "I do not know," and I found this a great relief. Sometimes I would understand a dream, and be able to offer a precise interpretation. But on other occasions when a dream was told, I would have no insight, and offer no response. There is a great freedom in not knowing, and trusting that if one needs to know, that knowledge will be present. Emptiness is central to the path. Sometimes understanding or knowledge will come into the emptiness; at other times one remains happily unknowing. I found that this also helped to keep me from becoming identified with the process of dream interpretation. Not knowing stopped my ego from feeling self-important.

Learning to listen in emptiness and then to verbalize what I heard was the real work. Also learning not to interfere, even if I felt that the dreamer was accepting an incorrect interpretation. At first I would inwardly react when this happened, but slowly I learned to give up even my idea that a dream should be understood. Yet just as Mrs. Tweedie said that it did not really matter if a dream is correctly interpreted, she also quoted her Jungian friend Werner Engel, who said that the dream will always make itself known. Trusting the wisdom and power of the dream gave me the freedom to step back and allow the dream to reveal itself. Sometimes different interpretations would add to the dreamer's understanding. Or the dreamer could be left in a state of confusion, having to look within rather than depend on others. The energy of the path made the dreamwork follow a hidden course, often confusing and strange, but always leading towards an invisible goal. The presence of the path within the dreamer and within the group allowed this contemporary technique of dreamwork to work in accordance with the ancient ways of the Sufi.

PROTECTING THE TEACHER

In the dream I had when Mrs. Tweedie was away in India, I was shown two aspects of my work with her: to bring people to her and to protect her. As more people came to the group, so the need to protect her increased. Anat helped Mrs. Tweedie with many of her daily needs, shopping, driving her to the doctor if necessary, working in the garden. I was needed in a different capacity. On a few occasions people came to the group who were disturbed or unbalanced, and if they disturbed the group I had to ask them to leave. Sometimes when the group finished in the evening people would want to stay to talk to Mrs. Tweedie, and I had to remain to make sure that they did not stay too long, or if Mrs. Tweedie did not want to talk to them, gently guide them to the door.

The room where I worked looked out over her front door, and I would always be aware if someone walked up the path and rang on her doorbell. As Mrs. Tweedie became known, her address seemed to become public knowledge, and people would arrive unannounced. Some even came with their luggage, thinking it was an ashram. If these visitors were not expected, and it was not the time of the group meetings, I would lean out of my window and ask them to our side door. Sometimes they would come upstairs for a cup of tea, or I would tell them when the group was open. We tried to protect Mrs. Tweedie's privacy and be responsive to the needs of those who came.

On occasion Mrs. Tweedie would close the group, or disappear for an undisclosed length of time. If she felt that someone was too attached to her to progress spiritually, she would throw him out of the group for a while, six months or a year. If she felt that the group had become too attached she would go on retreat without announcing either her departure or her expected return. People would arrive at her flat to find the door locked, and we would become the messengers. For many people this could be quite a shock, particularly if they had traveled from abroad to be with her. Some became angry or resentful, felt betrayed and let down. Others held the experience within their connection to the path, and realized the inner freedom that was offered.

We were there in the midst of each scene of the group's drama, each unfolding of the path. If Mrs. Tweedie disappeared on retreat she often did not tell us where she was going, so we could truthfully say that we didn't know where she was. One summer when she was lecturing in Switzerland she discovered that she had glaucoma, and was told by the doctor that she would go blind unless she had an operation to install a tiny valve behind each eye. She did not want the group to know and worry about her operation, so she simply pretended to disappear. She had two operations, one for each eye, and spent six months recovering in her darkened flat. This was a very difficult and painful period for her, during which she said that all she had to offer to God was her suffering. Nobody knew where she was, and some people even thought she had died. Knowing that she was downstairs in darkness and pain added an intensity to the inner silence that pervaded the house.

Holding the secret of our teacher's presence made us keep separate from our friends in the group. But living above Mrs. Tweedie created a quality of isolation even when many people came to the door. A spiritual teacher carries a projection that is unlike any other, because it belongs to the soul, not the personality. For those committed to the path the teacher is *the most important person* in their life, and this relationship is intimate, awesome, and impersonal. Anat and I had our projections onto Mrs. Tweedie, but we were also caught in the group projection. This group projection had many different facets, both positive and negative. People thought that we must be special, or particularly spiritual, to be sharing a house with their teacher, but there were also feelings of resentment, jealousy, exclusion. All these projections created an aura of isolation that was not easy. But it was also a training for the future, for the time when we would have to carry these projections alone.

I have always been a solitary individual, caring little for what others thought about me. This inborn quality was a wonderful safeguard against projections which could slip by me unnoticed. I also realize that throughout this time I was being inwardly trained not to identify with any projection—a positive projection is as imprisoning as one of resentment. In the Sufi practice of "Solitude in the Crowd" we are taught, "In all your outer activities remain inwardly detached; learn not to identify with anything whatsoever," and this was an invaluable guideline. One can feel the weight of someone's projection, and see whether there is any hook or response in oneself. I soon felt the burden of being thought of as particularly spiritual, and worked to free myself—simple human failings are a great help!

But one projection that often caught me was that of being a helpful masculine figure. I learned the danger of trying to help others by becoming entangled in their problems, or being a support that became a dependency. The knight in shining armor coming to the aid of a defenseless maiden, or someone else in need, is a powerful, archetypal hook. The ego feels gratified, pleased that it has done a good deed, or flattered by the response of those one has helped. But eventually I would feel trapped, especially if I took on responsibilities that did not belong to me. Once, feeling sympathetic to a woman in the group with two young children, I invited her to stay for a weekend. Those two days were very demanding, noisy, and exhausting, and her children became overexcited by the energy level of the house. (This was something we had to learn to be careful about, living above Mrs. Tweedie. The energy and power that permeated the whole house could disturb people who were not used to it, especially if they stayed the night.) The day after they had left, Mrs. Tweedie, who had felt the disturbance in the house, shouted at me, furious with my lack of discrimination, "Why did you invite them? You don't owe them anything!" Through my mistakes I had to learn the danger of being too kind and helpful, but discrimination, learning when to say yes and when to say no, learning what is the real need of the situation, is always one of the most difficult qualities to attain.

SPIRITUAL NEED

There is a line in a Sufi story which reads, "If you need enough and want little enough, then you shall find your way." The dynamic of need was strongly evoked in the group because of the nature of the spiritual process. People came to the group because of an inner need, a calling that they could not answer. The teacher is the doorway to this need's being answered, to the hunger of the soul's being fulfilled. The energy of the path further activates this primal need, which Abû Sa'îd calls "a living and luminous fire placed by God in the breast of His servants in order that their ego may be burnt."[1] The teacher and the path stoke the fire of longing until it becomes a burning hunger that one cannot ignore. The depth of this need is terrible because it is beyond the ego, beyond anything we have ever encountered. It cries with the infinite pain of separation, and is the quickest way to reach the goal. Rûmî advises the wayfarer to become needy:

> So, oh needful man, quickly increase your need! Then the sea of bounty will gush forth in generosity....
>
> Where there are questions, answers will be given; where there are ships, water will flow.
> Spend less time seeking water and acquire thirst! Then water will gush from above and below. [2]

I knew the potency of the soul's need, and how it carries a feeling of despair that it might never be met. My meeting Mrs. Tweedie resonated with a "yes" as my need found the path that could answer it. Need is what makes a seeker, what makes him turn away from the world and go Home. But it also has a shadow side, the specter of dependency, in which the need of the personality dominates. The teacher is the outer focus for the soul's need, but also easily evokes the feeling of dependency. To a detached observer the relationship with the teacher carries a dangerous dynamic, in which need is evoked but only partly answered. In fact, it is the job of the teacher to increase the need within the wayfarer, a need that can be fulfilled only by the Beloved. Only when we are free of the projection onto the teacher is the soul's need fully answered from within.

Mrs. Tweedie gave herself to her work of evoking and responding to the need of all who came. She made each person feel special, as she tuned in to each one's own hidden desire for love. Radiating love and acceptance, she was a magnet to keep each seeker's attention, until the path could hold him without any outer form as a support. But there was the added problem that she easily evoked the mother projection with all of its unconscious demands and fears of rejection. When the wayfarer was ready she would ruthlessly break any patterns of attachment, throwing him or her out of the group if necessary. But this work of preparation could take many years, and during this time, as the need grew stronger and stronger, she remained the focus. She had to walk the thin line of nourishing the spiritual need without being trapped in the limiting role of mother substitute.

People related to her through their own need, and because this need alone could take them Home, she could never say no to a seeker. As the keeper of the gates of grace, she could not reject a sincere wayfarer. Furthermore, although she was elderly and growing physically frailer each year, she had been taught to forget her own needs, especially those of her physical body. My work in protecting Mrs. Tweedie was to be sensitive to this situation, and to try not to allow people blinded by their own need to exhaust her unnecessarily. An added difficulty was that she could hide her exhaustion, and make her guests forget that she was old and at times unwell. As she became older we reduced the time of the group meetings from six hours (two in the afternoon till eight) to three hours (three till six), and tried to restrict people from seeing her outside of these times. But often people could not believe that this dynamic woman could ever be tired.

I also had to look carefully at my own feelings, for sometimes I felt resentment at what could seem like selfishness, people's inability to see beyond their own need. How could they be so oblivious to the needs of an old lady who gave herself so totally that she was forgotten both by herself and others? Why did they cling on, holding onto her when only the emptiness was real? Since the dream that allowed me to participate in the afternoon meetings, I knew that my own need could not be answered by her presence. At times I was jealous of those who could sit in her company and have the totality of her love answer their need. I saw in their eyes how they were held and nourished, and knew that this door was closed to me. Later every need within myself was answered, and I was held with a tenderness that is not limited by form or the danger of projection. But there were days when I felt an outsider, once again seeing others sitting, being warmed beside a fire that was forbidden me.

GROUP DYNAMICS

People came with their hunger and their dreams, arriving at the doorstep to be nourished by the energy of the tradition that flowed through Mrs. Tweedie. Within this space each seeker was accepted for herself, "warts and all," as Mrs. Tweedie liked to say. The only requirement was a desire for Truth, a need to find something within. To be accepted for oneself is a deep healing in itself, and combined with the energy of love and the presence of a teacher, the space provided a matrix of healing and transformation.

Some came to sit in silence, others with questions which were asked either directly or through dreams. Not everyone who comes to a Sufi group is a Sufi—Buddhists, Christians, all types of seekers would arrive. A group of women from Texas came who bred bees and were followers of Grandmother Owl. A Christian bishop sat in the corner for many weeks, while a Hindu healer would stop on his way through London. A young woman from New Zealand who was training as an opera singer came for two years while she was in London on a scholarship. She spoke little, but before she left I asked her about her time with the group, what it meant to her. She replied that she had learned to let her voice sing her and not the other way round.

People came for a week, a month, a year, or forever. Some came who had always belonged, while others allowed the energy to help them follow their own path. A few even came because they felt that they had an important message or teachings to impart. Mrs. Tweedie treated them with hospitality and, rather than reject their message, would sit them next to her, have special cups of tea brought to them, and give them space to impart their teachings. Many afternoons I have

sat with irritation building almost into anger as someone went on and on telling us about the future
evolution of the planet, or his own knowledge of the
path. We wanted only to listen to Mrs. Tweedie, and
these self-important visitors would easily evoke the
shadow. Mrs. Tweedie would watch us and our reactions, and we knew it was a teaching experience.

Everything was used to help us along the path, and
all the people who came were a part of a group drama
that unfolded, revealing the ego, evoking the shadow,
and pointing to the beyond. Part of the wonder of the
Sufi path is that this happens of its own accord. The
energy of the path constellates individual and group
dynamics, which are a teaching for those who do not
judge by appearances, who can honestly look at their
reactions and catch the thread—the real teachings
hidden under the surface.

Within the group there was a shadow figure for
each of us, a person who evoked a personal problem
or seemed the opposite of everything spiritual. For
myself those who expressed their neediness would
make me irritated, even angry, as I would think, "Why
can't they stand on their own feet? Why are they so
needy, so wanting to be mothered?" Finally I was able
to accept my own unanswered need, the shadow side
of my independent nature. Then the irritation passed.

I also saw how the shadow of jealousy was present
in the group, as jealousy is easily constellated by the
love dynamic of the path. Jealousy often appeared in
the feeling that others seemed to have more spiritual
dreams or experiences, that others were closer to the
teacher or belonged to the "in-circle" of friends from
which the individual felt excluded. So many times and
from so many people have I heard about these opposites of closeness and exclusion, and I came to realize

their origin. The call of the path is both the taste of union and the feeling of separation. Excluded from our own soul's closeness, we project this inner nearness we long for onto others; and because the teacher is at the center of the path, those who seem closer to her activate the pain of our own separation. But for Mrs. Tweedie the only real closeness was with the Beloved and her teacher, and a friend's apparent closeness was often just her response to his need.

The group was a hall of mirrors in which we learned to see ourself reflected. To some people Mrs. Tweedie was kind, to others hard. She would respond to the deepest need of the person, and the need of the group. Sitting in the group, watching this interplay, this flow of people, dreams, and lives, and seeing people change and evolve taught me so much. I saw the wonder of people's wounds, and the way the path allows them to be uncovered and shared in a protected space, the way these wounds could take seekers deeper within themselves. But I also saw the danger of being attached to pain and suffering. I saw the longing in people, and how that longing was invisibly fed, how people who arrived weighed down with burdens had these burdens lifted, how their eyes would slowly come to shine with the light of their true self. I observed that many people came, but only a few stayed, and knew that was how it has always been.

I also saw the work of the group: how it accepted and helped those who came. The love and devotion of fellow wayfarers wove a container that supported people in the group, both at the meetings and in everyday life, providing real friendship based upon something beyond the ego and personality.[3] The group had the strength to include the shadow and allow for the idiosyncrasies of individuals. As the group expanded, its significance increased, particularly for those who had just arrived and for whom Mrs. Tweedie seemed an unapproachable figure. People helped each other, listening to problems, working with dreams, and most important, bringing love into life. The company of "those who love one another for God's sake" is an important ingredient of the path. Those whose hearts are firmly fixed on the Beloved help others along the way. In the words of Rûmî:

> Be with those who mix with God
> as honey blends with milk, and say,
>
> "Anything that comes and goes,
> rises and sets, is not
> what I love."[4]

PUSHED TO THE FRONT

I liked so much being just a member of the group, but more and more Mrs. Tweedie pushed me to the front, first as an interpreter of dreams, and then as the one who would succeed her, who would continue her work. This was something I had never consciously expected, and it took a number of years to slowly digest what it might mean. I had never wanted any position, but just to be a silent wayfarer walking the ancient highway of the soul. I loved to be solitary and turn my attention inward, away from the world. For many years I had watched with awe the way Mrs. Tweedie taught, how she gave herself to others and kept their attention on the invisible goal. I also saw the projections that fell on her shoulders, how in her aloneness she had to carry so much.

When I was told that I would continue her work there was little inner response. There was no shock, no moment of awe. Just as when I first came to the group, my mind did not play with the situation. There was neither excitement nor doubt, as if something held back my ego from being involved. Meeting Mrs. Tweedie, coming to the group, and now knowing I was to continue her work did not belong to my everyday self. I knew from the moment she told me that it was not me, but a task, a duty to be lived, and that with the help of my Sheikh I would grow into it. But there was also a trepidation, a secret fear of the burden of the work and the danger of failure. Slowly I tried to consciously adjust to this future, but it was difficult and I often wanted to push it aside.

I now understood two dreams I had had a few years before. In one dream Mrs. Tweedie had said to me, "You ought to be a teacher." I thought that she was referring to my work as a high school teacher, but when I told her the dream she quickly dismissed my interpretation, and said it referred to being a spiritual teacher. I accepted her words, but at the time they had little meaning. In another, more symbolic dream, she asked me to get her a new pot for cooking one egg at a time. On this path each wayfarer is treated individually, cooked alone, and I now realize that this dream referred to the need for me to find within myself a new container for this ancient process.

A year after she told me that I would be her successor, she announced it to the group. People's reactions differed. Some did not believe her, thinking that it was just a test to see their reactions. For others there was the joy of the path continuing, the tradition of succession. I accepted the exposure, but part of me would rather have remained hidden. Also her announcement pointed beyond herself to a future in which she would no longer be alive. It set the stage for the next years of my life, to be living a future that had not yet arrived. For the group in London this situation evoked difficulties because her very presence embodied the path. For those whose hearts have been opened by her, she is the only one. And as I now represented a time when she would be no longer alive, I sometimes carried the shadow of their link to her—their resistance to having to consciously confront and accept that the real nature of this connection does not belong to this world, does not need her physical presence.

Yet I was also inwardly protected and held apart from the group dynamics. The very fact that we lived above the teacher had commenced a process of isolation from the group. We carried the stamp of her aloneness, of the teacher who can have no friends. Once a twelve-year-old boy came to the group for one afternoon, and then said to the woman who had brought him, "She has no friends." When Mrs. Tweedie heard this she was deeply touched by its truth. A teacher can have no friends because she has to stand alone, looking only to God.

CAUGHT BY APPEARANCES

A Sufi group is a dynamic, living entity, providing support, conflict, and teaching. The strength of the group comes from the inner bond of love and the power of the path. Wayfarers are accepted for themselves and do not have to adopt a "spiritual persona" for the group. Mrs. Tweedie would always see beneath the surface, and include within her heart the whole human being. Once, when I was accompanying her on an airplane, I looked down the aisle to see a heavily made-up, aging air stewardess walking towards us. I have always been prejudiced against heavy makeup, feeling that it covers the real person, and I inwardly reacted against the face I saw. As if responding to my thoughts, Mrs. Tweedie looked towards the stewardess and said to me, "Human beings are so beautiful, aren't they?"

Relating to the inner essence of the human being, she gave a space in which we could see many aspects of ourselves reflected. She allowed situations to occur and develop to help us see both our darkness and our light. Three years after she had told me that I was to continue her work, I was caught in a drama that was both humiliating and liberating. One morning I received a phone call from an American woman who had arrived at the airport. She was being held by the immigration officials because she did not seem to have enough money to stay in the country, nor an address of someone with whom she could stay. She said that she had come to see Mrs. Tweedie, and responding to a woman in distress, I vouched for her. Three hours later she arrived at our doorstep with a sad story of a husband who had cruelly taken away her children and money. She was destitute but wanted spiritual life. It was the only thing left for her.

I found her accommodation, and she came to see Mrs. Tweedie. Hearing Mrs. Tweedie talking about the practice of the *dhikr*, this new friend wanted to know the practice. So Mrs. Tweedie pointed to me, and told her that I should teach her. I felt flattered and encouraged. It seemed that here was my first disciple—my teacher had passed her on to me. I taught her the *dhikr* and told her about the path. She appeared very enthusiastic. She said that she was a massage-therapist and healer, and would try to make a living helping people. As it turned out she had considerable healing skills, and helped some people in the group with back problems and other pains.

That summer we had a two-week Sufi camp in Germany, with over six hundred people. I arranged for her to come and she had just enough money to pay her way. After a few days at the camp the trouble began. In the evening she would drink wine, and her spiritual persona would disappear and a darker side surface. She tried to seduce someone in the group who was married, and I had to tell her off. A Sufi group may accept the shadow but it has very high ethical standards, and such behavior is totally unacceptable. I was very angry but she convinced me that she was sincere and wanted the Truth.

Of course she did not change, and although she had healing skills, she was a corruptive influence in the group. After we returned to England she found her way to stay with someone who was quite wealthy, and we continued to hear how her sweet, spiritual nature would vanish under the influence of alcohol. She never again appeared at the group because she did not want to face Mrs. Tweedie, who she knew would tell her off. For myself it was all a profound teaching experience, as I saw how I had been caught by my own desire to be a teacher and have a disciple, as well as to be helpful to a woman in distress. Mrs. Tweedie had seen through her from the very beginning, when she first walked through the door, and also noticed my weakness. For a few months after she stopped coming Mrs. Tweedie would mention her name in different contexts and watch my reactions. Time and again I would inwardly wince, feeling humiliation and stupidity. When I finally no longer reacted, Mrs. Tweedie stopped mentioning her. I had been freed of any desire to have a disciple or to be a teacher.

INNER EXPERIENCES

A Sufi group is a stage of self-discovery on which as much as possible happens in the clear light of day. We are both loved and revealed, and the group contains and helps this process. Once Mrs. Tweedie turned to a friend and, referring to me, said, "He hated me for years." I had not consciously realized my hidden hatred for her until that moment. But now it was in the open and accepted. My ego's resentment of her power and authority, and of the fact that she was a woman, could no longer be hidden in the shadow.

Paradoxically, although so much was shared in the group, the real work of the path is hidden. Some people would come and just see an old lady talking and drinking tea, and think that silent meditation and dreamwork were all that was happening. But within the heart real changes took place; powerful, inner experiences were given. During those years when I was drawn into the center of the group, I also had experiences that remained secret for years.

These experiences often lasted just for an instant, and yet changed my whole perception. One morning in meditation I experienced the whole universe as being "inside out." The solar system and all the distant stars were within me, and their outer form just a reflection of their internal nature. This realization was stamped into my consciousness, profoundly altering my relationship to the outer world. I saw my physical self as a doorway between the two worlds, the inner being reflected in the outer. From this there came an indication that the external world is a creation of one's inner self, and that as one's inner psyche changes so does our perception of the outer world. Eventually the outer world becomes visible as it really is, instead of just being seen and distorted by one's personal psyche. Then one can see everything according to *its true nature*, rather than just one's projection. Suddenly I glimpsed the meaning of St. Paul's saying:

> For now we see through a glass, darkly; but then face to face: now I know in part; but then shall I know even as I am known.[5]

The "dark glass" that separates us from true perception is our own psyche, distorted by conditioning, desires, and thought patterns. As we work on ourself, polishing the mirror of the heart, so we can see more clearly, until we are allowed to see the real face of our own being and the true nature of life. One morning I awoke with the simple sentence, "Only saints and animals are realists." When I told this to Mrs. Tweedie she added, "and children."

As the glass between the two worlds became clearer, the nature of my perception of time also changed. We are brought up to believe in time as a constant linear progression. But as my meditation deepened and my consciousness became both emptier and more focused, I lived more and more in the present, with less awareness of the future, fewer thoughts of the past. Living in the moment expands the moment, gives it more space for the completeness of life to manifest. The moment became gradually richer and richer, not with events, but with a sense of being.

For much of my childhood I was very bored, with little meaning to fill the hours and days. Now I found that all residue of boredom had passed, and even when there were hours or days empty of content, meaning was present. As life filled itself, so it seemed to quicken, and inwardly everything speeded up. Sensing the seasons pass more rapidly may belong to growing older, but this was different. The more I lived in the present, the quicker the days passed, as if the substance of time had changed. Also the inner states changed more quickly; times of separation that had lasted for months now rarely lasted more than a few days. Outwardly my life continued with the routine of family life, meditation, study, and the group. But inwardly the rhythm was altering; my sense of time became malleable.

In meditation a moment can last forever, and gradually an awareness of the eternal permeated everyday consciousness. The eternal can be experienced only in the moment, because it does not belong to time. The expanses of the inner world became invisibly present within the moments of everyday life. The hidden relationship between time and eternity became a part of waking consciousness. Sometimes this could be confusing, as the mind would try to grasp a different dimension. Some days the infinite emptiness would be very present and everyday activities fade into the background. Then the inner would recede and the outer seem more real and tangible.

Living between the two worlds is not easy, but the physical presence of my teacher confirmed it as a definite reality. She lived like a dancer with the tip of her toe just touching the ground. Family life had forced me into this world, but the invisible inner became more and more present and as it did, time softened at the edges. Time was no longer a hard succession of minutes, hours, and days, but a fluctuating dance holding inner and outer experiences, a merging of the eternal with the present. The future was also there, particularly with the knowledge of the work that awaited me. But I had already felt the future evolving within me, and knew that it was not a static moment that would arrive, but a part of a fluid flow of events that first form on the inner planes. I had also come to realize that on the spiritual path things happen very differently from what we expect. The future is unrecognizable in the present, because it is an evolution that carries the seeds of the eternal moment which is outside of time. I could not have predicted any of the inner or outer events that had occurred since I met the path.

The texture of life changed; the two worlds came closer and time seemed to spin faster. Sometimes, talking to someone, I would suddenly be drawn into the inner world, to a different plane of consciousness. In that different state I would be given information to pass on, a helpful hint to the person in front of me. At first it would be confusing, almost embarrassing, to find my mind leaving me, even in the midst of a sentence. The train of thought would be gone, and I would be left open-mouthed. I learned to just say, "Please wait a moment, my mind has gone." And it would usually return with something helpful for the other person, an understanding or knowledge that did not come from me. The process was so simple that I could not identify with what I had to pass on. One moment my mind was blank; the next, certain information or a sentence would be there. I was just the messenger, but I also felt the wonder of how we are used.

Gradually, as I came to live more and more from my inner center, the feeling of "going somewhere else" subsided. There came to be less separation in the flow of the inner and outer. While talking, I see the inner that has to be conveyed, or it just unfolds in the course of the conversation. But there are also moments when my attention is turned elsewhere, into a silence permeated with light. I have learned to hold myself in emptiness with other people present, and wait for what is given. Sometimes there are words, or just a sense of stillness. Mostly I do not know how I am used.

Many experiences have been given, some silently within the heart. Suddenly, walking down the street, I would feel His presence, a love unexplained. Gradually all traces of the loneliness I had carried for so many years left me. One miracle of the inner world is that it carries a quality of closeness and intimacy that for most people is only a distant dream. As the path took me Home, this closeness became more real. It was not always present, and often there were days of desolation, struggles with the self. But once you know that nearness exists, then the heart sings a different song, and even the difficulties are not such a burden.

SAMADHI

During those years of living above Mrs. Tweedie I had two experiences in meditation that changed me more than I knew. The first happened soon after my father died. I had not been close to my father, but I loved him, and his death confronted me with the absolute nature of physical separation. He had been present all of my life, and now there was the strange knowledge that the seasons would pass without him, that my birthday would come and go without a card or call from him. The mystic knows that death does not exist, that it is just a change of consciousness. Meditation had given me this knowledge: I had seen the eternal nature of the soul. But I had not expected physical death to carry such a final stamp.

Two days after returning from his funeral I was lying in Mrs. Tweedie's meditation room when I consciously awoke somewhere else, to find myself in the presence of Mrs. Tweedie, who handed me a key. It was such a real experience that I was quite shocked when I came out of meditation to realize that I was in the meditation room, and all the time I had been meditating, Mrs. Tweedie had, on the physical plane, been in her kitchen next door talking and having tea with friends. When I told her of this experience she just said that it was "very auspicious" and that a key is an important symbol. Now I see this first experience of awakening on a different plane of consciousness as a turning point. In *consciously knowing* that I was not limited to everyday consciousness I had been given a key to the door to the beyond.

Soon after this experience my meditation began to change. For years I had loved going into meditation to disappear into *dhyana*, the complete abstraction of the senses, returning after half an hour or an hour, knowing nothing except that I had been into the beyond. But now an inner change took place: I no longer lost consciousness, but began to experience a dual consciousness. I would be aware of my surroundings, hear noises on the street, even have thoughts, and yet *also be somewhere else*, experience an inner space, a different quality of being. At first I resented losing the bliss of unconsciousness. I longed to totally disappear and know nothing. I resented the presence of my mind. But then I began to appreciate the consciousness in meditation that I was experiencing, the two levels of reality that were simultaneously present.

The outer reality was physical and mental. Yet I was not entirely present in either my body or my mind. For example, in normal waking consciousness there is no gap between the thought to move one's hand and the action: the movement is an instantaneous reaction to the thought. But in meditation I would feel my hand and want to move it, but find there was no response; the hand did not move. I could hear someone talk, but I could not speak. I knew that I would have to come fully back into the physical dimension to talk. Previously I had had this type of experience only in a dream state. Sometimes when I dreamed that I was meditating I would find that I could not move my body, and initially this was a frightening experience, to feel physically trapped in the state of meditation. Now I was experiencing this in full consciousness, but there was no fear. I gradually became used to being conscious of the outer world without being fully in my body.

I would also be aware of my mind and its patterns of thoughts, and yet be able to stop the thinking if I concentrated. Throwing myself into the emptiness beyond the mind, I could leave my thoughts behind. But there were also times in which I was not even consciously aware that I was meditating. I just was, and there were also thoughts. I came to realize that this lack of awareness was because my focus of concentration was not on the level of the mind. The mind remained, but it was not the center of my awareness as in waking consciousness. I was experiencing a consciousness quite separate from the mind.

Over the years the states of meditation have deepened and changed, evolved in ways beyond any understanding of the mind. Sometimes I am dissolved, taken outside of myself, leaving all consciousness behind. Then I awaken not knowing where I have been and it can take a few moments to readjust to the outer, to realize where I am. But there are also meditations which begin with an inner and outer consciousness, and I am then taken fully into the inner world where I retain a quality of consciousness. In this consciousness there is no duality, no subject and object; everything just is. There may be an awareness of oneness, or a light that permeates everything. Sometimes I am taken further, into an experience of nothingness, a complete emptiness and a sense of non-existence that carries tremendous freedom and security, and in which I feel I belong absolutely. I know that this is my real home, even though there is no self, just a fragment of awareness remaining. On occasions I consciously experience leaving the ego with its thought-forms and limited horizon, and expanding into this inner emptiness. Within this inner reality the values of the ego are left behind, its identity just a memory of constriction. But then, when one returns from meditation the ego is once again present, its patterns, anxieties and problems only too real!

I have learned not to desire these states of meditation, but to accept what I am given. Knowing that the inner world is so present, I no longer need to escape the outer world. Sometimes great longing will come and carry me away, and then I gladly give myself up to the unconsciousness of the beyond. But I seem to have accepted the need to hold the two worlds in my heart and carry this consciousness with me.

The experience of being given a key opened the way to these states of *samadhi*, a consciousness beyond the mind. Mrs. Tweedie told me that on this path one should not remain on the level of *dhyana* for too long; seven or eight years are enough. The path evolves within one, taking the wayfarer ever further. A few months after the experience with the key I had another important experience. I had just slipped off in meditation when I felt for a moment within my heart a love so complete that nothing more could be desired. Like a butterfly's wings touching the edge of my heart, love was present. Just an instant's touch within the heart and I *knew* that I was loved with a completeness that cannot be found in the outer world. The totality of the love included everything within me. This moment of love changed my life, because it gave me the absolute security I had been seeking. I *knew* that total love exists, and so I could live without the insecurity that had haunted me. The outer world no longer carried the threat of incompleteness.

The first instance of His touch carries the beauty of a first love. Other experiences of His love have followed, deeper and more intoxicating. But in that first moment everything was present and the foundation of my life in the world was changed. We all long for this total love, and seek it in a parent or lover. All my life I had been haunted by this longing, the need to be loved. Now it had found me, arrived unexpectedly, wonderful in its completeness. I no longer needed to look for it in the outer world, seek it in a physical embrace. I had been given my first experience of love's true wholeness, of a caress that carries the quality of union.

These two experiences imprinted within my consciousness the knowledge of a freedom and love that are not dependent upon the outer world. I now knew what my heart had always told me, and more and more I lived from this knowledge. "We are never given for ourself. It is always for others"; and what I had received enabled me to give myself without looking for anything in return, without seeking security or love in the outer world. My inner self had opened its doors, and I no longer walked the path dependent only upon faith. Deep within us we are all held in His heart, but this is hidden from consciousness. When the eye of the heart is opened, He whom we love reveals His closeness. He is always close, but one of the greatest mysteries is that we do not know it. We do not know what is hidden within us, as Ibn 'Arabî expresses:

"We are nearer to him than his jugular vein" (Qur'ân 50:16). In spite of this nearness, the person does not perceive and does not know... *no one knows what is within himself until it is unveiled to him instant by instant.*[6]

ON THE ROAD

Be in this world as if you are a traveler, a passer-by,
for this is not home.

Hadîth

WAITING FOR A DREAM TO UNFOLD

Sitting on the rocks above the Golden Gate Bridge, I knew I belonged in America. The destiny of my soul spoke to me, breaking through the barriers between the two worlds, bringing the meaning of the inner into the dimension of time and space. Looking out over the Pacific Ocean, I felt a sense of belonging that reached deep into the earth, a belonging that included the rocks, the plants, the sky. Then I had to return to London, to the grey streets that were my physical home. I had never thought to leave England. America, the most materialistic culture in the world, had never appealed to me. In my adolescence I had been drawn to the East, to the orange-robed monks of Thailand and the mist-shrouded rice terraces of the Philippines. Here I had found an external peace, a tranquility that spoke to me. But then I had returned to the city of my childhood, found my teacher, bought a house, and raised a family. There was no sense of looking else-where. The journey was inward and I was traveling in the company of friends.

Now everything had changed. Destiny had shown a different direction. Something hidden had been revealed, and I felt the wonder of a dream made conscious. Magic had unexpectedly entered my life, magic that belonged to a particular place, and which now made me feel a foreigner in my own home. I longed to move, to take my family and start living what I had felt. But destiny follows its own course, and I had to wait. It would be five years before we would buy our one-way tickets and pack our few suitcases. In the meantime I had a thesis to finish and two books to write. I also had to start to lecture, a work that would take me to America as a traveler flying back and forth.

WITH MRS. TWEEDIE AND THE GROUP IN CALIFORNIA

My first trip to California was in February. Four months later I was back, but this time I was not on my own. In June of 1987 Mrs. Tweedie came to the Bay Area to promote her book, *Daughter of Fire*. Fifty people from the group in London came with her. This was a month full of laughter, tears, and the unexpected. For the whole of this month I was in a state of inner freedom that had begun two weeks before we left, when I became conscious that *a human being cannot have a problem*. In this state I was taken beyond the level of the mind and psyche into the deeper core of my being where problems cannot exist. Problems by their very quality of conflict belong to the level of duality, while the essence of the human being exists in a state of primal simplicity beyond duality, beyond conflict. This liberating experience was imaged for me on an airplane flight with the simple realization that *up above the clouds the sun is always shining*. I had been thrown into a state beyond the clouds, into the simplicity and sunshine of my real nature.

This state carried a lightness and laughter I had never before experienced, and the California sunshine seemed to dance with the same sense of freedom. That month of June was also the first time I sat on the stage rather than in the audience. Promoting *Daughter of Fire* involved reading from the book, but Mrs. Tweedie's eyes were still painful from her recent glaucoma operation. So she asked me to read certain passages, which she would then expand upon. Sitting beside my teacher, reading from her book, was my introduction to lecturing in America.

At first I was nervous sitting beside her on the stage, facing hundreds of people. But soon I became caught in the energy of love that saturated the lecture. I saw the faces turned towards her as she spoke of her teacher and her time with him. She spoke with the passion of what has been lived with the blood of the heart, and this spoke directly to the audience. Here was no scholar talking about spiritual traditions, but an old woman shining with love, whose piercing blue eyes spoke of an inner mystery that had burnt her to ashes. Sitting beside her, reading passages of her book, I felt included in this trauma of spiritual training, in the depth of her lived devotion. I felt this ancient tradition sing in the air, carrying the smell and heat of the Indian plains, as well as the invisible fragrance of the heart. I saw the need in those who came, the unacknowledged need to taste what was real, what was lived and suffered for, the need to know love in its pure form, unadulterated by personality or ego.

What had been shared among a few friends in a small room in north London was now permeating this California audience. An ancient secret was being spoken in public, love was being brought into the open, and I was a part of this process. My English reserve seemed lost, pushed aside by the deeper currents of love that came from the inner planes. For a month I swam in this intoxicating sea that carried me through each day. Mrs. Tweedie quickly noticed the change in me, saying how I "sparkled along the pavement." She saw how my English conditioning had disappeared in the deeper joy that came from some hidden source. Every moment was permeated by the heart's song, by the joy of love being lived.

In this momentum were all the dramas of a month with our teacher. After a few days in Berkeley, where we were all staying, she telephoned the male members of the group, telling them each to buy a hat. She had decided that as Englishmen we were too reticent for California, and needed to stand out more. But at the time she offered no explanations; instead friends just heard her voice on the phone with the bewildering instruction that they needed to buy a hat. Because in England she did not have a telephone, most people had never heard her on the end of a telephone line. One friend was having a shower in the morning when he was told that Mrs. Tweedie was on the phone. He thought someone was playing a joke, but his attitude quickly changed when he heard her unmistakable Russian voice saying "Tweedie here. You should buy a hat." The shock of hearing her on the telephone, together with the incongruous instruction, was a Sufi teaching in itself: "Always expect the unexpected."

The hat store in Berkeley must have been surprised by the number of English customers, and soon the Englishmen in the group were easily visible in their Panama hats at all the events! We could no longer hide behind our shy reserve, but were out in the open. With one simple move Mrs. Tweedie had dissolved centuries of conditioning.

The incident with the hats at the beginning of the month was beautifully balanced by a group experience three weeks later at the Yuba River in the Sierras. We had all traveled to the old mining town of Nevada City, where Mrs. Tweedie gave a lecture. The day after the lecture we went swimming in the water holes of the Yuba River; the water was warm with the sun reflected off the rocks. The Yuba River flows through a gorge, and this is a place of natural beauty and simplicity. People had brought swimsuits, but Mrs. Tweedie said that everyone should swim naked. In this natural environment we should just be ourselves. This was a very refreshing group experience, in which more than physical clothes were put aside. So often we associate nudity with sexuality, but in this environment there were no sexual undertones, just the freedom of nature. One Spanish friend had to struggle between her fear of the Catholic church, which had conditioned her to oppose such nakedness, and her fear of Mrs. Tweedie! At first she just took off her bikini top, but when she saw Mrs. Tweedie walking along the dirt path towards her, the fear of her teacher proved stronger. She stepped out of her bikini pants and joined everyone else.

Part of the wonder of being guided by a spiritual teacher is that the whole human being is included, and there are no rules but those of love and commitment. So often we feel that we have to adapt ourself to follow a path, put on the clothes of a seeker. Here in the foothills of the Sierras, inner and outer nature reflected each other, and everything was embraced by the sunshine of the Self. There is a natural freedom that exists in America that is difficult to find in Europe, where nature has been cultivated for so many centuries. Mrs. Tweedie recognized the moment and allowed us to live it. Years later she told me that it was during that morning, standing on the dirt path overlooking the river, that she knew we would have a Sufi center in California, and that she would not be there.

THE STORM BREAKS

A few months before this lecture trip Mrs. Tweedie had received from the publisher the first copies of her book, and had given one to me. *Daughter of Fire* is the diary of Mrs. Tweedie's training with her Sheikh, but it is also the first time that this ancient spiritual system is described in writing. The book had a profound effect on me, not just because of the teaching made accessible, but also because in a momentary glimpse I saw that a curtain had been lifted on a new stage. In this instant I knew that this stage had deep implications for me and my work. Coming to America, Mrs. Tweedie was not just promoting a book, but bringing her teacher's path into the marketplace of the new world. I was sitting beside her on the stage, sharing in this work.

A spiritual path is a ray of energy that comes from the inner planes into the world. Its purpose is to nourish those who need it, and to help wayfarers make the journey back Home. That June in California, Mrs. Tweedie brought the energy of our line into a new time and place. During the lectures and afternoon sessions this silent work was slowly accomplished. The afternoon sessions took place in a church meeting room on a hillside, looking out over San Francisco Bay, with the city in the distance. I would read a few passages from the book, Mrs. Tweedie would talk, and we would share dreams. Significantly, during the first afternoon session a Native American holy man was present. He said nothing, but Mrs. Tweedie silently acknowledged him. He also came to the final session, when Mrs. Tweedie asked him to share with us something of his own spiritual tradition, and he spoke of how similar it was to many aspects of Sufism. We all felt that the presence of this man of power was an unspoken welcome by his tradition and the spirits of the land.

The sessions were full of the combination of the serious and the lighthearted that accompanies Sufi meetings. Sometimes Mrs. Tweedie teased the audience, as when she gave detailed instructions on how to magnetize water. The audience, grateful to be taught something so tangible, avidly wrote down these instructions, until the final sentence when Mrs. Tweedie told them, "But this will only work if you have total yogic control of the mind." Some people even continued to write, "Total yogic control of the mind," not realizing that this meant a lifetime's work. But under the laughter, dreams, and stories, a deeper purpose was unfolding, and by the final lecture the love flowed so effortlessly we were all drunk.

When something new comes into the world there is always a resistance, and Mrs. Tweedie contained the friction of this inner resistance. I sensed this happening, and the tension building up within her. Then, the evening before we swam naked in the river, the tension came to the surface. The group had driven up through the hot, dusty Central Valley, and we were camping on the publisher's property outside Nevada City. We didn't have any tents, but were assured that in June it never rains in Nevada City. There may be thunder on the horizon, but in June it never rains. So we had left our sleeping bags out in the evening air and had come to Nevada City where the lecture was to be held in an old Victorian meeting hall. Then, just as the lecture began, it started to rain, not just rain but a thunderstorm. It felt as if the tension that had been building over the previous weeks was being expressed through the thunder and lightening, the violence of the storm. Sitting beside Mrs. Tweedie, reading extracts from her book, rather than having spiritual thoughts I was thinking of our sleeping bags getting soaked, and the long, wet night ahead. It never rains in June!

The meeting hall had a metal roof on which the rain drummed almost deafeningly. As the rain came down I was reading a diary entry also from June, when the Indian monsoon had not yet come and the days were long and hot. When I mentioned the monsoon, Mrs. Tweedie motioned with her hands to the rain pounding on the roof, and the audience laughed. Someone from our group clapped, whereupon Mrs. Tweedie responded in anger, telling him that he should know better than to clap at a spiritual meeting. (The sound waves from clapping break up a spiritual atmosphere, which is why there is never any clapping at a spiritual talk or concert.) The moment passed and the storm seemed to subside, though dozens of bats flew out from under the eaves of the meeting hall, more bats than anyone in the town ever knew were in the building. During the interval there was a rainbow stretching over the building, and a pink cloud full of the light of the setting sun.

Then, when Mrs. Tweedie asked for questions, a woman stood up and angrily asked, why was she so harsh with the person who clapped? Mrs. Tweedie responded with force, "It is my business if I am harsh. You are nobody to criticize.... I had the right to be harsh to him. He is one of the London group and should have known better!" Then a man said that she lacked compassion. "I lack compassion?... Maybe this person doesn't deserve compassion. Sometimes it happens." The power of the rain on the roof was nothing to the strength in Mrs. Tweedie's response to this man. The power of her presence resonated in the old mining hall, and some women got up and left. Those who thought that the path of love was soft and sweet now felt a different energy, that of someone who speaks with the strength born of real experience, and saw how the teacher at times needs to be cruel to help the wayfarer. And yet during this dialogue, sitting beside her, I felt such love drawing me to her, penetrating deep into my heart.

Carrying the energy of the path needs power as well as devotion. Love's conviction is stamped with fire in the core of those who know. This was my real introduction to lecturing in America and to living my own truth. When I finally moved to California with my family, Mrs. Tweedie wrote out for me one saying: "The dogs bark, the caravan passes by." Looking towards the infinite, we travel only with those who dare to live their own passion, their heartfelt desire for truth.

MY FIRST LECTURE

We all returned to England exhilarated and saturated by the intensity of the month. The next stage of my own American odyssey took place a little over a year later when Mrs. Tweedie received instructions that Anat and I should have a holiday in the States. We had been married during my college term time and so had never had a honeymoon. Our children were now seven and eight years old, and we were to have our honeymoon, three weeks on our own in America! We started in Vermont with the magnificence of the autumn colors, the endless forests, and the beaver dams. Then we flew to Arizona, where we visited Hopi and Navajo reservations, and saw the vastness of the desert horizons and their empty beauty. On the Hopi reservation we felt the ancient sacred connection between the people and the land, and how the land carries the reverence of these early inhabitants. At the Hopi Mesa we were also privileged to witness a dance in which women made fun of men!

For someone coming from Europe where everything is contained and defined, the scale of the desert landscape in the Southwest impacts the senses with both beauty and grandeur. At the north rim of the Grand Canyon I experienced the closest to a mystical experience I have ever had on the physical plane. Looking out over the canyons I felt the absolute insignificance of the human form. In the vastness of that vista I was so insignificant as to be nonexistent. The nothingness of the human being before the scale and grandeur of His creation threw me out of myself. To have this mystical reality reflected so strongly on a physical level made me realize the potency of nature in a new way. Here the land holds a mystical quality both bare and beautiful.

From the emptiness of Arizona we went to Berkeley, where I had stayed during the month with Mrs. Tweedie. A small meditation group had formed since her first visit three years before, and supported by them, I gave my first public lecture on Sufism and dreamwork. All that I remember is that I was very nervous and that someone had had a dream in which Mrs. Tweedie was coming to Berkeley. This was a kind and gentle introduction to the work for which I was being prepared. A few months previously Mrs. Tweedie had suggested that as she was too old to travel again to the States, I should continue her work there, lecturing and promoting her book. This trip gave me a feeling for the land, and a first taste of lecturing.

One day during our stay in Berkeley, we drove north along the coast, to a small town beside the ocean. October there is a month of warm sunshine without fog, and the beaches were almost empty. We walked along the sand, with the sun dipping towards the water line and the sand stretching white into the distance. We loved this quiet country town, where people seemed to know each other in the grocery store and there was a sense of real community. When we returned to London, Anat mentioned the place to Mrs. Tweedie, who replied, "It has a good vibration. You should live there." At the time it seemed unbelievable, but destiny unfolds in its own way, and three years later we were living here, watching the hills turn golden in the early summer and then green in the first rains of winter.

On our way home from the West Coast we stopped for a few days in New York, whose energy and concrete mass hit me in the guts. In Brooklyn I had a meeting with a woman who was supposed to arrange my first lecture tour the following spring. I hoped that she knew what she was doing, but I was to discover that it was only the hand of my Sheikh that would help me. The following January Mrs. Tweedie asked me how many lectures had been arranged for the spring. Sadly I replied that no lectures had been confirmed. Two weeks later I received a fax from the woman in

New York giving details of nine lecture engagements from Esalen in California to Atlanta, Georgia. I happily told this to Mrs. Tweedie, who answered that she had said in meditation to Bhai Sahib, "If you want him to lecture in America, you had better organize something."

MY FIRST BOOK

During this time in London I had finished my thesis and was working on a book about dreamwork and Sufism. My writing was to provide all the material I needed for my lectures and be a focus for my work of integrating Jungian psychology, Sufism, and dreamwork. Like lecturing, writing came upon me unexpectedly. One evening I was invited to a talk in London on active imagination. I found the subject interesting, and asked many questions. When the talk was over, I spoke to the presenter, who, thinking I might be an analyst, said, "What are you?" For the first and only time in my life I responded, "I am a Sufi." "Oh," he said, "I am compiling a book on Jungian Psychology and Sufism. Would you like to contribute something?"

This conversation inspired me to write my first article on spiritual dreamwork, which, together with an article by Mrs. Tweedie, was included in the book, *Sufism, Islam and Jungian Psychology.*[1] During my study of Jungian psychology, I had come to realize that the dreamwork which took place in our group has a spiritual quality that makes it distinct from normal psychological dreamwork. Exploring the historical basis for Sufi dreamwork, I wrote about how our dreamwork integrates a contemporary psychological approach within a Sufi tradition. This article was the text for my first lecture in Berkeley, and when I showed the article to Mrs. Tweedie, she said, "This is a very good article. You should write a book."

Our London group was a wonderful source of dreams, which I compiled and interpreted, showing how spiritual dreams can describe the stages of the path. The analytic skills which I had learned writing my thesis were applied to my first book, *The Lover and the Serpent*, whose title came from the dream of a woman in our group. In her dream she is being kissed by a man. This kiss is a wonderful experience, not sexual, just a pure feeling of love in the heart. But then she feels a tongue in her mouth, and opening her eyes sees that she is being embraced by a serpent, and it is the serpent's tongue in her mouth, which fills her with fear. This dream combines the experience of a love affair, which is at the core of the Sufi's relationship with God, with the symbol of the serpent, symbolizing the depths of the unconscious, thus showing how the path of love will take the dreamer into the very depths of herself. The dream images how the spiritual and psychological aspects of the path combine, which is the central theme of my book.

Later I felt that *The Lover and the Serpent* was too analytic and lacked the deeper passion and feeling that belong to the path. Although I had no conscious intention to write another book, one night I had a powerful dream which pushed me to write *The Call and the Echo*, my second book, which is more full of feeling. This dream expresses the new quality which was to become part of my writing. In the dream I meet the anima figure who is my creativity, and show her a barrier of pain that separates her from her own creative depths:

Walking along a muddy road I see some keys in the mud and pick them up. I come across an old peasant man, who opens a gate and points out the path I should follow to return the keys to their owner. I follow the path across a landscape that feels ancient and magical, and come to a half-ruined stone building with arched windows, where a potter lives. She is sitting in front of her kiln which she has been tending all night. I can see the bright fire behind her.

I have met this woman years before and found her beautiful. She has long dark hair and wears thick oatmeal sweaters. Where she lives is remote and magical in an ancient Celtic sense. She is totally absorbed in her pots; they are all that matter to her. She comes towards me and we sit beside an arched stone window. I am a woman and I talk to her about her work, and how it makes itself in the depths of her being. It is here that her pots are formed. However, I tell her that she herself does not live in the depths of her being, but only on the surface. There is a barrier of pain between herself and her creative depths that is somehow connected to the magic of the land. She must go through this barrier, and then her pots will have an alchemy in their making. I see the pots she will make and they have sparks of color in them. Before, the form of her pots was perfect, but they had a colorless quality. These pots of the future are of clay mixed with the colors of red and gold.

As a woman I talk to her of the mysteries and the pain of the earth, and the alchemy of one's inner being. But then I feel to take her in my arms, and when we embrace and kiss I find that

I am a man. We kiss like lovers for a long time, and when she opens her eyes she says that she has never experienced a kiss like this before. I tell her that I loved her when I first saw her years ago. Arm in arm we leave the half-ruined stone building.

This dream, full of alchemical symbolism and love, is about the creative process, making pots. This creative process is a part of the magic of the land and its ancient heritage. Yet within me there was a block, a barrier that limited the alchemical potential of my writing. The feminine within me needed to confront a pain that was linked to the magic of the land, the pain that is caused by our intellectual rejection of the ancient mysteries of the feminine. Once I had crossed this barrier, accepted the wounding of this inner landscape, then my writing could carry the colors of alchemical transformation; the pots would be mixed with red and gold. Also, as the dream imaged, my writing would become a love affair: intoxicating, demanding, exhausting, and always unknowable. I would be drawn into the interaction with words, ideas, feelings, and stories that would demand total participation on all levels. Gone was any academic detachment; instead my writing evolved out of a deeply felt interaction between my conscious and unconscious self. I also allowed the lyrical music of the heart to carry the ideas I was expressing. After this dream I no longer planned my books, but allowed the inner to flow into the outer form of words. *The Call and the Echo* is not a book *about* Sufism and dreamwork, but an unveiling of an inner process, a dream unfolding into consciousness, a bridge between the two worlds.

WEARING WHITE

One afternoon when I was still a high-school teacher, I was sitting in Mrs. Tweedie's kitchen drinking tea when she passed by and said, "When you are thirty-six your life will change completely." Later, when I repeated this to her she had no recollection of it, which meant that it was a message just for me. The years passed. I finished teaching, wrote my thesis, visited California, and began my first book. Then, in April 1989, when I was just thirty-six, I was sent on a lecture trip across America. Mrs. Tweedie insisted that on the lecture fliers it should state that I had been named as her successor.

I was to travel with my friend Michael, and we were to wear white at the lectures. In the Sufi tradition women wear black and men wear white when representing the tradition. Mrs. Tweedie jokingly said that we should look like English cricketers, who wear white (once we were mistaken for paramedics when we were rushing to change planes at the Atlanta airport!). But it was a definite statement about our work of bringing the tradition to America. A few days before we left, we were in her flat when she suddenly turned to an American woman who was visiting for a few days, and, quoting Bhai Sahib, said, "I send my angels out into the world. They are tested with fire and spirit and never do they go wrong!" Later that evening the American woman told me that she felt that this saying was not for her. I knew that it was for me, and was a wonderful blessing for my journey.

Anxiety, unsureness, and excitement were present in equal amounts. But there was also the wonderful sense of something beginning; what I had felt as I sat on the rocks above the Golden Gate Bridge was coming into being. I am Aries; I love beginnings and challenges. There are moments in one's life when destiny turns a corner and an inner potential comes into being. I had my lecture notes and my white clothes, and I had the companionship of Michael, whose extrovert character was a perfect balance to my deeply introverted nature. Michael was a great help, both with all the arrangements and with my interaction with the American extrovert culture, which at times made me feel insecure. But beyond any outer help, I had the inner sense of my Sheikh, reflected in a vision in which I was given a chalice on which was engraved, *"Go in expectation. The help of your Sheikh is in your heart. That is all you need to know."*

The first talk I gave was at Esalen, the new-age center in California where they have mineral baths overlooking the Pacific. I spoke about the mystic marriage and the realm of the archetypes, but what amazed me was that as I began to talk an energy was present in the room. This was quite different from the first talk I had given on Sufi dreamwork in Berkeley, in which I was just sharing some ideas about dreams. Now the words were quite insignificant compared to the energy of the path that permeated the room. I knew that what was happening was greater than myself, that I was being used. This was a strange and wonderful feeling.

My next venue was the Whole Life Expo in San Francisco, a new-age marketplace that sold everything from "Psychic Safaris" to devices that retuned your brain. Lecturing at this convention full of new-age paraphernalia broke so many patterns of my conditioning in one afternoon. What had been so sacred and silent was now to be shared amidst the stalls of crystals, healing oils, and channelings. I remember that my lecture was followed by Timothy Leary talking about Psychedelics and Cybernetics. After my talk I held a workshop on dreamwork in a trailer behind the hall. Everything seemed so incongruous, and I wondered what I had to offer that people should pay to sit with me. But once I started to talk, this energy was again present. An atmosphere was created that had nothing to do with the external environment, but was full of the love and energy of the path. I was left in bewildered awe: such is the greatness of my Sheikh that he can bring the path into the present regardless of external surroundings.

Each time I give a talk I am filled with wonder as something happens and the inner world becomes present. I know that it is not me, as I have no idea how to make such an atmosphere. I just hold the audience in my heart and make an inner connection with my Sheikh. Then his grace is present, and a oneness holds the audience.

After the lectures in the Bay Area, Michael and I traveled to Georgia, to a Christian Jungian Conference called *Journey into Wholeness*. This was a totally different experience from the sophisticated new-age audiences of California. I had never been to the Southeast before, and I loved the accent and the warmth of the people. They had never heard of Sufism except in some strange connection to the Enneagram (a nine-pointed diagram of psychological and spiritual types), and Michael and I must have been very incongruous: two Englishmen dressed in white, wandering about the Methodist conference center. We became known as the "Sufi guys," and people would greet us in their slow drawl with the unforgettable phrase, "How ya'll doing, you Sufi guys?"

At this conference I met a family therapist who gave me two pieces of advice about working in America that I have always treasured. First, he said that the American culture is the most extrovert culture in the world, which makes any attempt at inner work difficult, as the nature of an extrovert is to interact only with what is external. Second, he warned me that this is a pioneer culture, which means that if things don't work out you hitch up your wagon and move on. Although this attitude was highly successful in settling the West, reaching Oregon and California, it is an impediment to inner work, as he had found in marriage therapy. A pioneer culture means that if one encounters a problem, the response is just to move on, to leave behind the relationship or problem. Those who are committed to the work of inner transformation know that "moving on" is usually just a pattern of avoidance, and that the problem reappears in a different form. Only when a problem and its accompanying pain are fully confronted and accepted does the alchemical process take place, in which the lead of our darkness is turned into gold.

During the *Journey into Wholeness* conference I was also able to hear the Jungian lecturer and writer Robert Johnson, whose books I have always admired, and who is the most introverted person I have ever seen lecturing. He shared some of his experiences as an introvert learning to lecture, which I found very helpful. He said that at first he tried to be extrovert, to begin his talk by telling an amusing story to create an interaction with the audience. But he found that the only way he could generate enough extrovert energy was to get himself angry by whipping himself with a wet towel in the bathroom before the lecture! Then one day he saw the Jungian Marie-Louise von Franz lecturing, saw her approach the lecture stand, and, putting on her glasses, plunge straight into her academic mode, "In the sixteenth century...." This freed him of any attempt to lecture in an extrovert mode, and his words reassured me. I have always found it exhausting to act in an extrovert manner. I came to discover that what I have to offer is a sharing of my own experience of the inner world, my spiritual experiences and the reality of dreams, which is often more tangible to me than the physical world. Rather than talking directly to the audience, I find it easier to let them share my own interior monologue, to draw them into the inner world as I experience it. I have found that this creates a sense of intimacy, and also introduces people to an inner reality which for them may be vague and intangible. Moreover, it allows me to be my introvert self even in front of hundreds of people. Only a quality of vulnerability is required, as I share with an audience of strangers what is most intimate and personal—my own experiences of the inner world.

Through my doctoral work on Archetypal Psychology I was invited to talk to Jungian audiences across the country, to whom I would speak more about Jungian psychology than Sufism, though always exploring the spiritual dimension of dreamwork. One advantage of lecturing on dreamwork is that everyone has had a dream, and so everyone can feel included. The wisdom of dreams is universal and the energy of love does not belong to any creed. In my interaction with the audience I saw again the importance of valuing the neglected inner world, particularly for an extrovert culture. I also saw how the hidden love touched people, opening a secret door within the heart that allowed them to be nourished by the grace of my Sheikh. That first lecture trip was full of wonder as I felt this grace descend and create an atmosphere of intimacy and love. People were touched without knowing why. I was just an Englishman dressed in white talking about dreams and some strange path called Sufism. But something else was present: a door was open to the inner world.

RESPONDING TO A NEED

During my first lecture tour, Michael arranged a schedule for the autumn. This second lecture tour was a different experience. The first lectures had just filled me with amazement that it worked, that energy was present and an atmosphere was created. Like being in the presence of an invisible magician, I was overwhelmed with wonder. But in the autumn I looked beyond this initial experience. I knew now that I was not just promoting Mrs. Tweedie's book because she was too old to travel. One morning, while I was staying in Berkeley, I inwardly asked to see the bigger picture. It took me many months to recover from what I was shown. I had always thought that I would become a part-time English lecturer, and have a meditation group meeting once or twice a week in my home. Suddenly I saw the immensity of the work in front of me, and in that instant I knew that this was to be a full-time commitment. The scale of the need, the hunger for what is real, flashed before my inner eye. I recoiled in fear because I knew the demand this would make—the role I would have to play. I have always liked the notion of a quiet, introverted life. I enjoyed being an English teacher, and have often thought of finding a quiet country cottage where I could write and meditate. What I saw in this instant blew away all these notions. Seeing my future life's outer stage, I was shocked and bewildered.

The autumn lecture tour continued. We traveled further, to a Buddhist conference in Los Angeles, to a small town in Vermont, to a healing center in Baltimore. I spoke about dreams and the inner journey, and how love unveils itself within the heart. Within me all the different lectures and places began to weave themselves together—the same story told in different ways to different people. Underneath the words, the questions, and the dreams that were shared, I began to sense the deeper need, the hunger that is the shadow side of material prosperity. At the end of six weeks my physical body was exhausted, so tired that after eight hours sleep I would awake still exhausted, having to drag myself through the day. I hated motels, and the food made me ill. But each time I was in front of an audience the energy pushed me aside, and I knew that I was not there for myself. Sometimes I felt like a tap that is just turned on and off, responding to the need of the audience. A tap has no feelings, but is just used for a purpose, and it was always the need of those who came that turned the tap.

Now, after seven years of lecturing, I have become almost used to the process. But it still fills me with awe. One moment I am empty, with nothing to say. Then there is energy, and love, and words come. The work is totally exhausting and totally exhilarating; the physical body is battered by the energy, the need of the people, and the traveling. Often I wonder what I am doing, but then there is one person in the audience whose heart is open, and I feel the wonder as the work takes place, the ancient work from heart to heart—the unfolding of love into the world. In this moment, time and place disappear; all the hours sitting in airline terminals and lying awake in motels vanish as a deeper purpose is made visible.

As well as this deeper need beyond any words, I also found themes appearing in my lectures that were a response to the audience. A central theme is that of allowing the feminine to be revalued. Before my very first trip to California, I had a dream in which I was flying over a desert landscape which I knew to be America. In this landscape I saw a primitive settlement of tents and simple shelters, whose inhabitants were women and children, dressed in ragged clothing. I came to understand the dream as a picture of the primitive state of the feminine in America. In this masculine, extrovert country, the feminine has been neglected, unvalued.

All inner work requires a feminine attitude, of nurturing and letting grow. The inner cannot be bullied into submission or given tangible goals. The process of inner transformation requires an attitude of receptivity, watching, and listening, containing in love and acceptance. The unconscious of the audience drew out of me the central theme of "allowing" in both a psychological and a spiritual context. Nothing is more natural than the journey towards wholeness and the heart's desire for its Beloved. Living this inner instinctual nature means holding a sacred space and allowing the divine to reveal itself.

As I heard different people's dreams and stories, I realized that not only the outer feminine, the woman, has been abused, but also the inner feminine, the sense of sacred wholeness and the instinctual wisdom that is deeper than the mind. Often as I discussed these ideas I felt an almost audible sigh of relief come from the unconscious of people in the audience, people who in sincerity were trying hard to work upon themselves, but felt that they must use only the masculine tools of effort and striving. Sharing dreams allowed this feminine wisdom of "work without doing" to surface and be valued, not just by me, but by all those who were present. I also came to realize how mysticism carries the shadow of our material culture. I came across many people whose mystical nature had been repressed by a desire to fit in. Often they confused longing with depression, or a need to surrender to God with feminine patterns of submission to the masculine. Dreamwork allows so many stories to be told, so many paths to one's innermost self to be revealed by the unconscious. Individuals sincere in their seeking had become conditioned by a masculine culture that says you must improve yourself, struggle to be other than what you are. But their unconscious told a different tale, of a unicorn that needs the healing herbs of the feminine, of a black panther whose spiritual power is a natural way of being. I felt honored to be able to listen to these dreams, to hear the wisdom of the inner world clothe itself in images and words and be told in public. I knew that the greatest healing is to be allowed to be oneself, and that we each have our own way of being with God hidden within us. In the words of Rûmî, "Open your hidden eyes and come, return to the root of the root of your own self!"[2]

A WEB OF LIGHT

For three years I lectured in America in the spring and the autumn, spending six to eight weeks on the road each trip. From Vermont to Florida, Vancouver to San Diego, I listened to people's dreams and felt their secret longing. Therapists will say that the security of the therapeutic relationship, or a well-established dream group, is necessary in order to allow unconscious contents to surface and be contained. But the power of divine love and the invisible presence of a spiritual tradition enabled strangers to share what was most precious. Their unconscious felt the protection that I knew emanated from the grace of my Sheikh, and their inner self could open and allow itself to be nourished.

Sometimes, inexplicably, an evening would carry a quality of magic that was almost tangible, and after the lecture dreams would pour from the unconscious, carrying the message of the soul. To feel a stranger's soul resonate throughout the room touches everyone. We would all sense the wonder of an ancient and intimate story being told, and leave the room caught in a shared aura of mystery and meaning. The outer surroundings were often incongruous in these moments, as a college classroom with blackboard and desks contained the atmosphere of a sacred temple. I remember a small gathering at a healing center in a town in Virginia. The building was concrete and beside a freeway, and when I arrived I shuddered at the idea of having to create intimacy in such an environment. But the evening transported us all to a different dimension, especially when people shared dreams and their archetypal stories unfolded, bringing wonder into that space. Finally an old woman sitting in the front row shared a dream in which white-clad figures helped her across a threshold. One does not interpret a death dream, but I told her that soon she would know what it meant. While her husband was quietly dozing beside her, she looked at me with shining eyes and nodded. Her heart had heard the confirmation it needed.

Each dream is always an adventure that awakens within me a quality of inner attention. Serpents uncoil, their potency and poison seen as transformation. Babies are born, carrying the meaning of a future, and boats make journeys across the waters of the inner world. Hearing these symbols come alive, watching the alchemical process continue its work within the psyche, I feel in awe of how the soul opens within each of us. The outer environment of freeways, motels, and shopping malls seems so at variance with this ancient inner process, but the inner work is not limited by the outer form of our lives. The soul does not need an outer temple to share its mystery. The sacred is always present, and the energy of love is the greatest protection.

Sometimes I sit with tears in my eyes as I hear the music between the words, the music of an infinite ocean and a distant shore that I know within myself. I feel like calling out, "Come, come, allow your heart to take you where it will. Leave the shore behind. Hear the cry of the soul's song, the seabird that flies beyond the skyline." On occasion I can hint that this journey is worth any price, and share the freedom of leaving behind the limitations of the known. But mostly I am a witness, recognizing the wisdom of a dream's images, just holding the sacred space where these travelers' tales can be told.

Then in the midst of these archetypal stories I hear a dream that touches something deeper within me, and I recognize a friend, a fellow wayfarer on the Sufi path. In a small town in northern Minnesota a woman tells of a lovers' embrace that led her to a warehouse where old men were carding wool. These men were masters at carding wool, and ran their fingers through their long white beards as they worked. The dreamer had no conscious knowledge of the dream's symbolism, but I remembered my favorite definition of a Sufi, "You are a Sufi when your heart is as soft and as warm as wool." The dreamer had been taken into the inner space where this work is always being done, where the masters of the path accomplish their work of carding wool, of softening and transforming the heart.

In a church meeting hall in North Carolina someone tells a dream of the caravans on the Silk Road to China, and in this dream there is a frightening image of a girl injecting herself with heroin. But as I sense from where the dream comes, I know that this heroin is no external addiction, but the deeper drug of longing and the addiction of the path—the one-way lane of love that the caravans of lovers have been traveling since the beginning of time. I feel the despair within the dreamer that this story has until now been unrecognized, the image of addiction misinterpreted even by herself. Then I can share with her memories of the journey, the memories of the soul that are always present, just hidden by the present patterns of conditioning. We can talk with the inner intimacy of friends who meet again in a different time and a different place, and who know that the purpose of this meeting is to inject even deeper the drug of our shared longing, the heart's desire to go Home.

Sometimes it isn't a dream but just a feeling in the heart that recognizes a fellow traveler, that makes me talk about my Sheikh until the tears start to run from the listener's eyes, as an inner connection is brought into consciousness. Or my heart opens and I go to hug a woman whom I have seen through a crowd, saying how good it is to meet again, although in this life it is the first time we have met. Sometimes before a lecture

I feel that I am waiting for someone, though on the level of the mind I don't know who, until the person enters and I know that I can begin the talk. Seeing such a connection reappear is always a miracle, as I stand at the threshold of the inner world and welcome an old friend. The incongruity of finding these friends in contemporary urban America touches me, but I also sense a purpose that belongs to the moment, to the time and place of the present.

In other times and places far distant, China, Tibet, India, we were together, following the path, sitting in meditation, sharing our longing. Now the path has reappeared in America and we are a part of this reappearance, waiting for the right moment to bring together the inner and outer, the silence and the song. What had been hidden within the heart can become known to the mind, as a traveler again picks up the thread of the soul's journey, looks inward to the heart of hearts where the Beloved is waiting. And I am a part of this process; my destiny is woven with those whom I have known long before. I am a very solitary person, a hermit happily alone, but now these friends reappear, carrying a quality of love, closeness, and detachment that does not belong to this world, but, like a half-familiar dream, has resurfaced.

The greatness of the path always amazes me, how people are at the right place at the right time when their heart needs to know its connection. So often we feel alone, solitary, sensing only our isolation. But through these meetings I have come to sense the underlying web that holds us together, the thread of a destiny that is beyond time and place and weaves itself through outer events. In a church meeting hall, a retreat center, or a bookstore, this web of light reveals itself as a group of souls that are inwardly together yet each making our own journey to the beyond of the beyond, a brotherhood of migrants whose work is to help bring love into the world. The destiny of a heart that looks towards God has the power to pierce through the veils of separation and make visible what is hidden. I feel so honored to have been drawn into this whirlpool of unveiling, into the moment when the heart calls to the human being with the ancient, irresistible call of the quest: "We were together before the beginning of time; now come, turn towards your Beloved and go Home."

Once in meditation I experienced this web of light as the feminine form of love in the nothingness which lies beyond the mind. I was shown that, like a woven basket, this web underlies and supports all of creation. I know that it is present in everything, in all of life, not just in the dance of souls going Home. But through these meetings with fellow travelers I first sensed this web of light, and saw how it is also a bond of love born outside of time. The heart's connection makes this web visible, brings it into physical form. From heart to heart love's potency and purpose are passed, a secret that belongs to life itself.

ORDERS ARE ORDERS

One November, soon after returning from a lecture trip, I had a strange and disturbing dream that described a change that was taking place within me, a condition of inner emptiness that carried a quality of desolation. The dream began in a primitive setting in which I am with a tribal people worshiping strange gods. Many strange rituals are going on as I wander through the tribe in search of my own tent. Someone points out my tent, but I never get there... I never find it. The dream then changes into an observer's voice describing me in the third person, saying how he was lying on a table and lost his mind in a mystical experience. Sometime later, weeks, maybe years, some people passing through found him, and took him with them back to their land. He became a hermit and lived in a cave. But that was all just on the outside because inside there was no mind.

Looking back over this dream, I can see how traveling through America was like wandering through a primitive setting with people worshiping strange gods. I had been with my teacher since I was nineteen, knowing little about other spiritual traditions and the gods people worshiped. My awareness of spirituality was contained by the invisible presence of our Sheikh and the feeling of totally belonging to his tradition. Only when people came to our group did I sense the different paths that people followed, whether Buddhist, Hindu, Christian, or other Sufi orders. But now, out in the world, I felt more strongly the different ways of devotion, different manners of seeking. Giving a lecture or seminar, one feels the psyche of the audience, its spiritual and archetypal qualities. Sometimes consciously, but most often unconsciously, I became aware of the different energies present in the audience.

So many paths, so many ways to follow, all leading to the same Home. Where do I belong in the swirling psyche of the new age? Within myself I tried to adjust, to find my tent amidst this tribal gathering. But the dream describes how I never found my place, and that a deeper process took place: I lost my mind, my sense of self. The dream changes into the third person because there is no one there to tell my story, only an outer form that used to be a seeker. Real experiences happen deep within, and often we are the last to know. There was no conscious knowledge of this annihilation, but then who would be present to know this new state? The dream says that something happened after which I am a shell of my former self. The dream tells its own story, and I become just an onlooker on my own life.

On the outside I become a hermit, an identity that carries some semblance of meaning. A hermit is someone whose solitary self looks only to God, someone for whom the outer world has lost its powers of attraction. I can identify with this image, with this way of being in the world. But something within me had been taken away, and any identity is only an excuse, a way to avoid telling the deeper truth: that the core of my being is empty. With this emptiness there was sometimes a feeling of desolation as the personality and ego struggled to find a point of reference. Emptiness is both wonderful and terrifying, like standing alone on the deck of a sailing ship in the ocean when all the sailors have vanished. The wind fills the sails, but there is no one there except a lone passenger, who looks towards the expanse of grey waters and the empty sky.

I no longer needed to find my place because I had become too lost: there was no one to find. About this time I came across a saying from the Christian mystic, the Blessed John Ruysbroeck, who speaks of "the dark silence in which all lovers lose themselves," and it echoed deep within me. Yet I did not know I was lost, sacrificed on the table of my Beloved. The dream describes an inner state of abandonment that gradually came into consciousness as an emptiness, a feeling of not caring what happens. One may think that being lost to oneself induces a state of bliss, intoxication, bewilderment. But then I felt the effect of non-being only as an emptiness of intention, in which the ego still functioned, but with no real connection to any sense of identity. I carried the form of a hermit looking towards God; but without mind, without sense of self, who can look towards whom?

Yet in the midst of this emptiness a very concrete purpose began to take form. When I returned to London after my second lecture tour, I told Mrs. Tweedie of the vision in which I had been shown the intensity of the work awaiting me, of my realization that this was to be a full-time job that would demand all of myself. This was the moment when she told me that she had known for some time that we would have a Sufi Center in America. Three times she told me, and still I found it hard to believe. Once again my spiritual conditioning that the path must be hidden, a secret shared among a few, blocked my way. A physical center, an organization, seemed to go against everything I inwardly felt about the path. But "Orders are orders." If this was His will I would live it.

To be "in the world but not of the world" is a cornerstone of the mystical path. I had now accepted lecturing, wandering from place to place with a handful of stories and Sufi sayings, listening to people's dreams. But a physical center and an organization were something quite different. Somewhere I knew that I could hide no longer, and that this future center would be both my life and my death. I had no desire for position, to be anything. The path had conditioned me to want to be nothing, to be in silence, unnoticed except by the Beloved within the heart. But now I was to be thrown into a different arena, into the bluntness of the physical world and the exposure this would bring. In reaction I withdrew into myself, to face my own inner demons. Gradually I had to surrender, to accept what was given and asked. I knew of no other way.

About this time I had a dream that pointed out this drama, and how it included both my reactions and my destiny. In the dream I am lecturing in a church when Mrs. Tweedie comes into the building and swears at a friend. This friend turns to Mrs. Tweedie and says, "You shouldn't swear in a church," to which Mrs. Tweedie replies, "I am so much in the presence of God that everywhere is a church. I am hung in the house of God." The moment I awoke from this dream I knew that it was my destiny to be "hung in the house of God." This was to be my death and my awakening.

What does it mean to be hung in the house of God? For me it carries the clear message that standing in front of people and carrying the message of the path is to be my crucifixion. This was one of the reasons I recoiled in fear when I was shown the work in front of me, the need of those who were waiting. I knew that all sense of my own self would be lost in this work, not just lost but thrown aside, trampled on and disregarded. I had seen how the people came to Mrs. Tweedie oblivious of her, seeing only their own need. I knew the total giving that the work involved, and added to this was my own introvert nature which rebels in fury against any exposure. Each time before I go on a lecture trip I withdraw into a kind of depression. I long to stay at home and quietly write and meditate. But inwardly I am driven beyond myself, not in any solitary seeking for truth, but by the power of the path that demands I stand in front of an audience. Once the lecture begins I am in love with the work, with the way the path touches those who come. I feel the power and presence of my Sheikh and am carried along by the currents of grace. But before this happens my little self screams in anguish and tries to hide itself in a corner.

After Mrs. Tweedie had told me about the Sufi Center, I consciously knew that my destiny was sealed, that it involved a totality of psychological and physical commitment. She even said that I should earn a living from this work, which was also a shock. Since I had stopped teaching I had been living off some savings, and I had thought that soon I would find a job as a college lecturer, and thus be able to support myself and my family. I knew that spiritual things must be free and never charged for. Mrs. Tweedie lived off her war-widow's pension, and money was never involved. But she said it is all right to earn money from lectures, for anything that you have studied for with your mind. For years I had been studying Jungian psychology and dreamwork, and I needed to earn a living. Bringing the two worlds together to such a degree would break down many patterns of resistance, and create a vulnerability that I had never experienced. Innermost spiritual surrender seemed easy in comparison to the future that awaited. The work of bringing the path into the physical world was what I dreaded, and so it was to be my fate.

But all these inner difficulties were more than balanced by a tremendous feeling of joy that came from the depths. This was the joy of the work becoming manifest, and my being a part of this work, of living the destiny of my soul to the utmost. The essence of joy is life flowing direct from the source, unpolluted, uncontaminated. The Sufi Center would contain this joy, as I felt in a prophetic dream:

> I am having a meal with Bhai Sahib. He is sitting at the head of the table and I am on his right. It is the first day of the Sufi Center. Many people are present and the atmosphere is full of joy. This joy is the central feeling to the whole dream. Mrs. Tweedie is there, and Bhai Sahib, and one of his disciples. The first baby is born at the center that day, and the first two gardens are planted. I have the key to the kitchen, which was also Bhai Sahib's kitchen.

From teacher to disciple the transmission of love takes place. I have been given the keys to my Sheikh's kitchen, where the food of divine remembrance is prepared. This food is for all those who need, who are hungry for nourishment on the long journey Home. In the company of my Sheikh I would share what I have been given, and the joy hidden at the center of life would be a part of this new beginning.

COMING HOME

*Then the pilgrim returns home, to the home of his
origin...that is the world of Allâh's proximity,
that is where the home of the inner pilgrim is, and that is
where he returns.... Beyond this no news can be given,
for beyond is the unperceivable, inconceivable,
indescribable.*

Al-Gîlânî

MOVING TO CALIFORNIA

One early-summer afternoon in London I was standing
in my kitchen with Anat, looking out over the back
garden, the green lawn, and the flowers Mrs. Tweedie
had so lovingly planted coming into bloom. In an
hour's time it would be three o'clock and soon people
would be gathering on the pavement, waiting for the
afternoon meeting. We had been living here for eleven
years, and although I knew that my destiny would take
me to California, it was our duty to be here and look
after Mrs. Tweedie. When she had finished her work on
the physical plane, then the next stage of our life would
unfold. This was an unspoken understanding that
belonged to our commitment to the path.

Suddenly, in a moment, everything changed. I was
hit by a blast of energy so powerful that it almost threw
me to the floor. With the energy came a shift in
consciousness, and I saw, clearly and simply, that it
was time for me to take my family and move to America

now—that the Sufi Center should start while Mrs. Tweedie was still alive. It was as if my inner direction was just shifted, and what had been hidden was made apparent. This new direction was so clear and obvious that there was no argument, no possibility of conflict. Anat had seen me stagger under the impact of this energy, and when I told her what I had been shown, she caught the shift in consciousness. One moment the prime function of our life was to look after Mrs. Tweedie and to help her with the group. The next moment, this was to be left behind and our work was to start a center in America.

If we were to move this year, the best time would be at the beginning of August, in two months' time. This would give us time to settle down before the beginning of the new school year and my autumn lecture tour, which had already been scheduled. Anat and I went downstairs, and, knocking on the sliding glass doors leading from Mrs. Tweedie's flat to the garden, stepped inside and spoke to her. I said that I had been shown that we should go to America this summer. At first she thought I just meant for a holiday with the children, but then I said no, it would be forever. Now was the time to move. On the surface she was shocked, but she also saw the inner clarity of the situation. She knew that the change was coming. When the group met that afternoon, she just announced that soon there would be big changes.

Although the moment of decision came so unexpectedly, even on the outer plane events had been preparing. The previous autumn Mrs. Tweedie had told Michael and me to look at different spiritual centers in America and see how they were run. We visited a yoga ashram that was also a health center, which functioned as a spiritual business and was very successful. We also spent time at a Vedanta retreat, where no money was charged but the organization raised one and a half million dollars a year through donations. We saw another center which was burdened by a property with too many buildings, whose upkeep they were no longer able to manage. The size and problems of the property took too much of the energy of the people who lived there. Traveling across America and looking at different centers opened our eyes, and showed us the middle road we needed to follow: a place large enough for people to come, but small enough to easily manage, a center that charges money for its activities, except meditation which is always free, but is not run as a business. We had been taught that if the inner attitude is right the money will be there.

The following spring we returned to America, and this time Mrs. Tweedie hinted that we should look out for a suitable property. We spent three weeks in California with our families, and kept our eyes open. We found a beautiful property amidst the redwoods and rolling hills of Northern California, lyrically called West of the Moon. My heart bounded when I saw the main building because it was just like a dream I had had a few weeks before: a large deck at the front of a wooden house, surrounded by fruit trees, shrubs, and flowers. The property itself had both woodlands and open pastures. Suddenly the center seemed no longer just a dream, but a physical reality.

Anat went back to London with pictures of the property, which she showed to Mrs. Tweedie, whose heart was also touched. We started an appeal to raise the money we needed, and began negotiations with the owner. I continued on my lecture tour, going on to Baltimore, Virginia, and then Georgia. Soon after I arrived back in England I learned that West of the Moon would never happen as there were complications with the owner. I was not disappointed, as I have learned on the Sufi path never to judge by appearances. The outer world is often used as a stage to enact inner experiences. Even though I had dreamed of West of the Moon before I saw it, the property served a purpose different from what I had imagined; it had brought the idea of a Sufi Center into the reality of the physical world, and the appeal had included the whole group in this process. There would be a Sufi Center, at a different time and in a different place. This was no longer just a dream.

A week after West of the Moon fell through I had the experience that showed me that it was time to leave home. When we were thinking of West of the Moon there was no time scale, and we still felt that our primary responsibility was to live with our teacher. Now, suddenly, this had all changed. The instructions had come to move, even though we now had nowhere to go. Then a friend in California offered us a house not far from the ocean. We bought our tickets, and cleared out all the accumulated possessions of eleven years. So much was thrown away, so little was taken with us: some books, children's possessions, and clothes. We found two friends to live in our flat and help Mrs. Tweedie. We left all our furniture, everything necessary for the flat to be fully furnished for the friends who would be living there. We just packed a few boxes and two suitcases each. I never find it difficult to leave things behind.

We arrived in California in the August fog. Although it seemed easy to leave, it was very difficult to arrive. The family had come to California twice for a holiday while I was lecturing, but this was very different. Having a dream of moving to California is quite distinct from the reality: spending days in shopping malls, buying everything from cups and knives and forks to sheets and beds—all the basic necessities—until finally I said that I could not go to another shop for at least a month. Combined with this I learned soon after I arrived that there had just been a change in the immigration law, and I would not be able to earn any money for at least nine months! A new place, a new school for the children, who were confronted with a small country town after city life and were now the new kids on the block. So much insecurity, and only a dream to live for! Luckily, when I left England I did not realize how difficult it was going to be. Then, eight weeks after we arrived, I had to leave for a six-week lecture tour.

ONENESS IN NATURE

A few days after the experience which resulted in our moving to California I had another important realization. I was made aware that I had made a mistake in identifying the Sufi Center with a physical place, West of the Moon. I was shown that in essence the Sufi Center is not a place, *but a state of being*, and that this state of being was within myself. Eventually, in the right time and place, there would be a physical center, but the real center was held on the inner plane, within the heart. I needed to live this state of being before it would become manifest.

We arrived in our new home amidst the silence and the trees. As the days passed I gradually became aware of a new relationship between my inner and outer world. For over ten years we had been living in the same house as our teacher, and had felt the support of our meditation group, which had in many ways been like a family for almost twenty years. Now, suddenly, we were alone on a hillside beside the ocean. We started a small group once a week in a friend's house in a nearby town, as the dirt road to our house could not support many cars. But throughout the whole winter and spring, apart from this weekly meeting I spoke to no one except for Anat and the children. The telephone never rang and no one knocked on the door. This was so different from our life in London, with a hundred people coming to our house every day. I spent my time writing, meditating, and walking. In the midst of this aloneness, nature opened her hidden self; the physical world became a part of my spiritual path in a way that I never expected. Among the trees and on the beaches I found a oneness revealing itself in the outer world.

That winter was a part of a six-year drought in California. In England I had been used to the months of January and February being depressingly grey, wet, and dismal. Here it was warm and sunny. In January I would walk on the beach, alone in the sunshine. In February spring came, with wildflowers opening on the headlands. With the unexpected spring came this new consciousness. Suddenly I found, walking in the woods or beside the ocean, an overwhelming sense of oneness. In meditation I have at times glimpsed the oneness behind creation, the oneness that contains everything and mirrors His oneness. But now I was experiencing this oneness *in full consciousness.* Wherever I was walking, looking at the multiplicity of nature, the different leaves, trees, rocks washed by the waves, a oneness was visibly present. This oneness was so natural, so much a part of what I saw and felt. It had always been there, only now I was seeing it for the first time.

I have always loved nature, particularly in the peace and quiet of early morning, with the mists over the English meadows, or in the softness of evening with the pigeons cooing and the ducks settling for the night. But nature was never central to my spiritual path. Instead I looked inward into the emptiness of meditation. Also, I lived for so many years in London, and despite the beauty of English gardens, and the wonder of the flowers Mrs. Tweedie planted and tended with care, even our leafy suburban street was enclosed in the aura of a city.

But now nature revealed something so wonderful that I still look in awe. The multiplicity is here, the tide-pools full of creatures, the hawks circling, the star-shaped flowers, but behind and around is this permeating presence. At the beginning I was just fascinated, expecting this oneness to be a passing mystical state. But gradually I sensed its permanence. After writing for a few hours in the morning I would go for a walk, and looking, find it, both visible and intangible. I sensed and saw the oneness, but not with my physical eyes. An inner eye had opened in which place and state of being were united—the inner and outer oneness mirrored each other.

My sense of the oneness around me was a container of my aloneness, a reassurance given by the Great Mother. I felt her presence, the power of the earth, the trees, the water. Here in California one senses a primal connection to life that is lacking in Europe, where nature has been cultivated for so many centuries. And this oneness was linked directly to my meditation, to my inner awareness where aloneness merges into oneness, as al-Hallâj writes: "Solitary, God loves only the solitary—One, He loves only he who witnesses Him as One."[1] In my aloneness I had found the oneness, the secret hidden within creation.

At first I thought that this outer oneness was only to be found in nature. But as the months passed, what I had found in nature permeated all of my life. I discovered that whenever I stopped for a moment in the midst of outer activities, I could feel the underlying unity. As I interacted with people or was immersed in everyday activities, my consciousness would necessarily be caught in multiplicity and the dualities of the mind. But I came to know that behind this activity a oneness was always present, a consciousness to which I could attune myself more and more easily. Ceasing my activities for an instant, I could sense the unity, feel the ever-present wholeness. Gradually this dual consciousness became so much a part of my everyday life that I would have to try to remember what it was like to live without it, to live solely in the isolating consciousness of the ego.

AN EMPTY SHELL

I knew that those months of silence and solitariness amidst the oneness of nature would not last long, and that people would return to fill my life. By the early summer we had found a house nearby for our meditation meetings, which we then held twice a week. People started to come, and my work also changed as we launched our own small publishing business, beginning with my third book *The Bond with the Beloved.*

During those months of isolation I had worked very intensely on this book, which was inspired by a saying in the Qur'an, "He loves them and they love Him," a saying which I found echoed within the Christian tradition in the Epistle of Saint John, "We love Him because He first loved us." *The Bond with the Beloved* explores the relationship of lover and Beloved which is at the core of every mystical tradition. This inner bond of love comes alive within the heart of the lover, a heart which at its deepest core is always looking towards its Beloved. A year before I began this book I had been invited to give a weekend seminar at a Roman Catholic retreat center in Florida, and for preparation had immersed myself in the writings of the Christian mystics. To my great joy I discovered the many similarities between these Christian lovers and the Sufis. In particular the work of Saint Teresa of Avila echoed within my heart, and *The Bond with the Beloved* is also partly based on Saint Teresa's stages of prayer, which I had found to reflect many of my own experiences and those of others in our group in London.

In writing *The Bond with the Beloved* I was moving away from psychology into the area of pure mysticism, which was also becoming more and more the focus of my lectures. The sayings of Sufi and Christian mystics speak so clearly of the link of love that underlies all of creation and which I discovered singing within my own heart. The book wrote itself in a few intense months, bringing into consciousness feelings and intuitions which until then had been hidden within me.

Writing about the stages of prayer, I understood something that had long puzzled me. Early Sufi writers say that the dervish should never sleep but be in prayer throughout the night. I had tried to stay awake, to meditate and pray the whole night, but found this was only possible when daily life made no demands. Sleep is a physical necessity, but what I discovered within myself is that the prayer of the heart does not belong to the physical world. This is not a prayer of words, but an inner state in which the awakened heart looks towards God, what Saint John of the Cross describes as "an effortless state of contemplation." When the heart is awakened *it is always in a state of prayer.* The heart's prayer is a state of consciousness which is always witnessing Him and praising Him. Because this consciousness within the heart does not belong to time or space, once the heart is awakened it never sleeps, as is beautifully expressed in the Song of Solomon: "I sleep, but my heart waketh: it is the voice of my beloved that knocketh, saying, Open to me, my sister, my love, my dove, my undefiled."[2] Inwardly the lover always looks to his Beloved, attentive to His will. The awakening of the heart is one of the central mysteries of the mystical path.

In the early summer, after the book was finished, I was on a camping trip with my family in the Sierras. One morning, in an area of desolate rock interspersed with lakes, appropriately called Desolation Wilderness, I was sitting in meditation on a rock, feeling the beauty of the bleak landscape, when I felt an inner hint that we should start our own publishing business, beginning with this book. The call to bring something into the world was pushing me from within, and it took me from my aloneness into a world of computers, distributors, and advertising decisions! Returning home, I still had time to walk in the woods, but my outer focus had changed, and the days full of outer emptiness belonged to the past. There was a need to bring together the two worlds, to express the mysteries of the soul in the marketplace, to sing the song of divine love on the stage of the outer world.

As my outer life became more busy, the oneness remained, always present at the borders of my mind. I also came to realize that whatever my outer activities, my real attention is elsewhere; somewhere I remain in the emptiness of inner space. With this awareness of an inner state of consciousness separate from my outer activities came the gradual realization that an essential part of me is *always elsewhere.* Mrs. Tweedie always said that the best part of herself was elsewhere. I had accepted what she said, but until now had not understood it. Now I knew its truth, because I was experiencing this state within myself; I was experiencing my own essential absence. Wherever I am, whatever I am doing, my real self is not here, is not interacting with people or events. There is an awareness of both an absence from this outer plane and a presence somewhere else, though this somewhere else cannot be put into words.

In human relationships I began to feel like an impostor, because I know that my essential self is not here, and thus I can never really relate to another person. There can be a semblance of relating, as the personality carries the appearance of a human being, and the thoughts and feelings that surround the ego interact with the outer world. But I know that this is not the real me, that I am somewhere else, being used for another purpose. I am aware that the part that lives here, talks, laughs, writes, is just a shell empty of my essential self.

In the dream I had had two years earlier I was shown that I had been made empty, that I had lost myself in a mystical experience. The sense of self, the consciousness that had been lost, had now reappeared, but not here, and not in relation to the outer world. In everyday life I still function on the level of the ego, relating to the physical world, yet at the same time there is a sense of absence that is also a sense of presence. Essentially absent to this world, there is a state of presence which is not me, in the sense that it is not my ego, but it is my real being. The Sufis call this state *baqâ*, abiding after passing away. The mind and everyday self can only feel that some essential part is elsewhere, is not engaged in the outer world. At times this feeling of absence can be disconcerting. Wherever you are, whatever you are doing, you are not fully here; there is an emptiness where the sense of self used to be. What remains is here just in order to make a connection to the real Self; that is the purpose of the shell I call myself. The work of the path requires this connection.

I have come to realize that it is the part of me that is absent that experiences the oneness and reflects this experience into my everyday consciousness. Part of me remains behind the veil of creation, immersed elsewhere. Slowly it shares its secrets with the servant who remains behind, with the denser part of me which embraces the physical, emotional, and mental world. The work of the servant is then to live in the world of multiplicity and yet follow the ways of oneness. Through this work the path of love can be brought into the world.

I had to learn to be always attentive to the inner state of consciousness that is elsewhere, experiencing a reality which my mind can never know. At times I have longed to join in with others, to be just a part of the play of forms, yet this door has been closed behind me. Because my real self is elsewhere I am always alone. I can never really interact with another person. On occasion this has brought a feeling of aloneness that is desolate beyond belief, but it also allows me to live from the hidden center of myself without restriction. The path demands that the only relationship which holds my real attention be with the Beloved and my Sheikh.

Yet somewhere, not on the physical plane, I am always at home. I began to experience this when I traveled for lecturing. In the airport, in the hotel room, I do not fundamentally feel that I am away from home. My body may travel and leave the house near to the ocean which I call home, but inwardly there is no journey. I am always somewhere else, so how can I go elsewhere? The real belonging remains inward, on a different plane of consciousness. And as this inner state unfolded, my life was interacting more and more with the outer world: being with people, lecturing, holding retreats, and engaging in the business of publishing. Yet this outer involvement is surrounded by a sense of emptiness, by a feeling of detachment. And there is always time for meditation, for leaving behind the ego and the mind, and dissolving totally into the emptiness, the only place where there is the feeling of absolute belonging.

A COLD, HARD COMMITMENT

Gradually more people started to come to our meetings, and a few friends even moved from different parts of the country in order to live nearby. As the group expanded I began to experience people thinking of me as a spiritual teacher. This projection increased when, six months after we left London, due to her health and age, Mrs. Tweedie closed her meditation group. In her own words she "officially retired," although she did continue to occasionally meet with a small group of friends with whom she still needed to work, to "take them to the threshold." In closing her group and retiring she announced that the work was continuing through the Sufi Center in America.

I have never referred to myself as a teacher, just calling myself a lecturer or an interpreter of dreams. I know that the real teacher is "without a face and without a name," an empty space through which the teachings of the path can be made known. The individual, the "I," can never be a teacher, and yet one cannot just dismiss a projection, especially the projection of the teacher, which carries the numinosity of an individual's Higher Self. Instead, one can allow the essence of what is being projected to be held in emptiness. Those who just want the security of a spiritual authority will find this emptiness too disturbing, and the projection will fall away. For those who sincerely follow the path, the projection will be held by the energy of the tradition until it is time for the wayfarer to withdraw the projection, as expressed in the words of Bahâ-ad-dîn Naqshband: "We are the means of reaching the goal. It is necessary that seekers should cut themselves away from us and think only of the goal."[3] If the individual is unable or unwilling to withdraw the projection, he or she is simply thrown out of the meditation group until this work is completed.

However, when I began to feel these projections, to see people looking to me for guidance, I looked within myself to see if I had any part to play. Knowing the importance of the projection, I felt that it should be reflected, honored by something within myself. What I found were two essential qualities stamped into the core of my being. One is the absolute nature of my commitment to the Truth. I saw how this is harder than steel and had been forged in a fire of intense spiritual training long, long ago. I knew that I had brought it with me into this life because it is deeper than my personal history, and I have always known it to be there. This commitment held me through the most difficult years of my life, in the chaos of my desperation and the tortures of longing. Within me it is the same as it has always been, and I discovered that it has a quality of cruelty, the cruelty that will push anything aside that stands in the way of my living this commitment. Like a knife of hardened steel it will cut away any obstacle barring the path, because this is its essential nature: nothing matters more than the quest for Truth. Seeing it bared within me, I felt the fire that had forged it, and I felt its cold, hard, unchanging nature which carries the stamp of the divine executioner—everything has to go.

I also found within me my connection to my Sheikh, a connection that is always present and which is my life's blood. Only this connection allows me to walk the path and tell others of the mystery within the heart. This connection is more precious than breathing because otherwise I would be lost, stranded in a world of illusion without any way Home. Once, for two weeks, he cut off this connection, and I felt like a ship without a rudder, with no sense of direction, wandering lost. The song in my heart was absent, the days held no promise, there was no light. When the connection was returned I felt unbelievably grateful. I know that everything has been given to me by my Sheikh, that I belong to him more than I can ever know. Through him the path has become my life.

My commitment to Truth and my connection to my Sheikh are all that I can offer. In order to honor another's desire for Truth I have to live these two qualities to the fullest. The projections of others do not belong to me. I am never a teacher, just a lover who has been given a glimpse of his Beloved.

The ways of the heart's unfolding are a tremendous mystery. The projection onto a teacher figure is a part of this process,[4] but there is also a deeper connection between teacher and disciple that belongs to the level of the soul. I had felt people have this link with Mrs. Tweedie, and seen how it brought a quality of lived devotion into their life. My link was always directly with Bhai Sahib, whom I never knew in a physical form, and so it does not include the physical dimension. But now I began to experience how for some people my soul plays a part in their connection with the path. I know that this connection is not with me, Llewellyn, but belongs to a different dimension, and yet is reflected into the dimension of space and time. I see the importance of this link of love, and how it keeps the wayfarer aligned with the path and allows His love to flow into the heart. Through this link the fire of longing is kept burning, as Rûmî describes:

> We have put a substance into you, a seeking, a yearning, and we are guarding it; and we aren't letting it get lost, we're bringing it to a certain definite place.[5]

Reflected from heart to heart, the path unfolds, bringing us always closer to Him whom we love.

Through this felt connection with others I have been taken so totally into the arena of love that I know

I do not belong to myself. Love uses me for its own purposes. I love my wife and children, but the deepest part of my heart is used for the work and the impersonality of the heart's connection to others. We are conditioned to associate love with attachment and with personal relationship. But the same impersonal fire that is my own commitment to Truth is at the core of these relationships. The ego and the personality have no part to play. There is only one Master to serve: He who is love Itself.

In the dream of the Sufi Center I had been given the keys of my Sheikh's kitchen. The food of divine remembrance can only be passed from heart to heart. Through the link of love the heart is opened to the beyond and the wayfarer is able to taste the mystery of his own being. For centuries the Sufi path has worked in this way, aligning the heart of the wayfarer so that the energies of love can flow through and out into the world. The inner connection of the soul is central to this work, a connection that is not limited by time or space. I will always remember when a friend from New Zealand had to return there, not knowing if she would ever see Mrs. Tweedie again. Mrs. Tweedie brushed aside her tears with the statement, "On this path we do not acknowledge physical separation."

LOVE'S INTIMACY

One of the wonders of the mystical path is its simplicity. Mysticism is a one-to-one relationship of the soul with its Creator. Everything else is secondary to this relationship of love between lover and Beloved. For many years I struggled through my own darkness and was torn apart by the almost unbearable pain of longing. Now it seems that these days have passed. There are still difficulties, painful struggles, and inner confrontations. But the desperate longing has been replaced by a relationship of love that is so present that at times I have felt almost guilty I am being given so much.

In the depths of every soul this love is always present, for it is the link of love that is at the axis of the world and within every heart. When this love reveals itself within consciousness, a sense of the deepest intimacy permeates everything. The heart is so happy, the soul sings with the ancient promise of the quest. Everything else in life is limited; every other relationship has boundaries and parameters. But when the heart of the lover is infused with the experience of His love, there is a fullness that increases, a bliss that always expands.

Sometimes I feel this love during the day, and the heart is so happy knowing that He is near. Then joy suffuses everything and there is a sense of sunlight everywhere. Not just the heart, but the whole body feels the joy of the sacred. There is a deep happiness that has nothing to do with external circumstances, and even difficult outer situations do not infringe upon this inner joy. Wherever I walk, each breath carries the beauty of an early-summer day, the invisible sweetness that draws the bee to the center of a flower. Only there is sometimes a slight sadness that this sweetness and joy cannot be shared directly with others.

But it is in the moments, even the hours, when I can turn inward that the love becomes so all-embracing that there is no lover and Beloved, just a fullness that becomes a merging and melting. Then I close the door of my room, turn my face to the wall, and experience the intimacies that are known only to lovers. Sometimes this love is like a secret calling and a coming near. The heart is open, and in the invisible emptiness I am contained, held, and embraced. A softness touches every part of my being, carrying a sense of belonging in which the lover knows the feeling of the heart's deepest contentment.

Yet as much as this love may be soft and tender, there are also times when it carries a penetrating ecstasy which makes the bliss of sexuality seem like a pale imitation. In these moments I have known the truth of Mirabai's statement that the soul is always female before God. The body arches in ecstasy as bliss explodes, bliss upon bliss, light upon light. The heart is pierced by His touch and the whole body is included, every cell seems a woman penetrated by her lover. The mind is lost in the rapture as everything is ravished. And what is left of the human being lies in wonder: how long can it last? how much love can be given? And you give your heart, and you give your heart again, until finally the waves of love subside.

One never knows when these moments will come, and then they leave, scarring the soul with sweetness and a knowledge of love that disperses every care or concern. His touch, that before had seemed so fleeting, becomes more and more familiar, yet always unexpected. What I have found most wonderful is, even when the intense states have passed, to look within the heart and find the trace of His presence in the sweetness of love. Then my lips will softly curl into a smile, knowing that He whom I love has not deserted me. So many days of darkness and hunger have brought their reward, so much calling has been answered. A moment's intoxication with this love dissolves every pain, leaving only the dimmest memory of the tears. And how many moments, hours even, has love been present...

Coming out of these inner states one returns to the ego, which remains with its old failings, psychological problems, and inadequacies. But the difference is that they no longer matter; they are no longer seen as an obstacle, but are accepted as a part of this world. Somewhere, something so precious has been given that one cannot ask for more, and the ego seems so insignificant. When a man has only a hundred dollars in the world, those hundred dollars are very important. But if he suddenly wins five million dollars in the lottery, the hundred dollars no longer matter. The problems of the ego remain, and in fact help to keep one's feet on the ground, remind one that only He is perfect. Only His love has real substance.

There is no end to this love, and maybe the longing will return. But my heart, mind, and body know the truth of His promise, know that He is a lover beyond compare. One feels only the tremendous gratitude to have been given so much, to have tasted the love for which everyone hungers. Sometimes I have thought with sadness, why are others content with so little, with the buying and selling of affection that they think of as love? Here there is so much waiting to be given, waiting to be poured into an empty heart. But what can one say? Once I told Mrs. Tweedie of these feelings and she replied, "Yes, Bhai Sahib said the same thing. We stand in the marketplace with our hands full of jewels, saying, 'Take them. It's free.' But they pass by because they think it is false."

When the heart is so full, one longs only to also be generous, to give and to give as one has been given to. But each seeker has to be left alone with her longing, with his deepest desire to taste this wine, to become immersed in the same limitless ocean. Words are so fragmentary, while the heart speaks a love that is whole beyond our understanding. Knowing this love, feeling this intimacy in which I am alone with my Beloved, I can only try not to interfere with the ways of love, the ways He wishes to make Himself known within the hearts of His friends.

Love is so simple and longing is so direct. Why does one ever look elsewhere, seeking this love in the forms of duality? These are the mysteries of life, while the path of the wayfarer is to find what has been hidden. When love comes there is no seeking, no effort, only the wonder that one has ever been absent. You know that this wholeness is always present, that love is the fundamental substance of creation. There are moments when even to think of separation is a defamation, when you know that the world could not exist if it were not permeated with His presence. But why was the way here such an invisible thread? Why did it take so long to find? Both questions and answers are left behind. There is nothing to say, only a tremendous thankfulness for what one has been given so freely. The real thankfulness belongs to the heart that looks in wonder and gratitude towards its Beloved, but also I, the ego, feel grateful to Him who has shown me His infinite love, who has allowed me to glimpse this aspect of Himself.

So much looking, and now I discover that love permeates everything. So much longing and nothing was lost. The circle of love holds the whole of creation, and within the heart this circle is always present. The heart holds this circle, holds the secret of love. And His lover can come to know this, can come to feel love's fullness which is our own real being. Within the heart so many mysteries reveal themselves, but the simplest and most wonderful is the fullness of love, a fullness which is simultaneously an emptiness without form. This fullness is the truth of His presence, a presence which is unveiled by love and which is love; for He has said, "Heaven and earth contain Me not, but the heart of My faithful servant contains Me."

TELLING THE STORIES OF LOVE

These experiences of love became the foundation of my work with other people, and the cornerstone of my writing. Heart is drawn to heart, the scent of sweetness an invisible attraction. When love is present the heart opens and something is shared beyond knowing. As a witness to this work I can only be amazed, like a child watching the dawn and wondering what is being born. I only know that I have to be vulnerable and give myself, not to another person, but to the divine that is hidden. In my vulnerability I have to listen, half in this world, half somewhere else, and to talk as I feel, not restricted by the inhibitions of the world.

Some people need to hear His love spoken of as a passion in which everything is included, while others need to share a sorrow that has been with them since the beginning. I need to be both present and absent, a stepping-stone that has no value in itself. And I must want nothing either for or from another human being, because otherwise I become an obstacle: freedom is a cornerstone of the path. What we are given is free beyond our understanding, because it carries the stamp of the Creator who is freedom Itself. Listening to the stories of love, and sharing my own experiences, I feel the need of this freedom to be known and lived.

Every other relationship in the world has strings attached, the strings of ego-dependence. Between lover and Beloved there is a giving and receiving beyond measure. The currents of divine love can only be contained by an unlimited heart.

Hearing people's problems, I always try to reduce these problems to what is simplest, to the deepest underlying need. For those who are born with a desire to go Home, this calling carries such an energy that if it is focused it can untie the knots of many seeming problems. Sadly, we have become a society of problem-solvers, always looking towards a problem and often fearful of the space around and beyond the problem. The ego easily identifies with problems, and diverts us from the quest. There *are* difficulties, problems that need to be addressed, and the tools of psychology are immensely useful. Psychology can help us untangle the difficulties our conditioning and childhood have woven around us, help us to confront the shadow and understand what we have repressed into the darkness. Yet the heart's cry for God is not a problem, but a living reality that is so often dismissed. The despair of separation and the need for real love can only be lived with the recklessness of those who remember their real nature, and have to bring this remembrance into their life.

For the mystic this world is a strange place, an environment whose codes and patterns of behavior never quite ring true. Learning to live one's deepest longing amidst the contradictions of the physical dimension can require help and guidance, particularly when we are immersed in a culture that asserts that the physical world is the only reality. On the inner planes the energy of the path spins the heart and takes us Home. In the outer world we may feel stranded, as the mind tries to reconcile the different realities. Learning to walk the middle way, to be in the world but not of the world, needs the help of fellow travelers, and of those who are one step further along the path. In this way we can help each other, pointing out the potholes that are most easily avoided.

In my lecturing and writing I attempted to create a contemporary context for mysticism, which is so foreign to our Western culture. Explaining its qualities and apparent paradoxes in today's language, I try to make it easier for those lovers whose hearts are turning towards Home, to help the mind and psyche understand as far as is possible the nature of this ancient journey, the states and stages the wayfarer passes through. For example, the opposites of love and fear, intimacy and awe, which are described in Sufi manuals, can easily be confused with psychological problems; but they belong to the nature of the relationship with a God who is both immanent and transcendent. The fear of the teacher, which can be misunderstood as solely relating to patterns of authoritarian repression, belongs to this relationship, and to the dynamic of expansion and contraction that keeps the wayfarer balanced—as the heart opens to the infinite, the ego bows in awe before its Master.

I have come to realize that even our concepts of spirituality are quite different from mysticism. Following a spiritual path, seekers often try to improve themselves, to become something: an adept, a yogi, enlightened. But mysticism is not about becoming anything, but about the one-to-one relationship of the soul to God, a relationship that is carried as an imprint within the heart. Mystics are born and not made, and the path of the mystic is to step out of the way so that this hidden imprint can be lived. The mystic only seeks to become "featureless and formless," to be annihilated in love until the union of "He loves them and they love Him" is experienced within the heart. 'Attâr beautifully expresses this central paradox of the mystical way:

> What you most want,
> what you travel around wishing to find,
> lose yourself as lovers lose themselves,
> and you'll be that.[6]

The eternal story of the mystical quest is of entering a darkness brighter than light, of losing everything and finding the nothingness that is our real essence. Every mystic longs to live the truth of "There is nothing but Nothingness," and it is a truth that demands only death, a complete giving of oneself. The path to the gallows of love does not belong to any creed or religion, for as Rûmî says, "Lovers have a religion and faith all of their own." But at different times this story needs to be retold, explained in the language of the day. When Mrs. Tweedie wrote her book, *Daughter of Fire*, she wanted it to be easily accessible, so that people could see that this path of love is not just a secret that happened long ago. Writing with the simple, direct words of the heart, she tells the story of her own experience, of a love that emptied her of herself. Those who are drawn to this destiny need to know that it can be lived, and that this crazy passion has a purpose beyond what one can even imagine.

PUBLIC HUMILIATION

As I work with people, the grace of my Sheikh is always present, giving the guidance and understanding that are needed. Sometimes this guidance is instantly present; sometimes I have to go into meditation and ask. I have come to know the truth of what I was told years before, *"The help of your Sheikh is in your heart, that is all you need to know."* However, during this time I also came to discover that I was still dependent upon the external support given by Mrs. Tweedie and the group. This outer attachment was to be broken in a most painful manner before I could fully realize that the only dependence and the only belonging were inward, to my Sheikh. No form of outer dependence could be allowed.

The outer stage for this inner process was set when the original publishers of *Daughter of Fire*, not wishing to reprint, gave the Sufi Center the publication rights for the book. As we considered the details of reprinting, someone offered to correct the spelling and other proofing mistakes that had occurred in the original book. As I was in California, I asked a friend who was traveling to London to ask Mrs. Tweedie if she wanted these corrections made. I received the answer that she did. We decided to delay the reprinting of the book while these corrections were made. This would entail scanning the text onto a computer program, correcting, and then reproofing the text. Because *Daughter of Fire* is over eight hundred pages long, the whole process, including the printing, might take as long as eighteen months, meaning that the book would have been out of print for up to two years.

About six months after we had begun the work of correcting the text, Mrs. Tweedie discovered to her horror that the book had been allowed to go out of print. We had made a fundamental mistake in not realizing that the book had to be continually in print. Because *Daughter of Fire* had been written under the orders of her teacher, and contains the teachings of this Sufi path, it was essential for the work of this path that it remain in print. Its energy belongs to the foundation of the work of our center, the work of bringing this Sufi tradition to the West. Recognizing our mistake, we made a short print run while the work of correcting the book continued.

One of the most painful experiences I have ever experienced is that of letting down my teacher. When I realized my failure in allowing the book to be out of print, I was torn apart from the inside, and was only partly relieved by the knowledge that soon her book would be back in the bookstores. I did not realize that this was only a beginning.

We reprinted in June, and then, in mid-July, a friend arrived from England with a message that Mrs. Tweedie was worried that the work of correcting the book would change some of the book's substance, that her teacher's words might be altered. Only much later did I understand how this depth of misunderstanding had arisen, how a friend's few misplaced words to Mrs. Tweedie had such an effect. Later I also discovered that there was more to this message, but the friend who delivered it from England was ill, and had not conveyed its full intensity. But outer events were now beginning to constellate in a most painful and devastating manner.

At the end of July, in the midst of these events, we had our first week-long Sufi camp with over a hundred people. This was an intense and exhausting work, during which I felt a strange and disturbing tension within me. At the time I thought this tension just came from my concerns about our first Sufi camp. But a few days after the camp was over, I received a fax from Mrs. Tweedie that made me realize that I had been picking up events that were continuing to unfold. She accused me of wanting to change her book, and that this was a criminal activity. How could I dare to do such a thing? A fax, like e-mail, can be the most impersonal mode of communication. Instantaneous and electronic, it bears hardly any semblance of the person behind it. The impersonal anger in her fax hit me in the solar plexus.

Recoiling from my teacher's anger, I tried to put together the pieces of what appeared to be a misunderstanding. It seemed that she had misunderstood the work of correcting the spelling mistakes. How could she think that I would ever allow her book to be altered, Bhai Sahib's words to be changed? It is difficult to even describe the depth of my feelings, the pain, the frustration that I was five thousand miles away and could not just sit and discuss the matter with her. I know only too well how misunderstandings occur, how confusions build up. But as I was being thrown around by the impact of her fax, I sensed that something else was happening.

That it was not just a simple matter of misunderstanding became apparent when I was hit by the next devastating news. At a recent meeting of her small meditation group Mrs. Tweedie said that I had deceived her, that I was trying to purposefully stop her book from being in print, that I was trying to undermine her work. She felt betrayed. Although I only heard some of what was said, I know that when Mrs. Tweedie wants to make something hurt she does not hold back; anger and invective were powerfully combined.

It was on a Sunday morning when I heard this news over the telephone from a friend who had been present at the meeting. I remember the tears and anguish coming to the surface, as the outer world became blurred by the impact of this public statement. It was as if I was naked in the marketplace, being pilloried by my teacher and my closest friends, feeling each rotten egg and tomato. The feeling of painful exposure, of being humiliated, was combined with the knowledge that I could not defend myself. The state of vulnerability was combined with an inner certainty that I *must* let this process just happen to me. I must allow myself to be torn apart.

In the midst of the anguish there was also a quality of detachment. This detachment enabled me to stay inwardly exposed and feel the full impact of the experience. I knew that I needed to stay open, and in this state I suddenly remembered an experience in meditation which I had had a few days before. I was shown a white light/energy of "meaning" coming from the inner plane, and then when it came into manifestation it took on the distortions of the outer world. So I tried to grasp the "meaning" of the experience separate from the outer expression, from what had been said to the group, and I was helped by a saying of Abû Saʿîd that came to me that day:

> The Oneness of God, which is professed by the Sufis, consists of: separating the created from the non-created, going forth from one's native land, rejecting attachments, and putting aside what one knows and does not know, so that in place of all this there is the Real.

I knew that the danger was to remain in the outer form of the experience, to think "How did this misunderstanding arise? How could I have avoided it? What should I have done?" I tried to separate the created from the non-created, turning away from the illusion of the outer form, and any attachments I might have, to the one reality that was within my heart.

What I realized was brutal but liberating, as I discovered that up until now I had been both supported and protected by Mrs. Tweedie's support and approval of me. Coming to America and beginning the work of the Sufi Center was with her blessing, and with the blessing of the whole group. I also realized that any such outer support is a limitation. What she had said about me to her group smashed this limited container, a container which had been necessary until now. There was a feeling of freedom and inner space. That night I had a simple dream in which I wanted to have my hair cut at a military-style hairdresser—"short back and sides!" I had paid for the haircut and was only surprised that it was to be announced in public that I was to have a haircut! Hair often symbolizes the personality. Her talking to the group had made public the process of my personality being cut shorter.

Then, a few nights later, while I was awake, I had an experience of being united with Mrs. Tweedie on the level of the soul. There was just oneness. I have never had that experience with her, only the feeling of merging with Bhai Sahib or the nothingness. It was so much more complete than any outer support. It just was.

I had betrayed my teacher. I had let her down and it had been made public. But something deeper and more lasting than any outer relationship had been given. I also had a powerful experience in the night in which I was thrown into a light so bright I was destroyed, annihilated. There was no way I could survive the brightness of this light. After being annihilated I found myself back on the ground.

HE WHO WAS LOST

Each September I visit Europe to lecture, and I used to spend a few afternoons with Mrs. Tweedie. The fax had arrived at the beginning of August, and although I felt that everything had been inwardly resolved—and we were making a full print run of *Daughter of Fire* without any changes or corrections!—it was still with trepidation that I rang on her doorbell. I met with her and her small meditation group, and, despite the residue of her anger still inside me, there was a feeling of deep love. During the meditation I felt together with her and the superiors of the path.

However, the next afternoon that I came to visit her she was alone, and it was one of the strangest meetings I have ever had with a human being. She began by saying that it was over between us. I had betrayed her. I had tried to change her book without her permission. Then she said that nobody had ever asked her about making any corrections, and if I said that someone had asked her, she would simply deny it. We both knew that what she was saying was untrue—she had been asked. But the power of her insistence together with my respect for her forbade any argument. I had to accept that "black was white." I also knew that people would believe her and not me.

Initially this threw me into a tremendous state of confusion. In any normal conversation or discussion there is an accepted framework of shared belief. For example, if you are talking to someone sitting in a chair, you both accept that the person is actually sitting in a chair. But what happens if the person in the chair absolutely denies that she is sitting in a chair? Then you find yourself in a situation in which there is no mutually accepted framework. This is the situation into which I was thrown. All normal patterns of truth had been demolished by my having to accept that "black was white."

The room was charged with tremendous intensity on all levels. There was nothing to hang onto. This was like an experience in meditation of being thrown into the void, except that I was experiencing it in full consciousness, sitting on the floor in front of my teacher. Everything in my outer relationship with her was torn to threads. In this instant I was thrown beyond the duality implicit in any outer relationship, the duality of you and me and the misunderstandings that belong to this duality. I *knew* that the only real relationship was beyond duality, and this was my inner relationship with my Sheikh, my total belonging to him. When all outer patterns are shown to be deceptive, one can either struggle amidst the destruction, trying to cling onto the ruins, or one can leave behind any outer form or identification, and turn inward where the only true belonging exists. Sitting in the presence of my teacher, I was turned away from the deceptions of the outer world with its limited perception of truth, to an inner reality in which there was only the oneness of absolute belonging. When belonging is total there is only oneness.

I had known this total belonging inwardly, a belonging in which I do not exist and only my Sheikh exists. But now I was being forced to acknowledge it in the full consciousness of the outer world. I also realized that my complete trust of him meant his complete trust of me. In this reality there could be no duality. The mind, the ego, and the body were included and were a part of this statement of trust and belonging. This situation brought both confusion and freedom as I was forced to consciously state to myself and to Mrs. Tweedie that I belonged only to my Sheikh and that nothing else mattered. I did not care about myself, about anything that might happen. I no longer cared if black was white, or if I had any relationship with Mrs. Tweedie. In that instant her companionship of so many years meant nothing. In the midst of this inner turbulence I rose from the floor to leave. As I walked to the door I knew that if I left now I would not see Mrs Tweedie again. I knew her character. She said that it was over between us, that I had betrayed her. I also knew that in this situation she would have to leave her flat in my house and find somewhere else to live, which would be very difficult for her as she was almost blind by this time, and she had become used to the flat. I also knew that the work would be split in two, as many people would feel that I had acted against her. Nearing the door a question came to my mind. I turned and said to her, "Is there anything I have to learn from this situation? All that matters to me is the work." This question immediately altered the atmosphere, as if she recognized the total commitment we had each made to the work, and that this was all that really mattered. She asked me to stay for dinner and a friendship was once again present. She remained living in my flat for the last four years of her life, but our relationship would never be the same. A dependence had been broken.

I left Mrs. Tweedie's flat in a state of bewilderment. Consciously stating both to myself and to her that I belonged only to Bhai Sahib brought this inner connection into the hard fabric of the outer world. The Sufi says that the only real relationship is with the sheikh, and this is an inner relationship on the level of the soul. Mrs. Tweedie had helped and supported me beyond measure, but on this path everything has to go: every outer relationship becomes an obstacle. In the words of the Zen saying, "If you meet Buddha on the road, kill him." The devastation that I had experienced inwardly in the previous month in America had now been enacted on the outer stage. A final outer attachment had been most cruelly destroyed, and I had been taken completely into the real inner relationship with my Sheikh.

I only began to understand the implications of this strange meeting later, when I had time to think and meditate. Then as the dust settled, I was amazed at the way events constellate to give us the experience we need. What appeared a crazy confrontation had thrown me beyond any patterns or identification. The outer teacher had been totally demolished, and the inner teacher established beyond the duality of truth or falsehood. I also came to realize that my seeming act of betrayal had been needed to break such a deep attachment, to be free of any desire to please my teacher. Only then could I stand on my own feet. And it needed to be done while Mrs. Tweedie was still alive. Some patterns need to be broken on the physical plane.

But immediately after my visit with her there was no respite, no possibility to withdraw and integrate what had taken place. Two days later I travelled to Switzerland to continue my lecturing, an intense weekend seminar with over two hundred people. Then, on the Sunday evening the weekend seminar was over, and I was sitting in a friend's house, physically and emotionally exhausted, watching television. Suddenly I was given an experience, so simple and unexpected that my whole being was full of wonder and gratitude. I felt my Sheikh make me conscious of the Self as a center of power on the inner planes.

I have always been wary of power, knowing how easily it corrupts and influences the ego. But this new consciousness was just a state of being, as natural as life itself. Within the Self there is not the duality which belongs to the dynamics of power, as one friend in our group described in an experience he had shortly before he died: "Just lowly me, and lowly me is all-powerful, but can't be bothered with power. Power over *what?* There's nothing to have power over." Beyond duality there is the oneness of being, which carries the masculine aspect of the divine, His power—as is beautifully expressed in the *Katha Upanishad*, "That boundless Power, source of every power, manifesting itself as life, entering the heart, living there among the elements, that is Self."[7]

The moment my Sheikh gave me this new awareness I knew that something was completed. I was reminded of the experience over twenty years earlier when he made me conscious I am a soul. This new awakening had a similar feeling, and I knew it was not a passing state. Something within me had been changed. Twenty years before, this new consciousness had been followed by an intense confrontation with failure, a reminder of my human nature. Failure is one of the simplest ways to destroy the ego's desire for inflation, which can easily follow a spiritual experience. Failure had again accompanied an inner awakening, as all summer I had to accept that I had failed my teacher, failed in my work. But now everything had changed as I felt the grace of my Sheikh, who gave me something so simple and so precious—made me conscious of what I was before I was.

Changes of consciousness are so natural and all-embracing that it can take time to realize their significance. But immediately I began to feel a sense of relief, as if in the deepest sense I could now be myself, without restriction and without compromise. What began so many years before felt that it had completed a circle. So much had fallen away and so much had been given. What remains I do not know.

I flew back to California exhausted and replenished, empty and full. A week after I returned, on a hot, dry,

October afternoon, a wildfire began in the hills behind our house. For four days the fire raged, destroying homes and thousands of acres. Much of those days I sat on the deck of a friend's house, our suitcases packed in the car, watching the smoke darken the sky, wondering if we would have a house to return to. A few years earlier we had arrived in California with a few suitcases; we did not have much to lose. In my life so much had been burnt, what was there left to burn?

But our house was unscathed, just the air heavy with the smell of ash, and nearby, vistas of devastation. Surrounded by burnt trees and a scorched landscape, I had time to slowly digest the past few months, how life and the path had tortured and transformed me, how so much confusion had given birth to something else.

I had come to know the totality of my belonging to my Sheikh, who is a spiritual being united with God. This totality of belonging was imprinted into my soul, brought from lifetime to lifetime. It has always been present, only forgotten, obscured. When everything was being destroyed, and the outer world offered only distortion, in despair I was drawn inward, to this eternal imprint. From any notion of duality I was thrown into oneness, and into a totality of belonging that is now lived in every cell of my body. Then, through his grace, I came to know myself, not the ego with which I have long been only too familiar, but my real being. A month later I awoke with the sentence singing in my inner ear, "He who was lost has come Home."

PART 4

EPILOGUE

EPILOGUE

Over ten years have passed since I wrote this spiritual autobiography, told the tale of my initial years on the path, the story of my first experiences of meditation and how they drew me to a teacher and deep within myself. Reading it now I can recognize the person who wrote it, remember some of the feelings, the traumas, the beauty, and the love. And yet it appears to me now as fundamentally the story of another person, of a fragmented self struggling to find something, to uncover and claim a deeper meaning. Yes, the journey took me to a sense of wholeness, to a deep coming together as psychological conflicts came to the surface and began to be reconciled. But little did I know ten years ago how this journey was just the beginning, and how the real pilgrim is not the person whose story was told.

In these pages I have told as honestly as I could the story of my spiritual journey as it appeared then. And this journey took me home, back to what was real and essential within myself. But now I see this journey from another perspective, from that of the divine pushing Itself through into ordinary consciousness, demanding to make Itself known. This autobiography tells the story of a seeker being slowly stripped naked, the painful process of the clothes of conditioning and self-image being removed. This spiritual uncovering is real and painful, and is a necessary journey—the journey to discover your real nature, "the face you had before you were born." But later one realizes that from the very beginning it was not about oneself. The deeper journey, the more real story, is how the light of the real Self pushes Itself through into consciousness, demands to make Itself known.

It is of course much easier to tell "our" story, our emotional, psychological, and spiritual journey, painful and intoxicating, demanding and tremendously rewarding. It is very difficult to realize that essentially it is not about us, that within our human drama a deeper drama is taking place, as the divine finds ways to bring Itself into consciousness, to be born again. Sometimes the divine works through subtlety and cunning, deceiving us into allowing It into our life. In many ways the whole image of the spiritual journey is a deception, a cunning contrivance to draw us into a divine mystery, to enable That which is Real to be born in us and into the world. And sometimes It comes with violence and seeming cruelty, forcing us to step aside, striking like lightning.

And yet few words can be said about this deeper journey, this real birth. Our language, our images, even our feelings belong to the ego and its relationship to the world. They help us understand *our* place in the world and *our* life's journey. The divine, that eternal presence which is always here and yet continually reveals Itself anew, is a mystery beyond words, something that can be hinted at but hardly told. But looking back on this story I have told of my journey, I feel more clearly the presence of that Other. I sense Its light behind the incidents and happenings of the way, how It was pushing me to make Itself known. And in some of the final pages of the book I am reminded of this real story, how love revealed itself within me.

There is also an innocence to this spiritual story which I no longer have. Since writing this book my teacher, Irina Tweedie, has died, and as her Sheikh said to her, many things are revealed only after the teacher's death. When I wrote this autobiography I still believed in the spiritual journey as something to be accomplished, a journey with a destination. And so I experienced my path through this image of a journey Home, a journey which I traveled with all of my longing and struggles. I now know that this journey was just an image, something that gave me a certain security and belonging, a sense of purpose. But the divine does not belong to our images—we cannot imprison Him within our beliefs or concepts. How all of my spiritual images were destroyed, how even the journey itself was tossed aside, is a story too painful for me to tell at this time. But I have lost my spiritual innocence in ways I could never have imagined, and I am left with a sense as much of human fragility as of His grandeur, light, and glory. There is laughter when I write this, but tears are also very near. The relationship between the human and divine, and how they are one, is one of life's primal secrets.

The human drama is real in its pain and bliss, but this is only one facet of something so remarkable, so wonderful and so terrible. Once the clothes of "you" and "I" have been taken or torn off, there can be a glimpse of another drama, Another's story. And yet in many ways this is also our own story, for what are we but a spark of the divine, and what is our journey but this spark being born into human consciousness, becoming a fire? If you can, on reading these pages, try to feel this deeper, more potent tale, see the traces of that presence and power. The real mystery is how It unveils Itself within us; how the Beloved makes Himself known to Himself in the fragile container of the human being.

And yet there is also something profoundly beautiful about the part we have to play in this process, the human side of the divine drama. I had hoped that the human being, the "I," would dissolve completely, the moth lost in the flame. And yet although there have been inner experiences of complete dissolving, being lost so completely it would appear that nothing could ever be found again, each time there has been a return to something essentially human, some segment of self. This particle is very different from the fragmented human being who began the journey those years ago, and yet at the same time there is an essential similarity, as if it carries the same unique stamp. The meaning of this return, the part the human plays in His unfolding, seems to be one of the great mysteries.

In the years since writing this book I have felt more strongly both the power of the divine and the human qualities, transient, almost evanescent, and yet so necessary for this mystery to unfold. What is the real nature of the human being in the midst of the divine drama? We know only too well human nature as it struggles to survive and how it so easily follows the paths of greed and desire. We see the ravages of this around us in our polluted and desecrated world. But what are the human qualities that belong to the divine drama? What do we bring to this marriage? I do not attempt to understand fully this question, one that has haunted me for many years. I know in every cell the intensity of the divine and the need to bow down before It. But there is something within the human being that is needed for Its revelation, for the mystery of divine incarnation. Maybe as I look back at those early years and see the struggle and longing, the despair and craziness, I can sense that my very human failing was an important partner. Possibly this is what we really have to offer, our inadequacies, our limitations, our longing.

Attâr tells a story of the great Sufi, Bâyazîd Bistâmî: "He called to me in my innermost interior: 'Oh Bâyazîd. Our treasure chambers are filled with approved deeds of obedience and pleasing acts of worship. If you want Us, offer up something which We don't have!' I said: 'What is it that You don't have?' The voice said: 'Helplessness and impotence, need and humility and a broken spirit.'"

In the midst of the drama of divine revelation there is a human story to be told. This is not a hero's tale and there is no spiritual ladder of ascent. What I saw as a spiritual quest I now sense to be closer to a partnership, in which we discover those qualities the Beloved wants and needs, those very human failings that are close to His heart. In this relationship we are nothing, a piece of dust blown on the floor. And yet it would seem we are also close to His heart, infinitely precious.

January 2009

APPENDIX
AN ARCHETYPAL JOURNEY
THE LOVER'S KISS

Imagine that you are sitting under the shade of a great tree that reaches up into the sky. You hear the birds singing in the branches, where they have built their nests. Many animals come around the tree. Beside the tree flows a stream in which you can see fish. Animals come to drink from this stream. You sit there and relax, feeling the roots of the tree reaching deep down into the earth. You feel that the roots are a part of you and that you are the tree. You feel the tree's strength and the wind in your branches. You watch the seasons come and go. The snow covers the land and then spring arrives and buds form on the tree. The leaves grow on the tree and then they turn golden in autumn. All this you watch, all this you feel within yourself.

You feel such joy in being connected deep within the roots of the earth. You feel the joy of just being and wanting nothing. You just are. Then you feel around you many other trees, like yourself, with roots deep into the earth and reaching high into the sky, each tree bearing fruit of a different kind, providing shelter of a different nature. You see how these trees form part of a great pattern, a great mandala. You are aware that all over the face of the earth this mandala is forming, as trees become conscious of themselves, feel their strength, and sense their beauty. Slowly, this mandala comes to life. It has a life of its own. The molecules in the earth are changing shape as this pattern weaves its way over the surface. Slowly something is waking in the depths of the earth, some new form. You feel this shift and change in the earth, in the substance of the earth, and yet you do nothing. But you feel as if all the trees are holding hands and dancing a dance of great beauty, as if gold and silver threads are being woven and interwoven. This dance has a music which you feel in the veins of your body. You realize that the whole earth is changing shape in a way you do not yet understand.

Slowly over the horizon a great new sun appears. It floods the land with sunlight. You feel that this dawn is somehow a call, and there needs to be an echo, an answer. You feel the answer come from deep within the earth, a great booming noise. Then about the tree stand twelve forms and they are twelve different ways this new energy can manifest. There are six men and six women, and yet they are all a part of one another. They begin to dance, to weave in and out about the tree. In this dance they tell you their names and you understand the different ways that this new energy will unfold. Yet deep within the tree you feel that something is missing, something which is needed to complete the dance. You know it is a word from a far-off planet that has been hidden from us, veiled in shadow.

With the dance of the twelve forms you weave yourself a coracle, a round boat made of light. You weave it with songs and with silence. You sit in the middle of the boat and it takes you far, far away. It takes you to the spaces between the stars, beyond the lines of any horizon. You touch galaxies with your fingers and realize that they are but painted pictures on a backcloth. You travel deeper and deeper, to the edge of the universe and beyond. You sing softly to yourself. You sing the song of the circle unfolding and the joy of being. Further and further you go. You pass beyond even the borders of emptiness.

Then you find yourself on a distant, distant shore.
This is the shore of the forgotten god where the sacred
syllables are born. You know that the new age needs
a new sacred syllable, so that its deepest meaning can
unfold and its purpose be known. Yet it is not yours to
ask and so, sitting on the sand, you wait. Across the sea
comes a flower with seven petals. It carries a perfume,
but not a sound; so you wait.

As you wait, just for a moment the veils between
the worlds open and you feel breath in your mouth.
You feel a stone being put in your mouth. You know
that this stone has a sacred syllable engraved upon it.
The stone is made of fire, though it burns you not. As
you wait there so the stone becomes part of your being
and its fire becomes part of your blood. You absorb
all of it until there is nothing left. Then out of that
nothingness there comes a voice which speaks to you,
saying, "Because you have waited with patience, here
in the place where the two worlds meet, I will answer
your question, a question which you do not ask for
yourself."

There is a great, magnificent green dragon breathing
fire and riding it with love and tenderness is a child.
They speak to each other and understand each other.
They know you also. Then you have in your hand a
small golden chain which is tied around the dragon's
neck. You become the dragon, and you become the
child also. You have this all in a ring around your finger.
It is a ring of green gold which is worn like a wedding
ring. You take it and put it on a chain around your
neck, for the hour of the wedding is not yet come.

Before you can return in your coracle made of
light, there is something else you must do in that place
where the two worlds meet. You are given the kiss of
the Lover, that all unfolding should be with love. This

kiss bears the Name of Him who kisses you, which is the greatest gift that He can give. Then you return to the tree.

Around the tree is a ring of fire. The fire burns and transforms the tree. In that space of transformation your partner comes to meet you. You two become one, and you give as a gift the ring that you wore around your neck. Then you kiss, and with that kiss the Name of the Lover is given also. This happens in each of the trees that form the mandala all over the world, and around the world is a dancing ring of fire. In that fire many things will be burnt. Many people will lose all that they had thought precious.

Then you find yourself sitting in the midst of an eight-petaled lotus which is born from the fire. On your forehead is engraved the Name of God, formed in fire. You are both man and woman. All this takes place in a pool in a garden, tended with love by a gardener. Standing by the pool, you wash your face with water from the pool and you drink from the water. So you come to know yourself. Others can drink there also and come to know themselves, for the doors of this garden are open to the four corners of the world.

NOTES

FOREWORD

1. Adapted from the foreword to the author's first book, *The Lover and the Serpent* (Shaftesbury: Element Books, 1990. Now out of print).

INTRODUCTION

1. Trans. John Moyne and Coleman Barks, "Who gets up early to discover the moment light begins," *These Branching Moments* (Providence, RI: Copperbeech Press, 1988), ode 19.
2. See ch. 2, "Meeting the Teacher," p. 40. See also p. 40, n. 5 on the Uwaysi initiation.

AWAKENING

1. However, I have since met other people who have had similar experiences as children and were not frightened by them.
2. The *kundalini* is a powerful energy which is needed for spiritual realization. It resides at the base of the spine, and, unless awakened, is only experienced in the form of sexual energy. Sexual energy is about one third of the *kundalini* energy.
3. In *Daughter of Fire* Irina Tweedie describes how the Sufi master Bhai Sahib awakened the *kundalini* within her.
4. The result of our work was an article, *Chartres Maze, a model of the universe?* by Keith Critchlow, Jane Carroll,

Llewellyn Vaughan-Lee (Research into Lost Organization Trust, Occasional Paper No. 1), which suggests that the maze is an archetypal image of both the planets and the psyche.

5. It was removed at the time of Napoleon.

MEETING THE TEACHER

1. *Daughter of Fire*, p. 3.

2. *Daughter of Fire*, p. 496.

3. She said that if someone called her by her first name, Irina, there would be the danger of making a personal relationship with her that could interfere with the spiritual relationship.

4. There is a story told in *Daughter of Fire*, pp. 551-552, in which the sheikh beats a young disciple to death in front of his family, and then brings him back to life as a *wali*, or saint.

5. It is not unknown in the Sufi tradition for a disciple to be guided by a sheikh who is no longer in the physical body. This kind of internal relationship, known as Uwaysi initiation (named after Uways al-Qarani, a contemporary of the Prophet Muhammad), is particularly evident in the Naqshbandi tradition. Bahâ ad-dîn Naqshband (d. 1390), the founder of the Naqshbandi order, speaks of being guided by two teachers in the spirit, Al-Hakîm at-Tirmidhî (d. ca. 907), and 'Abd'l-Khâliq Ghujduwânî (d. 1220). Ghujduwânî instructed him in the method of the silent *dhikr*, which is the central practice of the Naqshbandi path.

6. Quoted by Leonard Lewisohn, *Beyond Faith and Infidelity* (Richmond, Surrey: Curzon Press, 1995), p. 115.

7. For example, soon after she arrived she writes, "Doubts kept coming into my mind. Many doubts. Such ordinary surroundings. Such ordinary people around him. Is he a Great Man? There seems to be no glamor of a Great Guru, a Great Teacher, about him, as we used to read in books.... He was so simple, living a simple, ordinary life" (*Daughter of Fire*, p. 15).

8. Quoted in *Four Sufi Classics*, trans. David Pendlebury (London: Octagon Press, 1982), p. 191.

9. *Daughter of Fire*, p. 309.

10. *Daughter of Fire*, p. 404.

11. Trans. Daniel Liebert, *Rumi, Fragments, Ecstasies* (Santa Fe, New Mexico: Source Books, 1981), Poem 7, p. 16.

MADNESS AND BLISS

1. Quoted by Annemarie Schimmel, *Mystical Dimensions of Islam* (Chapel Hill, North Carolina: University of North Carolina Press, 1975), p. 199.

2. *Hamlet*, V i 279-283.

3. Quoted by C. G. Jung, *Collected Works*, vol. 5 (London: Routledge & Kegan Paul, 1956), para. 561.

4. Prince Hamlet's final words are "the rest is silence" (V ii 362).

5. *The Way of Individuation* (New York: Harcourt Brace and World, 1967), p. 109.

ROMANTIC LOVE

1. *Rumi, Fragments, Ecstasies*, p. 14.

2. *The Practice of the Presence of God,* trans. John Delaney (Garden City, New York: Image Books, 1977), p. 87.

3. Quoted by Laleh Bakhtiar, *Sufi Expressions of the Mystic Quest* (London: Thames and Hudson, 1976), p. 21.

4. Hâfez, quoted by Javad Nurbakhsh, *Sufi Symbolism*, vol. 1 (London: Khaniqahi-Nimatullahi Publications, 1984), p. 78.

5. *Collected Poems and Plays of Rabindranath Tagore* (London: Macmillan, 1936), pp. 441-442, slightly edited.

6. Told by Farid al-Din 'Attâr, *Muslim Saints and Mystics,* trans. A.J. Arberry (London: Routledge & Kegan Paul, 1966), pp. 93-94.

7. *The Psychology of Romantic Love* (London: Routledge & Kegan Paul, 1983), p. 3.

8. *Mathnawi*, III, 4160-4168, trans. Coleman Barks, *Rumi, We Are Three* (Athens, Georgia: Maypop Books, 1987), p. 12.

9. Song of Solomon, 6:10.

10. *C. G. Jung, Emma Jung and Toni Wolff, A Collection of Remembrances* (San Francisco: The Analytical Club of San Francisco, 1982), p. 53.

11. The passage about the two dreams is adapted from the author's *The Call and the Echo* (Putney, Vermont: Threshold Books, 1992), pp. 83-86.

12. Nurbakhsh, *Sufi Symbolism*, vol. 1, p. 75.

13. *Women in Praise of the Sacred*, ed. Jane Hirshfield (New York: HarperCollins, 1994), p. 138.

LIFE AS A HOUSEHOLDER

1. Quoted by Idries Shah, *The Way of the Sufi* (Harmondsworth: Penguin Books, 1974), p. 156.

2. Al-Hallâj, quoted by Louis Massignon, *The Passion of al-Hallâj*, vol. 3 (Princeton: Princeton University Press, 1982), p. 99.

3. *Daughter of Fire*, pp. 536-537.

THE ARCHETYPAL WORLD

1. *Psychological Reflections* (London: Routledge & Kegan Paul, 1971), p. 51 and p. 39.

2. C. G. Jung, *Memories, Dreams, Reflections* (London: Flamingo, 1983), p. 225.

3. This is why Jung was against unconditionally adopting an Eastern spiritual tradition.

4. Adapted from *Catching the Thread*, p. 77-79.

5. *Psychological Reflections*, p. 14.

6. The Greek myths are full of the tricks played by the gods upon humans.

7. *Katha Upanishad*, trans. Shree Purohit Swami and W. B.Yeats, *The Ten Principal Upanishads* (London: Faber and Faber, 1937), p. 34.

8. Henry Corbin, a follower of Jung, discovered the use of active, or "creative," imagination in the Sufi tradition. See Corbin's *Creative Imagination in the Sufism of Ibn 'Arabi* (Princeton: Princeton University Press, 1969).

9. C. G. Jung, *Man and His Symbols* (London: Aldus Books, 1964), p. 61.

10. See Appendix for an example of an archetypal journey.

11. For example, *Mother Holle* or *An African Tale*. See the author's *In the Company of Friends* (Inverness, California: Golden Sufi Center, 1994), pp. 46-48.

DREAMWORK AND THE GROUP

1. Quoted by R. A. Nicholson, *Studies in Islamic Mysticism* (Cambridge: Cambridge University Press, 1921), p. 55.

2. *Mathnawi*, II, 3274-3283, and III, 3210-3212, quoted by Sara Sviri, *The Taste of Hidden Things* (Inverness, California: Golden Sufi Center, 1997), p. 207.

3. See Llewellyn Vaughan-Lee, *In the Company of Friends* (Inverness, California: The Golden Sufi Center, 1994), for a full exploration of the Sufi group as a spiritual container.

4. Trans. Coleman Barks, *One-Handed Basket Weaving* (Athens, Georgia: Maypop Books, 1991), p. 108.

5. First Epistle of Paul to the Corinthians, 13:12.

6. Quoted by William Chittick, *The Sufi Path of Knowledge* (Albany: State University of New York Press, 1989), p. 154.

ON THE ROAD

1. *Sufism, Islam and Jungian Psychology*, ed. Marvin Spiegelman (Scottsdale, Arizona: New Falcon, 1991).
2. Quoted by William Chittick, *The Sufi Path of Love* (Albany: State University of New York Press, 1983), p. 339.

COMING HOME

1. Quoted by Massignon, *The Passion of al-Hallâj*, vol. 1, p. 614.
2. Song of Solomon, 5:2.
3. Quoted by J. G. Bennett, *The Masters of Wisdom* (Santa Fe, New Mexico: Bennett Books, 1995), p. 180. The Zen saying, "If you meet Buddha on the road, kill him," carries the same meaning.
4. See Llewellyn Vaughan-Lee, *Catching the Thread*, ch. 9, "The Relationship with the Teacher," p. 204.
5. Quoted by Michaela Özelsel, *Forty Days* (Putney, Vermont: Threshold Books, 1996), p. 21.
6. Trans. Coleman Barks, *The Hand of Poetry* (New Lebanon, New York: Omega Publications, 1993), p. 57.
7. *Katha Upanishad*, bk. II, 1.

ACKNOWLEDGMENTS

The author gratefully wishes to acknowledge: Coleman Barks for permission to quote from *These Branching Moments,* translated by John Moyne and Coleman Barks, from *Rumi: We Are Three,* translated by Coleman Barks, and from *One-Handed Basket Weaving,* translated by Coleman Barks; Jane Hirshfield for permission to use "O friend, understand" by Mirabai, translation © 1994 Jane Hirshfield, which first appeared in *Women in Praise of the Sacred: 43 Centuries of Spiritual Poetry by Women,* edited by Jane Hirshfield, Harper Collins, 1994; Threshold Books for permission to use "We have put a substance into you" by Rumi, quoted by Michaela Özelsel in *Forty Days: The Diary of a Traditional Solitary Sufi Retreat;* and Omega Publications (New Lebanon, NY) for permission to use material from *The Hand of Poetry: Five Mystic Poets of Persia.*

LLEWELLYN VAUGHAN-LEE, Ph.D., is a Sufi teacher in the Naqshbandiyya-Mujaddidiyya Sufi Order. Born in London in 1953, he has followed the Naqshbandi Sufi path since he was nineteen. In 1991 he became the successor of Irina Tweedie, author of *Daughter of Fire: A Diary of a Spiritual Training with a Sufi Master.* He then moved to Northern California and founded The Golden Sufi Center (www.goldensufi.org). Author of several books, he has specialized in the area of dreamwork, integrating the ancient Sufi approach to dreams with the insights of Jungian Psychology. Since 2000 the focus of his writing and teaching has been on spiritual responsibility in our present time of transition, and an awakening global consciousness of oneness. More recently he has written about the feminine, the *anima mundi* (world soul), and spiritual ecology (see www.workingwithoneness.org).

THE GOLDEN SUFI CENTER is a publishes books, video, and audio on Sufism and mysticism. A California religious nonprofit 501 (c) (3) corporation, it is dedicated to making the teachings of the Naqshbandi Sufi path available to all seekers. For further information about the activities and publications, please contact:

THE GOLDEN SUFI CENTER
P.O. Box 456
Point Reyes Station, CA 94956-0456
tel: 415-663-0100 · fax: 415-663-0103
www.goldensufi.org

THE PARADOXES OF LOVE

SUFISM:
The Transformation of the Heart

IN THE COMPANY OF FRIENDS:
Dreamwork within a Sufi Group

THE BOND WITH THE BELOVED:
The Mystical Relationship of the Lover and the Beloved

edited by LLEWELLYN VAUGHAN-LEE
with biographical information by SARA SVIRI

TRAVELLING THE PATH OF LOVE:
Sayings of Sufi Masters

by PETER KINGSLEY

A STORY WAITING TO PIERCE YOU:
Mongolia, Tibet, and the Destiny of the Western World

REALITY

IN THE DARK PLACES OF WISDOM

by SARA SVIRI

THE TASTE OF HIDDEN THINGS:
Images of the Sufi Path

by HILARY HART

THE UNKNOWN SHE:
Eight Faces of an Emerging Consciousness